Writing from Within

"Very deep . . .
very deep is the well of the past."

THOMAS MANN
Joseph and His Brothers

To Lowell and Mary, my parents

Writing from Within

A GUIDE TO CREATIVITY
AND LIFE STORY WRITING

Bernard Selling

Hunter House
PUBLISHERS

First U.S. classroom edition published in 1988, first U.S. paperback edition published in 1989, second edition published in 1990, third edition published in 1998 by Hunter House Inc., Publishers

    Hunter House Inc., Publishers
    P.O. Box 2914
    Alameda, CA 94501-0914

Photo credits: Leonardo da Vinci. The Last Supper. S. Maria delle Grazie, Milan, Italy. (Art Resource, NY); p. 59. Bruegel, Pieter the Elder. Landscape with the Fall of Icarus. Musee d'Art Ancien, Brussels, Belgium (Art Resource, NY) p.61. Cover photo by Karen Kemp © 1997.

Library of Congress Cataloging-in-Publication Data

Selling, Bernard.
    Writing from within: a guide to creativity and life story writing / Bernard Selling. – 3rd ed.
    p.   cm.
    Includes bibliographical references
    ISBN 0-89793-217-X (paper)
    1. Autobiography—Authorship 2. Report writing. I. Title.
CT25.S48 1997 97-15745
808'.066—dc21   CIP

Cover design: MIG/Design Works
Book design and production: Martha Blegen
Project coordinators: Wendy Low, Belinda Breyer
Editors: Mali Apple, Kiran Rana
Marketing director: Corrine M. Sahli
Marketing associate: Susan Markey
Customer support: Christina Arciniega, Edgar M. Estavilla, Jr.
Order fulfillment: A & A Quality Shipping Services
Publisher: Kiran S. Rana

Printed and Bound by Publishers Press, Salt Lake City, UT
Manufactured in the United States of America

9 8 7 6 5 4 3 2 1   Third Edition

Contents

Preface

When I was sixteen years old, my father died—an unexpected and painful event for me. He was an enigma: a prominent psychiatrist, the possessor of seven college degrees, an angry and charming man, highly ethical, overbearing, and accomplished. A heart attack eight years before his death caused him to stumble toward the finish line of his life like an exhausted marathon runner whose sole purpose in life was to stay alive until his children finished high school. He almost made it.

For weeks after his death, I read copies of all the letters he wrote during his years of public life. Nowhere could I find anything personal about him: who he was, where he had come from, where he thought he was going.

Beyond a few facts and remembrances and a few funny stories, I knew very little. My mother died a few years after my father and I reached young adulthood in the 1950s feeling like an existential anti-hero—free to make choices but not guided by an immediate past or a family history—truly alone.

In the intervening years, from Dad's death until the present, my father's sister, the one person who could reveal more of him, showed no interest in telling me more of his life, particularly his thoughts and feelings.

"People of our generation do not dwell on such things," she would say. "I don't have time." So it appeared that my father's history, both family and personal, would remain shrouded in darkness, consigned to oblivion. And indeed it has come to pass. This has saddened me enormously.

When asked to teach the classes from which this book was drawn, I thought how much it would have meant to me to know my parents well: how they were raised, the things they did, and, most of all, what they thought and felt as they experienced their lives. This became my touchstone for teaching the class—actions and events accurately described, feelings about them honestly and vividly captured.

As the classes developed over several years, I began to realize the importance of what we were accomplishing.

First of all, the writing process was immensely therapeutic for each person. It was plain to see that once the participants had overcome a fear of writing, the process of getting their life stories out and on paper had a revitalizing effect on them.

Second, being congratulated for good work and encouraged by class members to keep at the task was equally therapeutic.

Third, the warm acceptance of their work by family members revealed to each person that he or she was filling a genuine need within the family.

Fourth, and most inspiring, was the awareness that, as each writer became more skilled, the quality of his or her legacy would itself become a guide for the family and inspire histories to be written by generations yet unborn. Occasionally, someone would comment after a particularly good story, "What would it be like for us if our parents and forebears had left memories as well written and revealing as the stories coming to the surface in our workshop?"

Ultimately, this is the great lure of life story writing: to be able to affect the future of the families into which we are born; to give direction, amusement, and perspective to our children's children and their children; to write so well that a hundred years from now those who follow can clearly see the footprints we made and can begin to gauge their own paths by our direction.

I would like to thank the staff and class members of my writing class at the Professional Musicians Union Local 47 in Hollywood, California, for their support, advice, and encouragement. My Sunday afternoon workshop also provided me with a stimulating atmosphere within which I have been able to try out many new approaches to the craft of writing.

Following the publication of the first edition of this book, I received a great deal of valuable feedback about its effectiveness. A number of people responded strongly to the personal glimpses I had given my readers, so in this edition I have tried to provide a few more where they make my teaching a little clearer.

This new edition incorporates a number of new techniques that have become central to my teaching, such as experiencing the stories as mirrors of ourselves and ways to expand and manage our creativity. Also included is a new exercise section at the end of many chapters. These exercises have proven to be helpful to many of my students.

As I present my workshops around the country, I find that people are greatly interested in the unexpected and often unusual benefits of life story writing. The reader will, therefore, find in Chapter 19 a discussion of these benefits, including benefits to fiction writers, to the curricula of our school systems, and to the counseling and healing professions.

Finally, many of the stories from the earlier edition have been replaced by ones that more accurately reflect my current approach to life story writing.

I would like to give special thanks to my editor, Mali Apple at Hunter House, for her work on this edition. Her sharp eye and sensitivity to the material improved the book tremendously.

Bernard Selling
Venice, California, 1997

Introduction

In the years after World War II, America saw an unprecedented rootlessness developing. Easterners moved west, Southerners moved north, corporate Americans moved everywhere. But in the years since Alex Haley's *Roots* entered the consciousness of American society, we have seen a distinct shift toward respect for roots. And with it, we have witnessed an increasing respect for the wit and wisdom of those who have gotten us where we are—our parents and grandparents. For a writer and teacher who works with mature adults, this is a welcome change.

This volume, derived from the life story writing classes and workshops I have been teaching since 1982, is written for those who wish to inform their children and grandchildren about the life path that they, the writers, have followed. It is also a self-help text for those who wish to use this writing as a means toward greater self-understanding.

The book is divided into four parts. Part 1 introduces the writer to various techniques that will help him or her learn to express himself or herself fully and well on paper. It then guides the writer toward unearthing and exploring hidden memories. In Part 2, the reader is provided with something of a road map to follow in answering the question, What should I write about? Part 3 encourages the writer to find ways of harnessing and managing his or her creativity and discusses the many and unusual benefits to be gained from carrying out the task of writing one's life stories.

Part 4 is composed of life stories that demonstrate the various techniques that are developed and discussed in this book. These techniques allow the reader a much more intimate sense of the writer's thoughts, feelings, and experiences than is normally the case in journal, oral history, and life narrative writing. The selections give a real taste of what we mean by "writing from within": finding and capturing on paper the way life unfolds in vivid, emotional, intimate detail, experienced from the point of view of the writer at the age when the events occurred.

Some of you may wish to read this book through from beginning to end before starting to write. In that case, you may wish to jot down notes as ideas, incidents, and people from the past come to mind.

I encourage you to work in a leisurely manner; there is no need to rush. It may take weeks or even months to move from one chapter to the next. That is to be expected. How many stories you write while developing the techniques presented in each chapter is very much up to you. You may well take six months to a year or longer to work through the book.

In the first few weeks and months, you will be spending a great deal of time rewriting, time that you might prefer to spend on the next recollection. To achieve the intimacy and depth of feeling and observation that are possible using the techniques described in the book, allow yourself the extra time and effort. Reread the book several times, and you will gradually make the techniques you have read and thought about a part of you. Using them will begin to feel comfortable—and you will be happy with the results.

At the end of several sections on composing, I include a short personal note to the reader. These notes are intended to guide you into the actual writing, for I do urge you to begin writing when I say *now*. Don't bother fussing, worrying, or protesting. Whatever comes out is a first draft, which can be revised later. If you wish to read through the whole book before beginning to write, that is fine. But do allow the book to help you get down to the task of writing, not thinking about writing.

I am often asked, "Should I write my stories chronologically, or should I write as my inner urge dictates?" By all means, write as that urge dictates. Your stories ought, generally, to be arranged in chronological order if you print or publish them, but you, as the writer, need feel no compulsion to write them in that order. The vivid memories are the ones most likely to pop out at you at any time of the day or night.

I do suggest that you write several early memories first, learning to write from the child's point of view before skipping around and writing about different phases of your life. Writing a number of early memories enables you to start with simpler memories and to discover the power of writing "authentically," that is, writing in a voice that is consistent with the age of the person you were. By getting back to that person, you will discover much of your past that you have forgotten or remembered inaccurately.

The style you will be developing will be forceful, immediate, and intimate. It will be full of dialogue and your inner thoughts and feelings. You will be developing your own authentic writer's voice, while you learn how to "write from within."

PART I

Acquiring the Techniques

Introduction

As I walk up the steps to the second floor of the Musicians Union in Los Angeles, I wonder what this class will be like. For years I have been teaching people to write their life stories in classes and workshops around California, and I have been a musician since I was twelve years old. Now I hope to combine these two passions by helping musicians, mostly older and male, both black and white, gather together to share their stories of life on the road and in the studios with bands big and small.

The first session last week was fun. I had moved another class to this location in order to include these musicians, and the members of the old class welcomed the new members with a lot of warmth. The new members, the musicians, did a short exercise in which each shared his or her earliest memory out loud. Then I showed them how to tell their memories again in a way that would bring the stories to life. Now we will find out how the writing is coming.

"Good morning, Herr Professor." Dave Schwartz, a highly respected, retired violist, gives me a wry smile as I open the door.

"Hello, Dave, how are you?" I've come to see that he is not only one of the class wits, but a very sharp-minded man pushing eighty and looking sixty.

"Hey, Bernard, how's it going?" Eddie White's shy smile lights up the room. A small, kindly man with snow white hair, Eddie has been with me several months now and has shown over and over again remarkable storytelling gifts.

"Hey there, Edward, you got a good one for us?" I ask.

"It better be good," laughs Buddy Collette, the great sax, clarinet, and flute player who, with Charlie Mingus, Britt Woodman, and Chico Hamilton, formed the first postbebop band after World War II. "He called me at three o'clock this morning to read it to me." We all laugh.

"Well, I sort of lost track of time," Eddie chuckles. The smile never leaves his face.

"Eddie's always had a problem with time." Jack Burger, a long-time drummer in the Hollywood studios, laughs.

"Yeah, sometimes I play three beats to a measure and you guys are playing four." Eddie enjoys poking fun at himself. "That's why I hardly ever play in public."

"You're lucky. You played music because you loved it." Jack leans back in his chair. "The rest of us were cursed with talent and had to earn a living at it."

Dave nods toward Jack, a little smile on his face. "Not all of us who earned a living at it were cursed with talent, Jack."

I laugh again as other members of the class, the nonmusicians like Doris Argoud and Roz Goldstein from the earlier class, settle into their seats. Listening to musicians trade stories and gentle barbs is one of the highlights of my week, as it is for Roz and Doris.

"Buddy has a story," says Eddie. "I asked him to read it to me but he wanted to wait for your comments, Bernard."

"Well, let's hear it," says Doris, a whimsical, supportive woman in her late forties. "I'm dying to know his earliest memory."

"This is just a first draft, you know," replies Buddy. Tall and distinguished, a true elder statesman of jazz, he takes several sheets of paper from his briefcase and puts on his glasses. As he reads, I reflect on what I know of him: a superb musician, Buddy is (and has been for a long time) a force in the creative community of Los Angeles, conducting workshops, concerts, and performances for kids in schools. In the early 1950s, he was instrumental in bringing the black and white musicians' unions together to form a single, integrated union. He later became the first black musician to break into the studios. Thanks to him, our class is now held at the union.

I've known Buddy for several months, after a chance meeting brought him to the class in which Roz and Doris were students. Right away, he brought along relatives and friends, including Eddie. These new, creative storytellers have brought a wonderful energy to the class, and I'm impressed with Buddy's philosophy: "We're all moving forward, so let's move forward together." I find myself wondering, *What has enabled Buddy to become so positive and forward-looking, able to ease past obstacles that would stop another man?*

In this first story, he writes about a time when, at two years old, he sees something on the other side of the street and runs across the street to get it. A Model T Ford runs him down, and Buddy disappears under the wheels. Buddy's mother hurries to the scene and sees only the scarf in the spokes of the wheel. "My baby . . ." she whispers. A few moments later Buddy is pulled from under the car, stunned but alive.

As I listen, I imagine Buddy's mother growing hysterical and angry, as I imagine most parents becoming . . . as I myself became when my younger son ran out in the street.

But no, Buddy's mother sweeps him up in her arms, saying, "Oh, my little darling, I'm so glad you're all right."

How intriguing, I think to myself, as I listen to Buddy describe the little tests his father devised to teach him independence and resourcefulness. His parents' attitude seems to be, "If you want to do it, it must be worth doing."

I begin to reflect on the nature of parenting. From noncritical, supportive parents comes a sense of wholeness to our lives, the kind I see in creativity such as Buddy's. But for most of us, I think to myself, loving, attentive, supportive elders are, like wholeness and creativity, something for which we yearn, but seldom get. I feel a little sad.

Unlike Buddy, I grew up with a sense of something missing in my life. *What is it?* I kept asking myself all through high school. *What's missing?* I wonder whether it had anything to do with my parents, though they were pretty normal. Dad was my hero, a successful, highly educated psychiatrist who survived a serious heart attack when I was eight and who coped with my mom's emotional illnesses.

Of course, Dad was not always my hero. Highly critical, with a mind as sharp as a razor, he absorbed book knowledge with ease. The unspoken rule of the house was "read books, do well in school, win Dad's approval." As I looked around our library at home, I was intrigued and overwhelmed. How could I ever hope to read all those books? I became quite critical of myself, and Dad's occasional dark rages at me added a whole lower octave to the voices of my inner thoughts: *You won't be able to do that. You don't deserve to get that. You won't finish that. You've reached a plateau and that's where you'll stay.*

I reflect that my experience of my parents was probably not much different from that of most people: one parent highly critical, the other more supportive but often afraid to interfere. *Ah, that demonic inner critic, so ready to devour us. How sad,* I think to myself. *How sad.*

"What a wonderful story, Buddy," says Doris. "It gives us a lot of insight into you."

"My mother was a great lady," murmurs Buddy. "She gave a lot of thought to everything . . . like the music lessons we all got."

I glance around the room. Dave's face has a bit of a frown. "Dave, you have a question, I think?"

"I've always wanted to write about playing with Toscanini, Leopold Stowkowski, and Glenn Miller. But it just sounds like bragging. 'Big important me.' I get frustrated and stop writing."

"What voice is that?" I ask, expecting that those who have been with me a while will recognize it immediately.

"The voice of the critic," answers good-natured Roz. Dave still looks puzzled. "The voice that's telling you not to write or is finding fault with what you do . . . that's the voice of the critic."

Dave turns to me. "Is that right, Bernard?"

"Dave, when we were small, most of us were playful and we created endlessly . . . in the sandbox or at the beach, right?" The others nod their heads. "But too often our strongly critical mind, our 'critic,' simply overwhelms our 'creator' side. It makes it very difficult for us to see our deep-seated creativity and keep it going."

"So the perfectionist in me makes it impossible even to start writing," Dave muses. Roz and Doris nod their heads in agreement. "Very interesting . . . the conflict between my self-critic and my creativity is what's holding me back? Then how do I get unstuck?"

"In the course of writing our stories, we will often find these two sides of the mind fighting with each other. When this happens, we need to calm ourselves, to drain away emotions, particularly frustration—to allow our creative side to regain momentum." Dave stares at me intently. "I do a couple of things: I put a play-along jazz album on the turntable, pick up my clarinet, and accompany it. This calms me down, and I return more focused. Or I lie down and doze off. My mind calms itself down."

"You actually let yourself go to sleep?" asks Dave.

"He fell asleep during a story I wrote last year," laughs Roz.

"And he woke up and gave a great critique," adds Doris, racing to my defense.

"This balancing process has a very positive effect on the stories we write," I continue, "if we let it happen."

"It's had a positive effect on my life, too," adds Doris. Jack frowns at her. "Really, Jack. It's allowed a lot of my feelings to come out. Feelings that were buried for a long time."

"I was just thinking that nothing can help Dave put his life in balance," Jack chuckles. "He spends all his time carrying residuals to the bank."

"Don't I wish," laughs Dave. "But that does remind me of a story . . . anyway, go ahead Bernard."

Already I notice the men in the room becoming uncomfortable, joking and laughing as soon as we begin talking about feelings. This is not unusual. Buddy and Eddie are exceptions; Eddie's stories of growing up in the south are rich with feelings (see his story "Blind Lemon Jefferson Sings the Blues" on page 215).

"You know, when I was just starting to write," Doris offers, "I would sometimes get really emotional. A part of me would say, *Don't write this. It's too personal.* It took me a while to get up the courage just to go on and see where the story wanted to take me, what it would show me that I had forgotten."

"Writing isn't like playing the viola where I can just practice harder, is it?" Dave muses.

"Or listening to a record and stealing from the great artists," Jack smirks.

"Oh, Dave would never steal someone else's interpretation," adds Eddie with a sly grin. "He would make it his own."

"Don't bet on it," Dave laughs.

"Go ahead, Bernard," Buddy urges. "You were talking about feelings and writing?"

"Let me put it this way," I say. "When we are young, many things come along that hurt, embarrass, or frustrate us, yes?"

"You bet," Doris pipes in.

"Well, we soon learn to use language to keep that hurt at a distance . . . so we won't feel it as we write. As a result, we write in the past tense and use complicated words, anything to avoid reliving the pain of early childhood."

"So we actually use language to keep people from getting close to us when we write?" Buddy ponders this.

"Exactly," I answer. "Most of the time, we think we want to bring our readers into our stories; but in fact, we are filled with such fear of their discovering a lot about us that we actually keep them far away from the experience we are writing about."

"And the critic enters the picture, saying, 'You're bragging, don't do that,' and we silence ourselves even more," Dave adds.

"That's it," I answer. Dave is beginning to form an image of what has been holding him back. I turn to Buddy. "This is why we enjoyed your story about the Model T—because you let us inside the experience." I look around. They want more. "For example, many of us were taught in the early grades that it is self-centered to use the word 'I' in a sentence."

"I've never had a problem talking about myself," chuckles Eddie. "But go on. I like to listen to you talk, Bernard. Yes, sir, you sure can talk. Uhuhhhhh."

I suppress a laugh and continue. "Very often my students, in writing about themselves and their brothers and sisters, will say something like, 'We went to the creek and we were feeling good,' which is different from saying, 'My brothers and I went to the creek. I was feeling good.' There's a difference, yes?"

"A writer cannot make statements about the thoughts and feelings of 'we' and be believed, but he can speak about 'I' and be believed," answers Roz, who has been with me for several years.

"So it's a matter of belief, not exactness, that matters?" asks Dave. I enjoy the sharpness of his questions. "We have to make the audience *believe* what we are talking about?"

"Little differences in language, such as these, enable us to bring the audience closer to our inner experience or to push our audience out of our experience." I glance from face to face as each person digests these words. "We have so many ways of hiding our feelings and our thoughts from ourselves and from others."

"It's so true," says Doris, who writes vividly of growing up with an alcoholic mother. I hear the sadness in her voice.

"What we need is to find a way to express ourselves that keeps us in close touch with ourselves and our audience. In the next few weeks and months, as we go through the steps of 'writing from within,' we will learn how to express our experience of events and of ourselves in a way that draws our readers into our universe and keeps them in our orbit for the duration of the story—that allows them to believe what they are reading. A compelling story gets told and, at the same time, we have every opportunity to be at the center of our universe for a brief moment—and to make our universe interesting to others. 'I am here' rather than 'We were there.'"

"I'm with you Bernard," says Dave. "Open the door."

"Uhh uhh uhhh," murmurs Eddie. "Bernard, you sure can talk. You shoulda stayed in the air force. You'd have made a great general, or a politician." Everyone in the class laughs, including me.

"Just remember, some tears may flow," adds Roz. "And that's just fine." She smiles. "When I recalled the deaths of my mother and sister, tears were pouring out of my eyes the whole time. But I just kept on writing. I discovered a great deal about myself and my family as I wrote through the tears. I began to recover something I had lost a long time ago. It was wonderful."

"Let me just talk a bit more about how we can achieve this kind of wholeness and balance," I continue. "While discovering our creative side, a side many of us have never known, we may begin to recover something much greater, a part of our soul, the part that Roz is talking about."

Writing from Within: The Language of Intimacy

"Writing from within" is the act of exploring vivid moments in our lives from the point of view of the age at which we experienced them, and then writing those moments with an intimacy of emotional detail that balances the outer world of actions, relationships, and events with the inner world of thoughts and feelings.

Little by little, we will find "writing from within" to be a process that will take us into the center of our own universe, propelling us through time and space toward an experience of ourselves that brings the past into the present, allowing us to see ourselves in a multitude of ways, as if we were many selves, moons circling our larger self. Exploring these old parts will help us uncover and deepen our sense of importance and worth. It will enable us to find our own authentic writing voice, to step out onto the center stage of our own lives, and to take our journey of self-discovery in an unusual direction.

Using the "writing from within" approach, we will (1) learn a process of storytelling that yields a mode for getting at the truth of our experiences, which is different from what we could accomplish using other methods; (2) learn a process for creating a story that has quality as a work of art; and (3) create a product that can be shared, savored, reviewed, and rewritten in company with others, using the feedback methods taught in this book, and that yields a clear and unexpected view of important experiences too often hidden in a cloud of numbness and self-deception.

We will also learn to look at our stories in a way that allows us to gain insight and clarification from them.

CLARIFYING WHO WE WERE AND WHAT HAPPENED

One part of the self-discovery process is seeing ourselves and our reactions to life experiences as clearly as possible. For example, if we have had a loss of some kind in our lives, such as a death in the family, it is important to see that loss clearly, to understand what that loss looks and feels like, and then, perhaps, to see the patterns of behavior we use to cope with that loss.

This is not easy. Most inventories, as they are called in alcohol and drug rehabilitation programs and self-help books, look like unending pieces of sausage, narrative burdened with excessive judgments of the "shoulds" and "shouldn'ts" of life, without beginning, middle, or end. They often do not get very close to the actual events and the quality of the insights may not be revealing or stimulating.

In "writing from within," we choose specific moments to write about. Each story has a beginning, a climax, and an ending, so we do not have to assess more than we can handle in the course of the fifteen minutes to two hours most stories take to write. Yet in this short period of time, we are transported to another time and place, making it possible to see ourselves as we were decades ago.

RELEASING THE PAIN OF THE PAST

The numbness I mentioned earlier is only one way that we cope with emotional and psychic pain. When we have a physical wound, the tissue around it becomes raw, even infected, as red and white blood cells rage to fight off the invasion.

When we are wounded emotionally, there is a great deal of pain. We may try to anesthetize it, but unlike bodily injuries that tend to heal themselves, psychic wounds often grow if unattended. We look for ways to drain off the whirlpools of emotion long enough to enable us to go looking for the source. By seeing as clearly and fully as possible the experiences that haunt us, we are able to release ourselves from their weight and move on to handle other aspects of our lives.

For the past twenty years or so, the journal writing process has become a helpful outlet for people to release their emotions on paper without any form of criticism being leveled at them. Automatic writing, writing with the nondominant hand, and the like are other effective ways of draining off emotion while beginning the process of self-examination.

Sharing Our Experiences and Achieving Peace of Mind and Body

While the prospect of starting to write may scare us at first, we can learn to overcome our fear. As stories begin taking shape, we will see powerful feelings elicited in our readers. How immense is the satisfaction in store for us when we realize we have the power to touch others' minds and hearts. Likewise, sharing these stories unlocks for us, as writers, a greater unfolding of the experience (feelings, perceptions, more of the story), which would not take place were the story not told and shared with others. The more powerful and honest the story, the more penetrating the insights that come to us.

Deep within all of us there is a "protector" that exists to keep from us recollections it believes would be too painful for the conscious mind to bear. It acts as a kind of emotional circuit breaker in our unconscious, causing us to grow numb, to forget. Our protector keeps these events and experiences well hidden in our unconscious until it is convinced we are ready to handle them. "Writing from within," however, slips past the protective layers of "forgetting" and "selective memory."

In the fifteen years I have been doing this work, I have been fascinated by this process—bringing something hidden to the surface, facing it, and taking a giant step toward regaining a lost part of ourselves, a part of our soul that has been missing. When we do this as part of a group, it encourages us to see that what we experienced is much like what others have experienced: we are not alone.

However, when we get together in writing groups, we do not spend our time discussing the psychology of what has taken place in our lives—the motivations, causes, and the like. For the writer's protection, we, the listeners, only discuss our "feeling" responses to the writing. Guidelines are established about what is OK and what is not OK. In this way, we, as writers, are protected from intrusive scrutiny and from criticism of our work or the way we handled our experience. The sharing process, as outlined in the book, is positive and supportive as we continue to dig in the sands of life experience for the truth of what happened to us in the past.

When we write a story and dig for its truth, the characters come alive. Our thoughts and feelings are out there on paper as the listeners hang on the edges of their chairs to learn what happens to these people they have come to know intimately. There is a great satisfaction in this. Our greatest pain becomes a substantial asset.

USING "WRITING FROM WITHIN" AS A METAPHOR FOR MOVING TOWARD WHOLENESS

As a graduate student at the University of Michigan more than thirty-five years ago, I was introduced to a wonderful concept the fifth-century Greeks had for creating and maintaining a balance among the various parts of the self as well as the universe surrounding the self. This concept, *kalokagathia,* has stayed with me. I raised my two sons with it in the back of my mind—creating and maintaining a harmony among mind, body, and soul.

We might say that the *kalokagathia* of a good story is the harmonizing of three fundamental elements: narrative, dialogue, and inner thoughts and feelings. *Narrative* is the unfolding of events in the world through time; *dialogue* is the path by which we find and explore relationships among people (including ourselves) within that world; and *inner thoughts and feelings* are our deepest selves, as writers, made visible to others, giving us a sense that we are completely present in this universe of relationships and unfolding time. As we allow narrative, relationships, and inward-searching energies of our own thoughts and feelings to unfold and find a balance within each story, we also bring into balance our own life energies. In this act of writing and balancing, we reinvent ourselves. We discover our *kalokagathia,* our balance, of mind, body, and soul.

This balancing is not as easy as we might wish. After all, the world may be a stage upon which we are the players, as Shakespeare said four hundred years ago, but for a great many of us taking center stage is quite frightening. Our minds will distort recollections so that our fears are softened, our pain is pushed away, our anxieties are lessened. All of this is reflected in the way we write our stories, at least in the beginning. Some of us will relate a story and leave out all sense of relationship of the people involved and without including ourselves, as writers, in the picture. Others of us will write vivid dialogue but without a sense of a story unfolding. Still others of us will dwell so deeply inside our world of inner thoughts and feelings that we will appear to have little sense of relationship to the outer world or to the people in it.

These "unbalanced" ways of writing create distance between ourselves and the event and our audience, protecting us from the emotion of reliving the experience and the possible criticisms of our audience. They relieve us from taking center stage in our lives, from reclaiming our feelings, and from gaining the spotlight that we deserve, but of which we are so afraid.

Each step of the "writing from within" process will soften our fears and help us see and overcome the ways we create distance between ourselves and life around us, both as we live our lives and as we re-create it in our stories. Each step assists us in writing a more vivid story, but also helps us move past anger and rage, hurt and numbness, confusion and forgetting, past the need to keep life at arm's length. As we begin to use these steps over and over from one story to the next or from one draft of a story to the next, our memories will begin to yield different versions of each event. We will begin to persuade our unconscious that we are serious about learning what really happened way back when, and rewriting becomes our primary tool for searching out more and more of the truth.

This process of learning to use "writing from within" to create a more vivid story and to rewrite our stories to uncover more and more of the truth lures our energies away from our self-critic and toward our creator. We thus have an opportunity to discover a great deal about ourselves as we hold up the mirror of the ever-deepening story, asking, "Who am I in the mirror of this story?"

As we learn how to use the process of rewriting our stories to nudge to the surface more and more truths about events in our pasts, we set the stage for us to see life events with ever-more-innocent and inward-looking understanding and to value ever more deeply the profound dimensions of our own creativity.

CHAPTER 1

Overcoming Fear

To tell one's life stories, to explore the sad/happy, exciting/boring, fascinating/fearful experiences of one's long life, seems like a wonderful idea. But how many wonderful ideas have we had in our lives that never became anything more than ideas? Quite a few? What stopped them from becoming reality? Probably lack of motivation, or fear, or both.

If the idea of writing your life story strikes a chord within you, sets off a bell, causes you to salivate—or fills you with unspeakable dread— then you are ready to write your story. What is holding you back is not lack of motivation, but fear. Stark, naked fear.

Fear of what? Fear of being unable to write well and being criticized by friends and relatives? Fear of being unable to finish, of getting off the track? Fear that you might say too much and embarrass someone? Fear that you may dig up old, painful "stuff" that you can't handle? Fear that you just don't have what it takes to write well?

Research into the way the brain operates has revealed that there are two sides to the brain, left and right. Much of our fear of writing comes from the way these two sides do or don't work together.

We might term the right brain "the creator," for apparently it allows us to do creative things—make connections, manifest ideas, imagine situations, see pictures of events. The left side analyzes, categorizes, recalls words, and performs its learning functions in a step-by-step manner.

For our purposes, what is important to know is that the analytic left brain has a little attic on top that houses the "critic." He or she is the person in us who says, "Watch out! You can't do that! You'll fail, so don't even try. You know you're no good at that!"

Perhaps you would be right if you said the critic sounds a lot like dear old Mom or Dad: "If I've told you once, I've told you a thousand times, you may not do (something you really want to do) until you carry out the garbage"—or clean your room, wash the dishes, get good grades, and so on. Sound familiar? Believe me, I know. I, too, am a parent . . . and remember being a child.

Parents are great, but they do tend to be critical. They are our guides in the world, but too often they do more than guide us. They tell us not to do certain things, and we become afraid to do them.

Our critic becomes a problem for us when we want to create something out of nothing—say a story or a painting—because the right brain, in which our creator stirs every now and then, is very tender, very sensitive to criticism. So if our left-side, tough-minded, parent-critic brain says, "Forget it! You can't do it," our right-side, tender-minded creator says, "Fine! I'm going back to sleep. Talk to me in a few weeks."

And so our deep desire to create—in this case, to write our life's stories—gets buried once again.

How do we counteract the critic? We calm him. We stroke him. When he emerges, we become aware of his presence but we do not fight him. We can enjoy his antics, be amused by his swordplay as he cuts away at our confidence, but we must keep out of range of that slashing saber. And we must avoid a confrontational stance. "What do you mean, I can't do it! I can so!" To the critic, that is merely a call to arms. On the other hand, a flexible stance—something like "You'll be surprised what I can do" or "I've been doing pretty well, so I think I'll keep on creating, even if it seems hard"—will deflect the critic's thrusts and keep our creative juices flowing. So enjoy the critic, be amused by him, but don't try to duel with him. He will actually be valuable at a later stage when he is calmer and able to look at your work objectively, suggesting ways and means of changing and expanding it.

We human beings have an almost infinite variety of ways to censor ourselves. Fear not only keeps us from writing, it inhibits us from letting the world see our work when it is done. We tend to be very hard on ourselves as writers. In fact, some very good work may be lost because of our pessimism.

Following is a fine story that the writer had tossed in the garbage. The writer revealed what he had done, and the class responded by insisting that he resurrect the story and bring it in. Here it is, complete with stains from coffee grounds and fried eggs.

My Friend Jake
by David Yavitts

From a small town in eastern Russia, our family arrived in the Midwest of the United States, in St. Paul, Minnesota, a short distance from the banks of the Mississippi River.

Our house was on two and a half acres, partly in a hollow. The front of the house, that is, the parlor, living room and dining room, were on street level. The kitchen and bedroom were on the hollow portion, held up by posts.

It was there that life for me began in this country. In the next couple of years, we had acquired a cow, horse, chickens and ducks. My responsibility was the ducks, keeping their quarters clean and feeding them.

I became very fond of them, gave them names and learned to recognize them by color and size. My favorite duck I called Jake, because we got that particular duck from our neighbor Jake's farm.

As I spoke the English language poorly, I did not have any friends, and I adopted Jake as my friend and confidant. He listened to me and would cock his head and did not move until I was through speaking. He would always wait for a while.

Jake grew faster than the other ducks and his feathers, especially around his neck, were a ring of black. The rest was white.

That winter the ducks became full grown and plump. In the spring, I was assisting my mother in cleaning the stovepipes. They were full of soot and as I removed the soot much of the black powder made my face and hands black.

DAVID YAVITTS   David, who is in his eighties now, grew up along the Mississippi River. His fondest childhood memories are of the rough and bawdy riverfront life of the early 1900s. David was a professional gambler for a time aboard the riverboats that plied the river.

It was time to feed the ducks and I couldn't find Jake, my duck. I looked everywhere and called him. There wasn't any response. I finally went into the house; my mother was at the stove baking what she said was a chicken. I explained to her that Jake, my duck, was lost and that I couldn't find him. My mother told me, if the duck was lost she would get me another one—not to worry!

At this point, my older sister came in the kitchen and said, "Is the duck done yet?"

The sky fell down and I shouted, "That's Jake!" They could not pacify me. I cried and told them they were mean and bad to kill Jake and I ran out of the house, saying I didn't want to live there any more. I said I was going to my uncle's house across the bridge, over the river.

They didn't believe it, but I started my journey.

I knew where the bridge was; I could see it from my home and headed in that direction. Here was a dirty-faced kid about three and a half who cried as he walked toward the bridge. In my mind, I knew my soft-hearted uncle would solve my problems.

Well, I didn't get very far on the bridge when I was stopped by a policeman who asked, "Where are you going, young man?"

He repeated that question many times. I did not understand too well. I spoke Yiddish and that soft-hearted Irish policeman spoke English with a brogue. He took me to the police station. There, an officer who understood me got my story, figured out where I lived, left me at the station and eventually called my mother. She got my older sister out of the classroom at school and sent her to the station. My sister thought she would have to bail me out. There I was, my sister said, sitting on a table with an ice cream cone in my hand and crying. The tears ran down my face, washing the black soot off in white streaks. The ice cream washed my lips. I was a sight! My mother said, "Come home, dinner is waiting."

I said, "Mother, I don't eat duck!"

— • • • —

Having read the story, we can see that it is complete and effective. The details and observations are sharp; the dialogue is appropriate. It has a beginning, a middle, and an end; it is personal and deeply felt. Yet, despite its obvious excellence, the writer had dumped it in the trash. Imagine what would have happened, not only to the story but also to the man's future as a writer, had the class not insisted that he retrieve it.

Once we understand how our left-brain critic operates, we can begin to work on our memoirs, knowing that we can defuse our fears by identifying the pressure of the critic when he appears.

You may say, "I don't really have any fear and I don't think I have much of a critic." That's wonderful. But let's give ourselves a little test in order to find out. Let's suppose we've been given a writing task and have about a paragraph written. Myself, I am inclined to stop at this point and review what I've written. What about you? Do you go on? Or do you keep working on your first paragraph until you feel it is "correct"? In the next chapter, we will see what the answer to this question tells us about ourselves and our critic. We will also begin to work on our first life story.

CHAPTER 2

Finding Your
Earliest Memories

"So, Bernard, let me ask you a question." Dave Schwartz has a thoughtful look on his face as we walk into the conference room at the Musicians Union.

"Sure, Dave, what is it?" I reply as we settle into our chairs.

"As you know, I want to write the stories of my experiences playing viola with Toscanini and the NBC Orchestra as well as the Glenn Miller Army Orchestra and the Paganini String Quartet."

"Yes?"

"Well, you mentioned that it is important to start with early memories of our lives," Dave continues. "But I want to write about things that happened to me from the time I left the Curtis Institute when I was twenty."

"First of all, writing early memories is important in the same way that every musician has to learn *Twinkle, Twinkle, Little Star* before he can tackle Bach, Beethoven, or Brahms."

"I see. Well, that makes sense," Dave replies with some uncertainty in his voice.

"But," I add, "there are other, equally important reasons, one of which is that in writing early memories we have a chance to see what the world was like from the point of view of a child, which is the place where we begin the search for our own artistic voice."

The other members of the class are listening, so I continue. "Your earliest memory is a good place to begin writing because it is something you see in your mind's eye, but it is not too complex to describe. It will probably be a fragment of something, a piece of a picture. That is just fine. It doesn't have to be a story. Even a few lines will do.

"You may be surprised how interesting, revealing, and important that little fragment really is. One of my students had been told all her life that she had hit her baby sister over the head with her bottle. What a traumatic memory to live with! But when she went way back to the incident, she recalled hitting the bottle on the side of the crib, and the bottle breaking and then hitting her sister. Suddenly, she was relieved of a guilt that had haunted her all her life, and the relief was wonderful!

"Earliest memories are often dramatic—a birth or death in the family, leaving or arriving at someplace special, a medical emergency. Sometimes, though, they can be as simple as remembering a shiny thing that hung over your crib. No matter how simple, write down what you see in your mind. Just that. Nothing more."

Getting Ready to Write

First, find a journal or notebook that you will feel comfortable writing in. I suggest using a standard-size notebook (8½ by 11 inches) so that you don't feel cramped. Even if you plan to do most of your writing on a computer or typewriter, you may find that at times you will feel more relaxed writing the old-fashioned way, so having a journal on hand is still a good idea. Then, before you actually set pen to paper, take time to consider the following things.

RELAX YOURSELF

Even if your mind is racing with solve-me-now problems, your childhood memories are not very happy ones, and your youthful writing experiences were also unpleasant, you can relax into writing. Here are a few tips.

CREATE A BACKWARD-LOOKING CEREMONY. Don a favorite shirt or dress from twenty or forty years ago; reread a beloved novel from childhood; cook a meal from childhood (French toast for me); revisit a beloved place from long ago (Maine, in my case); talk to friends and relatives from years past; or gather pictures that bring back the happy memories of earlier times (railroads, particularly narrow-gauge ones, do it for me).

CHOOSE A COMFORTABLE PLACE AND TIME IN WHICH TO WORK. Find a quiet, comfortable place in which you can work undisturbed (although European writers often prefer outdoor cafés, where the noise seems to be strangely comforting); something relaxing in which to sit—a bed or a chair; and a place where the light is adequate and not distracting. It is equally important to find the right time to write. Our brains often whirl with problems to be solved; we need to find a time when we can put problems aside. For many people, sometime between eight in the evening and noon the next day is the best time to do this. Our right-brain creativity is most at work during these hours, whereas during the afternoon our left-brain, analytical, problem-solving energies are at their peak. So, if you don't feel like writing in the afternoon, don't force it.

GET OUT OF TOWN. If you are willing to invest the time, energy, and money to get a good start on this project, reserve a room for yourself at a quiet bed and breakfast in a peaceful town well away from the care and concerns of everyday life, or go visit a childhood haunt. (As I write this, I'm sitting at a table in my cabin beside a pond in southern Maine looking out over the water.)

EMBRACE YOUR IMPERFECTION. Remind yourself that your writing does not have to be perfect. It is a part of a process to be learned. Fears are natural, and overcoming them is possible. (I used to believe that improvising a jazz solo, like writing, was something God-given and useless to try to learn. Twenty years of studying music and putting words and pictures on paper have taught me otherwise.)

PUMP YOURSELF UP. Create an image of yourself as a knight in shining armor poised to seek adventure, like Lancelot and Percival or Joan of Arc going out into the world to do battle with their fears.

DRIFT OFF. Perhaps you find yourself growing sleepy. You resist the urge, battling it for ten or fifteen minutes until finally you fall asleep. You awaken some time later feeling depressed; you have let yourself down. But you really have not. The next time the urge to sleep strikes you, give in to it. It's OK. It is your brain's way of switching from the everyday, problem-solving, left-brain mode to the creative, right-brain mode.

CALM YOUR MIND. Close your eyes, take a deep breath, exhale, do it again . . . and again. Listen to your breathing. This technique is used by professional athletes—tennis players waiting to receive serves, batters standing at the plate waiting for the pitch—to relax and focus at the same time.

RETURN TO THE PAST

Use your daydream or reverie to channel your thoughts back toward the deep past. Now that you are comfortable and relaxed, and perhaps semi-sleepy, allow your mind to float back in time, way back to your first memory. It really doesn't matter whether you were three months old or three years old. It doesn't matter if it is not a story. It may be just a fragment of a picture. That is fine, as long as you see something.

Composing

Composing is the first phase of writing your life stories, and it involves the following elements.

START WRITING AND KEEP ON WRITING

Once you have begun your story, keep writing. Resist the urge to go back and make that first paragraph perfect. That urge is your critic speaking. Just plunge on. Don't stop.

WRITE FROM A CHILD'S POINT OF VIEW

Write down what you have just seen in your mind's eye from the point of view of the baby or child you once were. If you were in a crib, the reader would expect to see a bit of the crib and perhaps Momma and Poppa staring down at you. Create a strong and vivid picture of what you see: the place where the event is occurring, the sounds and smells around you, and the atmosphere of the scene. It is important to record all these details. Seeing the world through the eyes of a child, when the world was new and fresh, makes fascinating reading.

Here are some topics that may trigger your earliest memories:

- My earliest happy experience

- My earliest sad or shocking experience

- My first experience with a birth in the family

- My first experience with a death in the family

- My first day in school or the first day I remember in school

- My first experience of being all alone without Mommy or Daddy

- My first experience in the hospital—tonsils out, or illness

- My first experience eating, or playing, or riding on a train or a bus, and so on

At this point, we are ready to write. To make this easier, I will give you a little prompt to follow so that your self-critic—the urge not to write—will recede into the background. If, however, you would prefer to take a more step-by-step approach to this writing moment, please turn to the "Exercise" section at the end of this chapter. After you have completed that, you may wish to return to study the material in between. Following is your first writing prompt:

I know what to do, so it is time to do it. I am ready to begin. I am in a favorite, comfortable place. There are no distractions. It is quiet outside and in. There are important objects around me and I may even be a bit sleepy. My mind begins to drift back, way back. I am very relaxed. I am beginning to see the first thing that I remember. I am going to write it . . . <u>now</u>.

Reviewing

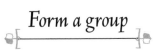

Form a group

Working with a group of friends or acquaintances who are also interested in writing their life stories is very desirable for several reasons. Reading your memoirs aloud to a group will tell you whether your stories are coming across well or not. It is also fun to share remembrances with friends, and often someone else's stories will remind you about similar experiences of your own. Another benefit is that sharing stories with friends who are also interested in writing is less intimidating—everyone knows that his or her writing will be reviewed.

Having found your earliest memory and written a first draft of it, you have completed the initial writing phase. The next phase is to review what you have done to see how your work comes across to a listener or reader. Like composing, the reviewing phase has several steps.

RESIST THE URGE TO MAKE CHANGES

The urge to make big changes and to be critical is always strong at this point. ("It can't be any good—I better change it.") Resist that temptation. Read over the story and make only a few corrections, such as cleaning up grammar and spelling. What you need most at this point is some feedback about the quality and effectiveness of what you have written.

GET FEEDBACK

Writing is 50 percent self-expression and 50 percent finding out what the audience needs to know. At this point, you need some responses from friends about what you have written. It's rather scary to ask for reactions, but it will turn out OK. My own preference is to have a group of like-minded people review it. Friends and relatives may be either too critical or too patronizing, and neither of these attitudes is helpful for a beginning writer. So find a friend and read it aloud to him or her. (See the appendix "Developing Supportive Feedback" for assistance on how to do this.)

WRITE VISUALLY AND FOR IMPACT

Ask those who listen to your stories two things: Are the stories visual (can they *see* them clearly in their minds)? Do they have an emotional impact (what do the listeners *feel* as they listen to them)? If a story has impact, listeners will often tell you it reminded them of a similar time in their own lives. This is a very good sign.

Rewriting

We are now at the final phase of putting together your first memoir: rewriting. The first phase, composing, frees you up to get your story on paper without stopping, that is, without letting the critic grab hold of you and drag you back to redo that first paragraph, as so often happens. The second phase, reviewing, helps you to get some objective feedback about your work by having a friend or group listen and respond to it. In the final phase, rewriting, you will learn how to make your story more vivid and substantially clearer to the reader, while deepening its impact.

Later we will explore rewriting more thoroughly, but this first memoir needs only a bit of tinkering to make it work. It is, after all, just a moment from your childhood, probably not even a complete story. Like a pianist learning to play the scales, a note at a time, your present task is only to make this moment dramatic and believable.

Following are some guidelines to keep in mind when rewriting your first memoir.

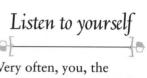

Listen to yourself

Very often, you, the writer, will respond to listeners' comments, both positive and negative, by mentioning incidents, colors, objects, observations, and reflections that you consciously or unconsciously left out. This is almost always vital information that needs to be in the story. So listen to yourself in class or with your friends, and flesh out the story with this information.

Write in the present tense

In the rewriting phase of our work, we can explore using the present tense (using "is," not "was"), which gives the reader a wonderful sense of being present at or in the event. When we read a story written in the present tense, the events seem to be happening now; they seem to be happening around us rather than far away as if recollected through a tunnel. Small details suddenly become clearer and more vivid in our memories when we write in the present tense.

A child knows only what is directly in front of its eyes. Therefore, we believe a story written from a child's point of view more easily if it is written in the present tense. We may lose some information, but we gain a great deal in dramatic impact and believability.

Writing in the present tense is not easy for some of us. We have been accustomed to writing in the past tense for so long, we can hardly conceive of another way. It also forces us to use our imagination. An additional advantage is that writing in the present tense somehow puts our critic to rest for a while. We get out of our reflective, all-knowing, critical adult self and into a seeing, feeling, more innocent self.

If you can use the present tense, do. If you are not comfortable with it at first, keep writing your stories in the past tense. Then, from time to time, experiment with the present tense. Just change all the past tense verbs to present tense: "I walked" becomes "I walk" or "I am walking."

Write in the first person

Some of us find writing in the first person ("I was/am" rather than "he was/is" or "we were/are") troublesome. Many of us were taught in school that it is self-centered to say "I." This makes it a bit difficult to write one's life story.

In one of my classes, a tall, burly ex-Marine named Joe Page begins reading:

> Joe P. got on his wagon and went down the hill really fast and then Joe P. nearly bumped a lady crossing the street. Joe rolled the wagon on its side. Joe really hurt himself.

"Joe," I say, after he has finished, "how long have you been out of the Marine Corps?"

He gazes at me for several seconds with his sad, tired eyes. "'Bout thirty-five years," he answers in a soft voice.

I glance around the room. The fifteen other members of the class, all women, are very quiet. "Well, Joe," I say, "It's OK to say 'I.'"

"You ever been in the service?" he asks, eyeing me closely. I nod. "Then you know." He pauses for a long moment. "When 'a first went in, 'bout 1926, my first sergeant, he says to me, 'You boys ain't people no more, you're part of the Corps. It's 'we' and 'us' and 'the Corps,' hear? I catch any you sayin' 'I' this or 'I' that, I'll bust your a___. So don't let me hear that d____ word from any ya!!'"

"It's another time and another place, Joe," I say. "It's OK to say 'I.' Try it."

He nods, looking down at the page in front of him. "Mmm . . . mmm . . ." he stammers, wiping his face with a large red handkerchief. "Mmm got in the wagon and went down the hill." He glances up at me for an instant, then goes back to reading. "I got in my wagon and went down the hill," he mutters. His eyes meet mine for a moment, a hint of a grin on his face. "I nearly hit a lady and I turned my wagon over on its side . . . and I fell out."

Joe looks at me, then at the others in the class. The silence turns into relaxed, amiable chatter. "I know just how you feel, Joe," says one lady, touching his sleeve. "I was raised the same way." Many of the others nod in agreement.

WRITE FROM A CHILD'S POINT OF VIEW

Writing from a child's point of view—stripping your story of adult language—is perhaps the most important consideration for this early story. Be sure your memoir sounds as if it were experienced by a child.

You are probably asking, "How in the world can I write as a child would when I'm not a child? Shouldn't I just write as an adult looking back?"

The answer is no. You may not be able to write exactly as a child would, but you can *avoid certain writing patterns that mark the passages as those of an adult.* You are, after all, trying to recapture the world as seen through a child's eyes. *Avoid using vocabulary, diction, and phrasing that a child could not possibly use.* Consider the following passage:

There were times, I suppose, when it seemed as if one would never be permitted to mature at a pace which was reasonable for my age. No, I was forced, albeit in a kindly fashion, to repeat *ad nauseam* the chores and duties attendant upon childhood: taking out the garbage, playing sports, minding my manners, and obeying the strictures of my parents.

No one reading this passage would suppose for a moment that a child had written it. Why? Because children don't talk or write that way. Let us look at specific parts of this passage to see what is unchildlike about it.

VOCABULARY AND PHRASING: "permitted to mature," "reasonable for my age," "ad nauseam," "attendant upon" are all phrases no child, other than one attending college at a remarkably early age, would ever use.

QUALIFICATIONS: Statements that are qualified or modified are virtually never used by children. "I suppose" is a qualification, as is "albeit in a kindly fashion."

THE OBJECTIVE VOICE: "One" is the objective voice and is virtually never used by children.

LISTS: Cataloging chores and the like in an orderly manner is an adult way of organizing. Children may do it, but they are less orderly and logical.

Now, let us look at the passage after rewriting it in a way that may not be childlike but at least is not obviously adult.

From the time I was six or seven until I was eleven, my dad insisted that I take out the garbage every Thursday. What a chore that was! It seemed as if he'd never give me any real responsibility, just chores. But I remember one time when he . . .

Here you have a voice that could be adult or child. The passage is simple, straightforward, and visual. The narrator's voice and point of view do not intrude on the action or the progress of the story.

Let's take another look at the garbage incident, now written in the present tense:

I am twelve years old. Dad makes me take out the garbage every day. Yuk. Every day for six years. *When do I get a chance to do something important?* I wonder.

Suddenly, the story is more intimate, more vivid, more personal. This is a direction for us to explore.

In the first and second drafts of the story below, you can see the differences between a childhood story and a rewrite told exclusively from a child's point of view.

Willem ——— FIRST DRAFT ———
by Jade

I have no recollection of the first years of my life. Looking way back into my early childhood, I come up with this little picture, a picture that has surfaced every once in a while whenever I am thinking of the old days.

I must have been three or four. There was a big sprawling backyard. A tall hedge concealed the main house, some distance away. The house was quiet; my mother must be resting. It was siesta time, the time after lunch when the shimmering tropical heat made people drowsy. It was also Sunday, the drone of my father's machines was not there. My father must also be resting. My father had a house-industry at that time. He bought up spices such as pepper, nutmeg, cloves, cinnamon, etc., from the farmers overseas on the other island, then he ground and bottled them in a special building on the grounds. To assist him he asked Willem to come over from his hometown on a far island to work as his foreman. Willem also lived with us in an outhouse.

I liked Willem, because he always spent time with us, whenever there was a chance. That afternoon was no exception. He showed my

JADE   Jade (a pseudonym) grew up on a Borneo rubber plantation in the years before World War II. She came to the United States in the 1960s. She is married and a mother, and she came to life story writing to "review her life and leave something for the grandchildren."

brother and me some magic tricks and then he said, "Kids, I am going to show you how strong I am!" He asked Joni, another workman, to go fetch the bicycle. Then he lay down on the grass and Joni was told to drive over his chest. I was greatly impressed when Willem stood up unhurt. Then he said, "And now the van will drive over me." Again he lay down on the thick grass and supposedly the car drove over him. I was in awe that nothing happened to Willem. This was where I got befuddled. I am sure I had not told my mother then and there, because she would have taken some action regarding Willem's way of entertaining us and she would have remembered the incident. As it was, when years later I talked about it, my mother said, "Nonsense, he must have tricked you." But I still wonder, did it really happen or was it just my imagination?

• • •

After hearing the story, members of the class suggested that the writer simplify the vocabulary and tell the story exclusively from the child's point of view, letting go of the inclination to set the stage, which takes the reader out of the child's experience. We also suggested she write the story in the present tense. Here is the result.

Willem ———— SECOND DRAFT ————

I am sitting in the grass. The grass is cool and green and very thick and soft; I sink in it. I like to sit there. The sun is very bright, but the hedge behind me makes a shade.

My brother is there, too. He is bigger than I. Papa and Mama are not there. I know they are in the house a little far away behind the hedge. But Willem is there. He is very big, almost as big as Papa. I like him. He always has something nice for me and my brother.

What will he do today? He is lying in the grass. There is also Joni. I do not know him too well, but he does not matter. Willem is there!

Willem is saying: *"Anak mau lihat Willem digiling sepeda?"* ("Kids, want to see the bike run over me?") Joni already goes to fetch the bicycle. There he comes—straight at Willem lying in the grass. Then the bicycle is already on the other side of Willem and Willem is standing up and laughing. He laughs at us kids. And then, with a laugh in his eye, he tells us, Papa's big truck will now run over his chest. Again he lies down in the thick grass—the car comes and it is over him—only his head sticks out—he is laughing at us. I hide my head. I am afraid and I grab my brother's hand. But I still look. Willem is already up again. Willem can do anything!!!

Years later when I talked about it, my mother said, "Nonsense, he must have tricked you." But I still wonder, did it really happen?

— • • • —

This rewrite of "Willem" is a much simpler story than the first version, isn't it? This version gives us the feeling of being "in" the event rather than of watching it from a distance. In fact, we feel as if the event is happening to us, as if we are the child watching the truck go over Willem, wondering how such an awesome thing can happen.

An approach that works well if you have a group around you is to tell your earliest memory aloud, then tell it again, consistently using the present tense. Notice how you suddenly remember more of the incident. Then write the incident down on paper.

If you find yourself avoiding "I," perhaps by saying "We did such and such," remember: the days of your being unimportant are over. You are at the center of your autobiography. You may report what others are doing, but you are the person through whose eyes and ears we, the readers, experience the event. You are important. It is another time and place. It is OK to say "I."

If, at the end of your memory or subsequent early memories, you would like to add some background information or some of your present adult feelings about what happened back then, do so. But keep the adult reflection on the event distinct from the child's point of view. Jade's last line, "Years later when I talked about it, my mother said . . . but I still wonder," is a good example of including an adult reflection while keeping it distinct from the child's experience.

In successive stories we will continue to write from the child's point of view, although as we begin to write our more recent stories, we naturally know more of past and present and can set the stage more fully.

Please see Eddie White's story "Blind Lemon Jefferson Sings the Blues" (page 215) as an example of a powerful memory seen from a child's point of view.

Exercise

PART 1: MY EARLIEST MEMORY

STEP 1: Think of the first thing you remember when you were really young. Do you have a picture of it in your mind, perhaps just a very vague picture? Picture it even if it is just a fragment.

If you are having trouble remembering an early, early memory, turn back to the topics list on page 27 to jog your memory.

Now, if you are working in a group, tell your story out loud to the others.

STEP 2: Write it down. Begin your story now. Start with "I was ___ years old." Tell your story in the *past tense*.

PART 2: MY EARLIEST MEMORY (FIRST REWRITE)

STEP 1: Once again, tell about the first thing you remember. Tell it out loud to your group or to a friend or a family member, and this time in the *present* tense ("I am," not "I was"; "I remember," not "I remembered"; "I do," not "I did").

STEP 2: Think about what differences you feel when you tell your memory in the present tense rather than in the past tense.

STEP 3: Now *write down* what you remember of your earliest memory. Write the story in the *present tense,* beginning with "I am . . . " (giving your age when the moment happened to you).

Here is an example:

> I am four years old and I am learning to tie my shoe. I keep trying. I have finally done it. Now, I can go tell my mom I've learned to tie my shoe.

You can see from this example that your first memory does not have to be lengthy. It can be very short and still be a good place to begin.

Now that you have finished writing your earliest memory, you have done what every writer does: composed, reviewed, and rewritten. These are the same three steps you will follow with every story you write. As you write your earliest memories, you will find that even earlier incidents and experiences will come to mind. The process of putting pen to paper seems to call up memories. Write these as soon as they become vivid and significant. Many life experiences block feelings. Writing unblocks these feelings and allows you to move ahead, free and unencumbered.

CHAPTER 3

Uncovering Your Most
Vivid Childhood Memories

"You know, Bernard," chuckles Eddie White as the Musicians Union class draws to a close one afternoon. "I just have no idea what story to write next. After all, a lot has happened in my seventy-five years."

"Oh, you'll learn," smiles Roz.

"What would you tell him, Roz?" I ask.

"Search out a memory between the time you were born and when you were about twelve years old." She turns to Eddie with a grin. "A memory that's really vivid. Find the climax to it, then begin the story just before the climax."

"Very good, Roz," I reply, tongue in cheek. "You remembered."

"This is my seventh year," she chuckles.

I turn to the other members of the class. "Remember, almost everything we write is a story of relationship—you to your parents, you to your loved ones. Pick out the relationships that remain vivid in your mind, whether they were happy and loving or not."

Composing

WARM UP BY WRITING

Begin composing by following the steps that were outlined in Chapter 2, directing your mind back toward your earliest *vivid* memory, one that truly stands out in your mind.

This new vivid memory should not be confused with your earliest memory, which may simply be a tiny fragment of a recollection, like some archaeological relic from a prehistoric time. Now we are looking for an early memory that has power, a memory that is very strong.

Up to now, I have suggested you begin the story with, "I am ___ years old and I am . . ." Many of you will tire of this beginning before long, and well you should. "Where *should* I begin?" you ask. A good method is to establish what the climax of the story is, and then begin just a little before the climax.

"What about background information and setting the stage?" you ask. "Isn't that important?"

Setting the stage is less important than you may think, and background information, or *backstory,* can be provided in the second paragraph of a story. What is important now is that you begin the story and then build momentum.

The details are coming back to you. You are *warming up.* That is, you are doing what every artist must do: musicians play scales, actors do voice and facial exercises, writers write. You work your way into the story, establish where the events are taking place, who is there, and who you are in the story. We are not worried about crafting the beginning of the story, only about building momentum. After all, the best way of handling your self-critic—who is saying *you can't do this, you shouldn't do this*—is to pick up the pen, or sit down at the computer, and begin. Later, we will find out how to establish the beginning of the story from the material that you have created as a warm-up.

Here are a number of "firsts" that may bring to mind some of the vivid moments of your life between, say, two and twelve years old:

- My most vivid memory of Mom or Dad

- My most embarrassing moment in school

- My first adventure

- My first time being really afraid

- My first success in school

- My most vivid recollection of Grandpa or Grandma

- My first kiss

- My first time getting into trouble

- My happiest time in school

- My best friend in school

If you wish to take a step-by-step approach to writing and rewriting, turn to the "Exercise" section at the end of this chapter.

• • •

*I am ready to return now to my storehouse of childhood memories. I am sitting in the right chair . . . the music may be playing . . . perhaps there is a fire in the fireplace . . . I am ready to return to the time tunnel. Back I go . . . to a distant moment in time, keeping details in view, searching out lost ones . . . stripping away the wrapping around my memories until I can see the moment clearly. I am ready to write . . . **now**.*

• • •

Write down everything you saw and experienced, all at once. Don't stop, even if the pieces are disconnected. Don't stop, even if the memory makes you want to cry. If you begin crying, cry. But keep writing.

Now, how does the story read? Is it one story or fragments? Are the details sharper than in your first memoir? Are the feelings stronger? If you have written a series of fragments, would you like to fill in the gaps? If not, OK; go ahead and take this memoir to your group or chosen friend. Read it aloud and listen carefully to each response.

Reviewing

During this second phase, we will learn more about what to look for when evaluating our own writing. I will also talk about how to listen and offer helpful critiques when other people read their stories to us.

Let us begin with a checklist of the first steps in reviewing:

- Resist the urge to change, to be too critical.

- Get feedback: go to a friend or group to get responses.

- Ask if the work is visual and emotion-producing.

- Listen to your own comments to see if something was left out.

- Express your stories as experiences seen from a child's point of view.

Let's go into some of these concerns a bit more thoroughly. It is very important for a story to have an emotional impact on the reader. So the first thing to do is to add your feelings to each story. From there, you can enhance the visual clarity of the story by focusing on actions, by bringing the story closer to the reader with appropriate dialogue, by focusing on one incident at a time, and by listening carefully to feedback from the group and from yourself.

ADD YOUR FEELINGS

One of the first things you can do to make your stories more vivid is to incorporate your feelings. "I am nervous," "I am sad," and "I am excited" are the kinds of feelings that will make a story more interesting. They glue the reader to the page: through feelings, the reader connects to the writer's experience.

What you need to remember is that feelings—our feelings (that is, the feelings of the narrator) and those of the characters—have to be added *to each moment* of the story. It's not enough to mention a feeling at the beginning of the story and another at the end. That's not really adding feelings to the story—it's more like showcasing a feeling just to make your teacher happy. So, come on, add feelings each moment of the way.

> I am walking down the road to my house. I know Papa will be angry when he sees my report card. I'm a little nervous *(narrator's feelings)*. As I get closer, I see him on the porch of our farmhouse. He has his arms crossed over his chest. Oh, oh. He's mad *(other character's feelings)*.

In the course of teaching life writing for more than fifteen years, I've noticed what great difficulty men have in writing down their feelings. It's not that we men don't have feelings. More likely, it's a matter of us not being aware of our feelings even as we are possessed by them. After all, we are human and we do have feelings.

If you are a man, you may have to work on becoming aware of your feelings and making sure they are in each story. You can start by simply adding feelings in a mechanical way.

> He has his arms crossed over his chest. Oh, oh—he's mad. Now I'm really scared.

If you add feelings mechanically, you will reach a point where you will be able to unearth your real feelings, even the more painful emotions, without a lot of difficulty.

In Chapter 5, we will explore this question in more depth: How do we get our feelings into the story as fully as possible?

Create vivid details

The first objective in writing good narratives is to make the events visible. The easiest way to do this is to bring the events into sharp focus by including little details that make the picture unique. Look at the following passage from "Uncle Eli" by Rose Rothenberg, the complete version of which appeared in the second edition of *Writing from Within*.

> Uncle Eli is a dapper man and extremely meticulous about his person. His shirts are always pure white, at least until they yellow a bit with age. His dark serge suit is always well-pressed and clean. It does not yellow with the passage of time, but takes on a shine that competes with the gloss he maintains on his high-button shoes. In the summer months he sports spotless white buckskin oxfords—the same pair year after year. His straw hat is worn at a rakish angle and, rain or shine, he is never without an umbrella.

The details in this passage—the shirts "always pure white until they yellow with age," the suit that "takes on a shine," and the umbrella that is carried "rain or shine"—tell us a great deal about the man's character: his stubbornness, inflexibility, and pride in the face of changing circumstances.

Now let us look at another passage rich with revealing details. This is taken from a longer story, the complete version of which appeared in the first edition of *Writing from Within*.

Life on the Railroad ——EXCERPT——
by *Eugene Mallory*

The year was 1904. Not a good year for the overbuilt, midwestern railroads or the ever-distressed farmer either.

The Missouri Pacific Red Ball freight was two hours out on a night run west. The nearly new Baldwin 4-8-2, burning clean Colorado coal, was really showing what it could do.

Conductor William Sidel was riding the high seat in the cupola of the darkened caboose and pondering what he should do with his upside-down life in general. First as a boomer brakeman, so called because he and many other bold young men had followed the railroad expansion of the late 1800s wherever the new rails led. Always moving on to new runs, new towns.

Then a bit of luck, and a bit of the old blarney, and he had his own train on the Hampton, Algona and Western, riding the varnish, not a crummy caboose. Even if the varnish was only an old combination coach; half seats, half mail and baggage, and his little conductor cubbyhole. The coach had to be there to satisfy the franchise, and he had trundled it up and down the 90 miles of lightweight rail that was all the Hampton, Algona and Western ever amounted to. No matter that many grand names had been painted over or that the old coach was hung on the end of an untidy string of freight cars and seldom exceeded 20 miles per hour, it was varnish.

A perfect old man's job, while he was still young, had perhaps made him old in too few years. God forbid!

But why was he uneasy on this perfect prairie night? True, when he had totaled his manifests, the weight of this train had shocked

EUGENE MALLORY   Gene was born in Iowa on a farm near a town hard-hit during the Depression. He has always loved writing, and traces his forebears back to Sir Thomas Mallory. Eventually, Gene moved to Los Angeles, where he worked for North American Rockwell.

him, and now his certified reliable watch said they had covered 40 miles of track in the last hour. Things had changed while he had vegetated on the "branch."

● ● ●

The phrase "riding the high seat in the cupola of the darkened caboose and pondering what he should do with his upside-down life" gives us a vivid picture of a man perched up high, looking out on the moving train and looking inward on his life in the darkness. Another phrase, "no matter that many grand names had been painted over," gives us an equally vivid picture of time passing.

These phrases are good examples of the power of using well-chosen details to convey information and feeling. What you will want to avoid is giving lots of details about objects when you are describing, say, a room or a place. Select details carefully, or they can become repetitive and boring. The most interesting and useful details seem to be those that give a glimpse into the character.

SEEK OUT YOUR AUTHENTIC WRITER'S VOICE

For many years, I was a college English teacher (as you can tell by the way I write sometimes). Student after student wrote lengthy sentences, inflated with high-sounding phrases. "Why do they write this way?" my colleagues and I asked ourselves. Years later, when asked to teach senior citizens to write their life stories, I was struck by the fact that many of them wrote the same way, using complex sentences that reflected their thoughts, not their feelings or what had happened.

Little by little, it began to dawn on me: most of them didn't *want* to relive the past and bring it to life. They wanted to keep the past, and their feelings about the past, at arm's length. In fact, a great many of us do the same thing—adding a lot of "head stuff" to our writing to keep our vulnerability, uncertainty, and hurt well away from ourselves. To cope with trauma of any kind, we explain, analyze, psychologize, and bury the event under a barrage of jargon. Sometimes we romanticize it with wonderful literary-sounding phrases that give it "quality." It's a neat way to put as much distance between ourselves and the experience as possible.

"I would have loved to write purple prose of the kind popular in my day," George Orwell once wrote, "but the age [of the struggle between

Fascism and Communism] did not permit it. The age demanded a clear look at things, expressed in language that did not prettify."

If we intend to view an event clearly without editing or injecting our adult point of view, we need to eliminate anything in the story that sounds adult or literary. This is particularly important as we go back into our childhoods seeking out our experiences of an early age.

It is also true of our stories from a later time in life. The innocent, uncluttered, direct point of view that we will develop in our early stories is essential in our later stories as well.

Why is this voice so much more reliable as an indicator of the truth? Because the child in us knows how to feel. The adult in us is always cautioning us to be careful. "Hold it back," it says; "that may not be acceptable to others, and to ourselves." The voice that echoes the darkest and deepest criticisms we've felt (often the voice of our parents) may be the voice that does not want us to see that we can be ourselves, not mere echoes of someone else.

The act of stripping away the adult language in a story is not something to worry about as we first begin writing. It is part of the rewriting phase of the work.

For an example of a story made more vivid and believable by stripping away anything that sounds adult, read both versions of "My Mother's Death" by Stephanie Bernardi, found on page 105. For a discussion of these two versions, see pages 102–107. Here, the truth of the event becomes clearer as the "adult" voice is stripped away and the honest, more childlike voice is heard.

Some of my students ask, "Why am I writing in this childlike way in later years, when I'm not a child?" The answer is that the pure, direct, emotional language we find in ourselves as children is our voice as an artist. I am not asking us to write as children when we are adults; I am asking us to eliminate anything that *sounds adult,* which is synonymous with *distant, intellectual, analytical.* Simple, direct, emotional, visual language that creates pictures and feelings will aid us in finding the hidden moments from our past.

This step of the process helps us tell a story more effectively and gives us a path to the secrets we hold inside ourselves. We get our cake and we get to eat it too. But we will need courage when we write to do things a bit differently than we normally do them and to face the truths that lie inside.

Uncovering
Your Most
Vivid
Childhood
Memories

◄ 45 ►

Go ahead and reread your story now. You may find the event coming back to you a bit differently, perhaps more fully.

Get and give supportive feedback

Most of us think that artists, particularly writers, create in isolation, that they are intent on expressing themselves at all costs and to heck with what the world thinks of their work.

Some writers do create that way. But an equal number rely on trusted friends to give them feedback that will inspire their next steps. I, for example, could not have written this book without the feedback of a group of valued friends.

For most people who are not writers, their self-critic is so strong that they must actually reeducate it. The inner critic might say, "This work is no good, forget trying to do this story" or "You are revealing too much, it's too personal" or "You have nothing to say, so don't expose yourself to criticism."

However, a group of friends trained in giving feedback "from within" would probably take a different approach. "Good, not good. What does that mean?" I can hear one of my students, Judy Klein, saying to a member of the class. "It's all about the impact the story has on us, the readers. If you write about just one moment in your life and tell it in the present tense, with feelings, add some dialogue, and get rid of all that adult stuff, we will feel something."

I suggest that those giving feedback pay attention to three things.

1. Does the story create a picture you, the listener or reader, can believe?
2. Are the feelings of the characters and the narrator in the story?
3. How am I experiencing the story?

The third aspect is far and away the most important: to help the writer in a positive way, we do not give feedback about the story. *We give feedback about our experience of the story.*

In other words, when we listen, we must give our attention to the story and how we are reacting to it—where we are touched, where we are pushed out of the experience, where we are fully with it, where we find our minds wandering.

We need to avoid such judgmental statements as, "I was bored in the beginning, but then it got better." A fairer comment would be, "I found my mind wandering in the beginning, but later I got scared and worried about would happen to you, the central character." This kind of feedback helps us take risks in our own writing, for the gentle but accurate way we give feedback to others is the gentle, accurate way we will begin to give feedback to ourselves.

Writing in the present tense and eliminating anything that sounds adult launches us into the child's world of experience, well away from our own. It helps us get around our fears. It also creates an artistic distance between our listeners/readers and the child's world. The present tense helps us leap into this world of the child. The challenge for the writer is to keep us there. Getting rid of anything that sounds adult helps that happen.

T. S. Eliot, quoting Wordsworth, once said, "The artist's task is to create a willing suspension of disbelief," and that is exactly what we are after. The present tense and the use of simple language propel us from adult skepticism and disbelief into another world where everything is new and rich and never experienced before, a world where it is safe to feel again, where no one will criticize us, only support our expressing all the powerful things we feel inside but have been afraid, as a person and as a writer, to express.

Sometimes, when we fall into the old habits of using adult language, we cause the reader to come out of this rich world we have created. The belief is broken, perhaps just for a moment.

The other steps we will be exploring—writing dialogue, expressing inner thoughts and feelings, finding a vivid beginning and climax—also help create belief.

Dialogue, in particular, is a powerful way of transcending the gap between the listener's world and the writer's experience. Characters come to life through dialogue, which in film terms is a way of creating close-ups.

When we have accomplished writing from the child's point of view, we want to continue to express ourselves in this simple, vivid, emotional, unsophisticated language and style. This is the language of the artist that burns within us, the artist in us who sees things in a fresh, real way. It is the language of the artist in all of us who refuses to be bound by psychological jargon and other ways we have of keeping distance between ourselves and our experiences. It is the language of the artist who wants to risk seeing the self as it truly was at *vivid* and *critical* moments in our lives, a language that can touch our subconscious and provoke it into giving up its protections, so we may at long last pull the scrim of fear from our eyes and see ourselves clearly.

Gather together a group of friends and practice giving feedback from within about your stories. Can you see the picture? Can you feel the feelings? These are the two important questions to ask. Be sure each member of the group is giving feedback about his or her own *feeling experience* of the story, not what he or she *thinks* about the story. Did the story take you, the reader, somewhere, and keep you there? Did it cause you to feel something along the way?

The highest compliment you can pay a writer is, "I was there with you every moment of the way. Nothing caused me to come out of the moment. I saw every picture and felt each feeling." (For more information on giving feedback, see the appendix, "Developing Supportive Feedback.")

RECOVER VOICES AND FACES FROM THE PAST THROUGH DIALOGUE

Another important step in getting to know our past is to grasp, as fully as possible, the relationships in our circle of experience as they swirled around us when we were children.

One of the most effective ways of seeing this is to begin adding *dialogue* to our stories. Dialogue is what people say to each other. It usually comes out of vivid emotional moments in the narrative. Most of us begin to write dialogue quite naturally at the high point in the narrative, which is also the point where we most want the characters to speak for themselves.

We may say, "I don't remember what was said," but in fact we have within us worlds of hidden experience that we may uncover. To illustrate, I like to tell of the time I was taking classes in directing from Lee Strasberg of the Actor's Studio. One evening he was giving demonstrations of how an actor can get hung up in the process of merging himself with the character he is playing. A young actor was reading a part, and it wasn't going well. Strasberg stopped him.

"Where is the problem, young man?" he asked. Strasberg was a wizened, intense little guy. The actor was terrified. His fear of displeasing the master was written all over his face.

"What part of your body?" Strasberg asked. The young man pointed to his shoulder. "And what is the memory?" continued Strasberg.

The young man then told a story having to do with his father, the same sort of experience the character in the play was facing. Rather than being able to identify with the character's problem, the actor was paralyzed by his similar experience. After he finished telling the story, the actor returned to the scene and did it beautifully.

In this way I learned how we carry around our memories in various parts of our body. So let's improvise some dialogue. Suppose I write the following: *Momma yelled at me to get up the stairs in a hurry.*

The line cries out to come from Momma's mouth, as: *Momma yells, "Get up the stairs! Now!!"*

This is a big improvement. It becomes even more effective if we put the "he says" or "she says" at the end of the first phrase of dialogue, or at the end of the sentence if the sentence is short: *"Get up the stairs! Now!!" Momma says. "And no back talk!"*

Before long, we will find our dialogue sounding like what Mom and Dad actually said. On the other hand, if we try to re-create dialogue and it just doesn't sound like what took place, we need to drop it and move to another place in our story.

Anytime we wish to get closer to an event, we can try improvising and adding dialogue. One caution: if in reality we could not have heard what was said, we need to avoid trying to re-create it. The reader must believe what he or she is reading. There is no point in trying to fool him. The reader's belief in our narrator's honest telling of a story is our greatest asset.

We will also find that adding dialogue will make the story far more interesting than telling it all in narrative. The following excerpt is an example of good dialogue, well remembered.

Jefferson Barracks, Missouri ———EXCERPT———
by John Strong

We stepped outside for some fresh air. As luck would have it, the pigeon air corps was practicing dive bombing with Ford's new green sweater as target.

"Why did those damn pigeons pick on me?" lamented Ford, as he tried to wipe the droppings from his sweater with his handkerchief.

"Because they knew we were headed for the air corps and wanted to show us some expert bombing!" I joked.

"This isn't funny, John," protested Ford.

"Maybe they hate Irishmen and you're Irish and wearing green," I laughed.

"But you're Irish and a bigger target. Why didn't they pick on you?" asked Ford.

"Oh, can it, Ford," I yelled. "I'll give you the money to get it cleaned. This is trivial compared to the army life we've gotten into."

"Maybe Jefferson Barracks will be better," offered optimist Bill. But when we pulled into St. Louis next morning, Ford was still talking about the big stain on his sweater, the size of a pancake.

I went to a phone in the station, collecting my thoughts for my official call to Jefferson Barracks as the officer at Harrisburg had instructed.

"Sir, this is recruit John Strong, with recruits Bill Bee and Ford Smith. We are coming from Harrisburg, Pennsylvania. I have all the necessary papers," I recited in a good strong voice, trying to make a favorable impression.

On the other end of the line, I heard a childlike voice squealing, "What son-of-a-bitch stole my comic book? It was a Dick Tracy one, too. Come on, cough it up." Then he grumbled to me, "Say that again," which I did.

His next words really startled me. "What the hell do you expect me to do about it?" I thought I had a captain's young son on the phone, so I remained silent for a moment. "You got a tongue, ain't you? Now tell me what you want me to do," the brat ranted. "I have no papers on you at all."

"Maybe you can suggest how we can get to Jefferson Barracks," I offered, with a slight sneer in my voice.

"No one told me you were coming. The only way you can get here is in the mail truck. It's due at the station in about fifteen

JOHN STRONG   John is a strapping man, six feet three inches and two hundred and forty pounds, from a patriotic family of Pennsylvania coal miners. Many of his ancestors fought for the Union during the Civil War, and John was brought up on stories of war and heroism. He writes vividly of his boyhood years growing up in Pennsylvania, of his young manhood as a coal miner during the Depression, of his disappointment at not gaining an appointment to West Point, and of his days as a soldier during World War II.

minutes, so get your asses to the entrance or you will have to walk the fifteen miles to get here. If you don't get here by midnight, you will be AWOL." With that, the jerk slammed the phone down.

• • •

Notice that new characters are introduced quickly through dialogue: "I heard a childlike voice squealing, 'What son-of-a-bitch stole my comic book?'" Soon we learn that this is his new commanding officer—a quick, unexpected glimpse of a new character. This is good dialogue at work.

FOCUS ON A SINGLE EVENT

A vivid memory may in fact be a *series* of vivid memories, so you must develop a sense of where an episode begins and ends, and write only one episode at a time. This is called *focus*. Classically, in an Ibsen play for example, the story begins after some important event has taken place—a death, a crime, or the like. In your work you may start with a similar event, or just before the event. What is important is to express the reactions of the major characters throughout the episode and to know when the incident or event ends.

Focus is also related to finding the "spine," which we will discuss in greater detail in Chapter 6 under "Form and Structure (1): Find the Spine of the Story." For a good example of a well-focused story, see George Small's "Doctor, Oh Doctor" on page 223.

Focusing on what the episode is about—where it begins and ends— and writing visually using details makes up what we call *narrative,* or storytelling. Ultimately, you will be seeking a balance among narration, dialogue, and your inner thoughts and feelings.

Rewriting

You are now ready to begin rewriting your second story. You have a greater fund of techniques at your disposal and a more thorough grasp of what those techniques can do. You have the responses of your friends or classmates to help you. Likewise, you have a better grasp of how to look at your own work after writing that first draft.

We tend to think of rewriting as very taxing, perhaps boring, maybe even painful. But the results are almost always worth the effort. To have one's work go straight to the mind and heart of the reader feels wonderful, as you are no doubt finding out. At this point, let's review the steps we discussed in rewriting your first memoir—

- use the present tense

- write in the first person ("I")

- include your feelings to create emotional impact

- write from a child's point of view (eliminate adult-sounding vocabulary and phrasing)

- and add the concerns we have just mentioned in our review phase: details, dialogue, and focus. Do not try to rewrite on a step-by-step basis, however. Once you have given thought to these various areas of improvement, read your story over and make gut-level changes where it feels right to do so.

Having done your rewriting, take your story back to your friends, relatives, and classmates. I think you will be pleasantly surprised. And if you want to write several more "vivid memories" before going on to the next chapter, please do so.

Exercise

PART 1: MY EARLIEST VIVID MEMORY

What memory of your life between birth and twelve years of age do you have that is more vivid in your mind than any other, one that you remember better than any other? Tell it in the *present* tense.

Here is an example:

I am twelve years old. I'm walking into my brand new school. As I walk into my homeroom, I feel as though everyone is staring at me. I think to myself, "What if my friends get lost and don't meet me at the lockers—then who am I going to hang around with?"

I hope I don't arrive late to any of my classes cuz I'm afraid that the teacher might tell me something in front of the whole class.

The day goes by pretty fast and I have no problems. I finally go home.

The writer wrote about a very common vivid early memory—the first day in a new school. Other common vivid memories may be a birth in the family, a death in the family, a separation or divorce, or a special family event, such as a birthday or a religious celebration.

If you are having trouble remembering something vivid, try remembering the "first time" something happened, such as the first time you went with your father or mother on an adventure, or the first time your schoolteacher told you to behave.

Now, *write* your earliest vivid memory. Start with these words: "I am ___ years old and I am . . ."

PART 2: MY EARLIEST VIVID MEMORY
(FIRST REWRITE)

Now you will write your vivid memory over again. First, be sure it is in the present tense, then add the steps below.

STEP 1. Ask yourself, "Are my *feelings* in the story?" If not, *add your feelings* ("I feel sad," "I feel happy"). As before, begin with the words "I am" and tell us your age when the event happened.

Below is the revision of the story about the first day at school, incorporating the narrator's feelings.

I am twelve years old. I'm walking into my brand new school. *It seems so big and scary. I can feel the butterflies in my stomach* as I walk into my homeroom. I feel as though everyone is staring at me. I think to myself, "What if my friends get lost and don't meet me at the lockers—then who am I going to hang around with?"

I hope I don't arrive late to any of my classes cuz I'm afraid that the teacher might tell me something in front of the whole class. *How embarrassing.*

The day goes by pretty fast and I have no problems. *I feel relieved* to finally go home.

Do you see how much more interesting the story is when it includes feelings? It grabs you and pulls you into it. Try to do more than put your feelings in at the beginning and the end of your story. Every time an action takes place, bring your feelings into the picture.

Remember, you may know how others feel from their actions or the expressions on their faces, but you know *your* feelings from the inside. Tell the audience what those feelings are. After a while, you will begin to include your feelings as you write your first draft, but for now adding them into the rewrite is fine.

STEP 2. Take out any words or sentence constructions that sound adult and would not be very believable coming from a child.

STEP 3. Get some feedback on your rewrite from your classmates or friends.

PART 3: MY EARLIEST VIVID MEMORY
(SECOND REWRITE)

Now we will add another step to the writing process: we are going to add *dialogue,* which is *talk between people.*

We can often make dialogue out of narrative. For example, *Mom told me to go to the store* can easily be turned into *"Go to the store," Mom told me.*

Now, let's learn how to separate speakers. Try to rewrite the following passage so that it is clear who is saying what.

How do you know if I am speaking or you are speaking when writing looks like this I ask my students. It sure is confusing one girl answers. So Mr. Selling tell us, huh? Huh? another student says.

"When a person is speaking, use quotation marks so readers will know that he or she is speaking," I tell my students.

"How do I know if you are speaking or I am speaking?" one of my students asks.

"Each new speaker gets a new paragraph," I tell her. "And put quotation marks around the actual words a person says."

So, every time a new person speaks, he or she gets a new paragraph, and quotation marks around the words tell us someone is speaking.

Try adding some dialogue to the second draft of your story. You may not remember exactly what was said, but that's OK. You can invent what was said, as long as it feels like the truth. When you have finished writing, ask yourself whether or not your story is improved by your use of dialogue.

Uncovering
Your Most
Vivid
Childhood
Memories

◦ɬ 55 ɬ◦

CHAPTER 4

Uncovering Your Most
Vivid Teenage Memories

I walk into homeroom the first day of school in the eighth grade and look at my schedule for the year. I am stunned. Fourth Period—Senior Band. *Senior band?? Me? Why me?* I wonder. *I'm not a very good clarinet player.* But it's true; the bandmaster has promoted me along with a half dozen other eighth graders into the senior high school band. I feel so proud—and grateful—that I practice hard. By the end of the year I am very close to the top of the clarinet section. Also, during the year I go from mooning over the ethereal Sue to liking the curvaceous Gail. I discover basketball and swing dancing. More often than not, my father and I come into conflict with one another. I want to do things my way; he wants things done his way.

Hormones have struck, as they do all of us between the ages of twelve and twenty. Those are exciting, often difficult years, filled with change. To grasp the excitement of those years and to embrace the depth of what we felt at the time, we will need to expand our range of storytelling techniques. Therefore, in this chapter we will explore more fully (1) how to start writing a story and (2) how to define the characteristics that make the people in a story interesting.

Composing

Establish yourself as character and narrator

One thing you can do to help yourself as a writer while you are warming up and looking for the point at which to enter the story is to be aware that *you, as a character, must be in the story at all times.* Why is this so? Well, if you are not in the story, the audience will have great difficulty knowing through whose eyes they are seeing the action and they will not believe what they are reading. Consider the following story.

> It's a hot summer day here in Macon, Georgia. A light breeze is blowing and my aunt is sitting on the porch fanning herself.

Suppose somewhere in the early part of this story we add the line: *I am sitting on the porch playing with my toy trains.* This awareness helps the readers in many ways. They will know where you are and from what point of view they will see the action, that is, close to the ground because you are small.

Now let's suppose you look for some details to fill out the picture. Oh, yes. There is a newspaper with a large headline. Let's see if we can make it out. Ah, there it is. "Wall Street Crashes." So let's add that. *A newspaper lies at her feet. It says "Wall Street Crashes."* So now we have:

> It's a hot summer day here in Macon, Georgia. I am sitting on the porch playing with my toy trains. A light breeze is blowing and my aunt is sitting near me fanning herself. She has a funny look on her face. At her feet a newspaper says "Wall Street Crashes." I wonder what a walled street is.

Here we have a wonderful paradox: the writer as character is innocent and wide-eyed; the writer as narrator is giving powerful details to which the character responds in this believable, whimsical way. (Later we will find out that we can go one more step and place the line *I am sitting on the porch* at the beginning of the story—but that's yet to come.)

How do we create a sense of belief in the audience? First, we begin by making sure that the narrator's voice always sounds appropriate for the age at which the events are happening to the narrator. Thus if you were seven years old when the event happened, the audience wants to

When we begin a story, we as artists have one purpose: to carry the reader on a voyage from where they are to where we wish them to be—in another time and place.

At that point our objective is to create *belief,* which is about the only way we have of keeping the reader in that altered time and place. In our day and age, readers tend to believe only a particular person's point of view, not a general perspective. This is why the great nineteenth-century writers like Herman Melville fell into such disfavor with readers in the twentieth century. The educated readership of the early years of the twentieth century did not believe the world to be orchestrated by an all powerful, God-like power, and therefore refused to believe anything written from an omniscient narrator's point of view. Thus, the most powerful charm we take with us on our story-telling voyages is our amulet: *belief.*

believe that the event is being experienced by a seven-year-old.

When you as the narrator are a little older, say nineteen or twenty, the audience will believe your experience if you keep them in touch with your feelings at every point in the story, while continuing to keep the language simple—emotional, not intellectual. If you were, in fact, an intellectual nineteen-year-old, let that be reflected in the dialogue.

These three things—level of language, presence of feelings, dialogue that is appropriate to the characters—will create a strong sense of belief in your reader.

ESTABLISH A POINT OF VIEW

Take a look at the paintings on the next two pages. In each painting, notice the perspective from which the viewer sees the action and how the perspective helps the viewer comprehend and believe the painter's meaning and message.

The first is Leonardo da Vinci's *The Last Supper.* We are placed directly in front of Christ, able to see the effects, on either side of him, of his statement, "One of you shall betray me." We are neither below nor above the action, neither awed by nor superior to it. It is happening directly in front of us, in a clearly defined space in which a fifteenth-century Tuscan valley unfolds behind the head of Christ. We know where we are and from what position we are seeing the action. It is "real" to us.

In the second painting, Pieter Brueghel's *The Fall of Icarus,* we are high on a hill overlooking a distant harbor in a place that resembles northern Europe. It is early in the sixteenth century.

We are placed near a peasant whose chores will take him down and to the left in the painting. Our eye is led to distant vistas: to the new "round" world beyond. Because of our position near the peasant, we

would most likely ignore anything in the lower right portion of the painting, such as the leg of Icarus, who has just fallen out of the sky. (You may recall that Icarus and Daedalus escaped from the labyrinth of King Minos by making wings of wax. Though advised by his father not to fly too close to the sun, Icarus disobeyed and plunged into the sea when his wings melted.)

What is the meaning of this painting? Perhaps something like, "We are all so preoccupied with our daily tasks, we hardly see the truly important events in life taking place. We are distracted by the boring necessities of life (the peasant's tasks) and the world's concerns (opening up the world and viewing it, not as flat, but as round)."

The settings of these paintings and the perspectives from which we view the action have a great deal of influence on their message and impact on us, and it is similar with stories.

The writing techniques I am suggesting are cinematic. Many modern films begin with a tight shot and then widen to include everything important, so your establishing shot might come after a line or two of dialogue or some action at the beginning of the story. I often advise my students to begin with action or dialogue to get the reader into the story quickly, and then "widen out" to bring more into view.

Another technique, which early filmmakers often used, is this sequence: first, the establishing shot, a wide-angle shot encompassing a whole city or village; next, a medium shot, bringing us closer to the dwellings or places we are going to inhabit; and finally, a closer shot of the characters important to the narrative. If you are writing stories of your life when you were less than ten years old, that is, writing from a child's point of view, establishing shots might actually be unbelievable at the beginning of a story. The child's world is tiny and narrow, though fascinating. So an establishing shot—a more comprehensive, adult view—might come at the end of the scene or story. After the story ends, you may also wish to tell the reader how the event described has affected you over the ensuing years.

As a young child, I see the world through a very small window. I know little of what others are doing. I know nothing of past and future. It is a very particular stage setting. As I mature, the window through which I see the world widens. I know more of past and present, of life beyond myself; therefore, I can set the stage more fully.

As a writer, I ask my reader to suspend his or her normal disbelief and believe what I have written. From a child, the reader can believe the

world only as seen through the tiny window of a small child's aware-ness, but from a more mature youngster or an adult, the reader can ac-cept a much more fully set stage.

Reviewing

In reviewing our stories, we want to continue to add to our techniques and concerns, so we will now address an additional aspect of writing: creating interesting people.

CREATE UNFORGETTABLE CHARACTERS

Unlike the Lilliputians in *Gulliver's Travels,* into whose world a big per-son was suddenly cast, we are all born into a world of big people. Moth-ers and fathers, in particular, loom especially large in our lives and our imaginations. Sometimes they appear distorted. My father, for example, appeared to most people as a strong-minded, humorous, thin-skinned, and occasionally imperious man. As I was growing up, he appeared so powerful to me that, until well into my thirties, I had dreams in which he appeared as a pursuing monster and I was a frightened Lilliputian.

Family members, many of whom have great power over us, must be dealt with in our memories honestly, clear-sightedly, and fearlessly. Since our view of them changes as we grow older, it is both appropriate and necessary to see them as they were experienced by other members of the family and by ourselves at different times in our lives.

Let's consider what makes a character in a book, a play, or a movie "interesting," and see how it applies to our parents and the rest of the family. We might begin with the following definition: An interesting per-son is someone who wants something badly (*what* she wants is usually very clear) and takes an interesting, unusual, or difficult route to reach that goal (*how* she is going to get it is also clear). To the degree that the goal is dangerous and the means employed involve risk, the person might move up the scale from interesting to heroic.

UNCOVER CHARACTER QUALITIES

How a person goes about getting what he or she wants reveals certain character qualities. Charm, determination, humor, honesty, self-assurance, dependability, opportunism, and perfectionism are all qualities that get us what we want; they may also, tragically, defeat us in other ways.

After you have had a chance to think about and discuss several kinds of interesting characters, take some time to write about one yourself. Follow these six steps:

1. Think of a character you consider interesting.
2. Recall an incident, event, or series of actions that were typical of this character.
3. Find a word for the memorable quality or qualities he or she possesses.
4. Ask yourself if the incident you recalled really brings out the quality you have identified. If it does, go ahead and write about it; if not, you may wish to select a different incident.
5. Remember that the most interesting characters have several strong qualities, sometimes contradictory ones.
6. Include yourself in the story, making certain that your character qualities—as the narrator—are also evident in the story.

Here are some interesting or important people you might want to write about:

- My grandparents
- My parents
- My sisters or brothers
- My best friend from the time I was __ years old
- My first teacher, mentor, or guide
- My first boss
- My "black sheep" relative
- My companion through a difficult ordeal

If you wish to use a step-by-step approach to writing and rewriting a story from your teenage years, turn to the "Exercise" section at the end of this chapter.

• • •

I lean back in my chair. The images of the past rise up to meet me through the murky depths to the present. The place and person become clearer. I begin to write . . . __now__.

Rewriting

Many of you may be feeling that rewriting is still beyond you, that it takes time and you are not sure what the benefits will be. Virtually all writers go through a rewriting process that involves considerable change. Many of us write first drafts that are undistinguished and uninteresting. What counts is what we do *after* we have made it through the first draft.

DEVELOP YOUR OWN WRITING PROCESS

So that you can see what I myself go through, I am going to write about an interesting character using the techniques I have given you so far. What you are about to read is exactly what comes from my head and my typewriter. Will it be any good? Will it be interesting? I have no idea. I will follow the steps I outlined for you and see where they lead.

1. Think of a character you consider interesting.

   My father . . .

2. Recall an incident, event, or series of actions that were typical of this character.

   Hmm . . . I'm not ready for that . . .

3. Find a word for the memorable quality or qualities he possesses.

   His curiosity . . . his desire to know . . . but the way he died? Ah, there's the incident . . . his death . . . what kind of curiosity could kill him . . . uh, hmm . . . pickiness, his insatiable desire to pick at the surface of things. That's it!! His intellectual curiosity and the way he died, together.

Dad's Death
by Bernard Selling

My father had an insatiable desire to pick away at the surface of things. Intellectually, it caused him to be unendingly curious, devouring books, thoughts, and concepts hungrily. He loved learning and absorbing and analyzing, acquiring two Ph.D.s and an M.D. As director of the Recorder's Court Psychopathic Clinic, he was an innovator in the field of traffic offenses, alcoholism, and emotional disorders. Yet this insatiable desire to pick away at the surface of things had another outcome.

In the winter of 1955, he found a wart on his foot, a wart that bothered him. He picked up a razor blade from his shaving kit and began to pick away at the wart. The razor was dirty and infected. By the end of the month he had blood poisoning and was hospitalized. Shortly after, under the threat of having his leg amputated, he got up in the middle of the night, slipped, broke his hip, had a heart attack, and died. My mother and sister and I could hardly believe what had happened.

• • •

Now I've finished this first draft and I look it over. I realize I'm not in the picture, nor are my feelings. I begin to look for me in the picture to see where I am and how I'm feeling. I go back to the time he was in the hospital and see how I feel. I begin to write:

I am sixteen and bewildered. *How can he have done this?* I wonder. *He is smart. He has two Ph.D.s and an M.D.*

I think back to how I feel after his death. I am so angry at him for dying. I can almost burst. *Why?* I wonder. *He and I have been battling with each other,* I answer myself. *Only recently does he even begin to know who I am, sort of.* Am I only angry? "I miss him," I write. "The funeral is a blur."

I review the story again. Yes, I'm in the story and so are my feelings, but the whole thing sounds rather academic and feels kind of remote. *How can I put this in a book on writing?* my critic asks. *It's OK,* my creator answers. *I'm letting them see how I get past the first draft.*

If this were one of my students writing, what would I suggest he or she do at this point? "Find out where the story begins." So I look over the draft again. Ah, there it is: "In the winter of 1955, he finds a wart on his foot." *Maybe it's going to be a different sort of story,* I say to myself. *Go on, make changes, see what happens—and try it in the present tense.*

Dad's Death ——— SECOND DRAFT ———

One day, Dad finds a wart on the bottom of his foot. It is winter, 1955. He is fifty-three years old and not too well. He coughs a lot during the winter. I know he had a heart attack eight years ago. I worry about him. We all do. With a razor blade from his shaving kit, he begins to pick away at his wart. Nobody tells him not to. Nobody can tell him anything. A month later he has blood poisoning and is hospitalized. Shortly after, he is told that he may have to have his leg amputated. I am sixteen and bewildered. *How can he have done this? I ask myself. He is smart. He has two Ph.D.s and an M.D. His brain cuts through stupidity, error, nonsense, and people's bullshit all the time. I'm afraid he'll cut through mine sometime.*

Mom and Lee, my fourteen-year-old sister, go to see him in the hospital. I don't. It's Saturday and I play tennis with the guys instead. Afterwards, Lee tells me that Mom and Dad were like young lovers.

"He was telling all his old dirty jokes," she says, "and Mom was laughing and giggling like a schoolgirl. It was so . . . erotic, you could cut it with a knife."

I nod, feeling numb, wondering what I have missed.

Sometime after New Year's, he is still in the hospital. The doctors want to operate. He's outraged, I'm told later by my mother. He gets up in the middle of the night, slips, breaks his hip, and . . .

No, that's not quite how it is. I look back to see where I have gone off . . . *Ah, that last paragraph.*

Sometime after New Year's Day, I am in my room. I am working on a model train. The phone rings upstairs somewhere. I hear Mom answer it. A few moments later she comes into my room.

"Lopo died this morning," she says quietly. "He got up in the middle of the night. He was angry at the doctors. He slipped, broke his hip, and had a heart attack."

I listen. I walk away—or does she? We say nothing to one another.

I go to school the next day. Everyone knows he is dead. His picture is on the front page of the Orlando paper. I can see they are shocked that I'm here in school.

Finally, Bill Bledsoe comes up to me. "I'm sorry to hear what happened," he says. "I liked your dad." I mumble something. Later in the day, Bill Nichols comes up and says the same thing. No one else says anything about my father. Friends say nothing. Teachers say nothing. Mom says nothing.

Dad is dead. No more arguments. No more fights. No more misunderstandings. No more laughter. Would he have forgiven me for my breaking his prized Spike Jones records in a fit of anger if he had lived? Could I have found out why he got so furious at me for holding hands with Jeri B. when I was thirteen and staying out in the canoe with Pat C. when I was fourteen?

I was so angry at him, so humiliated, I would have loved to have knocked him down but, no, I couldn't. He might have died. So many questions, so many feelings haunt me. *Why this? Why that?* I am so angry at him I can hardly see straight. The funeral is a blur.

The rest of the year I go inside myself.

"Do you want to play the lead in 'Dangerous Dan McGrew'?" the bandmaster asks me. It's the part in the band skit that had the audiences howling when I played it the year before. Dad was laughing so hard that even from the stage I could see him wiping the tears from his eyes.

"No," I answer. I play in the band. I get decent grades. I go through the motions. I don't want to be noticed, and no one does. Dad is dead and part of me is too.

— • • • —

Now, looking back, going through the feelings again, I find it hard to believe that Dad would place himself in such a vulnerable position—a man with diabetes and a history of heart disease, a doctor and a man of science, a man with a family he cared about so deeply, picking at a wart on the bottom of his foot with a dirty razor blade. That insatiable desire to pick away at things got him.

From this example we see that the rewriting process begins when I ask myself, "Am I in the picture? Are my feelings present?"

Then I ask myself, "Where does the story begin?" as I encourage myself to soften that critical voice of mine, the one that could so easily stop me from writing.

Then at the end of the second draft, I realize there is a point at which I have created distance from the experience—where I have gone off the track, perhaps where the event is too painful. This time I return to the event, keeping it close to my experience, no matter how painful.

This, then, is the process: keep close to our feelings, hold our self-critic at bay, review the event to explore our actions and feelings more closely with each rewrite, and expand moments with dialogue, inner thoughts and feelings.

Keep a checklist

As you review and rewrite, you need to keep in mind all of the things you learned earlier, while adding new items to the "stew." In fact, you might want to make a checklist of questions to ask yourself, as do pilots, who go through a list of procedures before takeoff and landing. At this point, your checklist might look like this:

Life Writing Checklist

1. Is my story written in the first person and in the present tense?
2. Have I stripped the story of adult, intellectual language?
3. Are my feelings in the story?
4. Do the details and actions make the story clearer and more interesting?
5. Does the dialogue help tell the story and make the characters more interesting?
6. Have I kept to one well-focused incident at a time?
7. Are the characters interesting, perhaps unforgettable? Are their qualities evident?
8. Are my feelings about the events clearly expressed?

Rewriting now becomes easier because you know what has to be done and you have a variety of techniques with which to approach the task. At this point, look over the checklist, begin to visualize any changes you may wish to make, and then make them.

Exercise

PART 1: MY MOST VIVID MEMORY
BETWEEN TWELVE AND TWENTY

Think about something else that happened when you were young, something you see vividly in your mind. When you start writing, keep going until you finish. Don't stop for anything. Use the *present tense*. How do you feel about what happened? Include your *feelings*. Use *dialogue* if you can.

PART 2: MY MOST VIVID MEMORY
BETWEEN TWELVE AND TWENTY
(FIRST REWRITE)

Now you will rewrite the memory you have just recorded.

STEP 1: Form a picture in your mind of the memory you just wrote. Did you write it in the *present tense*? If not, rewrite it in the present tense. Did you add your *feelings*? If not, add your feelings. Does it contain anything that does not sound like the child speaking? If so, make the changes now. Did you add dialogue? If not, go ahead if you can.

Don't worry about spelling or grammar when you are writing. After you have finished your story, you can check your spelling.

STEP 2: Ask yourself, "Am I clearly in the story as a character?" If not, make your character clearly visible. We do this by making sure the audience always knows what the narrator of the story is thinking, feeling, and doing even as he or she is listening to another person speaking.

"Go to the store," my mother says, "and pick up some eggs."
I shrug my shoulders. *Why do I always have to do the chores?* My head hurts and my stomach aches. I think I'm getting sick.

Uncovering
Your Most
Vivid Teenage
Memories

"Come on!" she demands. "Move those feet."

"Yeah, yeah," I mumble.

PART 3: MY MOST VIVID MEMORY BETWEEN TWELVE AND TWENTY (SECOND REWRITE)

Read over your first rewrite.

STEP 1: Ask yourself, "Am I clearly in the story?"

STEP 2: If the answer is yes, ask yourself, "Is there a separation between what the *character knows* and what the *narrator tells us* through the dialogue of the other characters?" As an example, consider the following story.

> I am playing with my train set on the floor in the living room. The train goes round and round. "Whee!" I laugh as it goes so fast that it falls off the track. I look up at Mama. She stands in the doorway, silent . . . looking down the street. There is a letter in her hand. I put the train back on the track and make it go faster this time. "Whoo Whoo!!" I laugh, making train sounds. In the background, I hear a car drive away.
>
> "Get up, little one!" Mama whispers.
>
> "Mama, I'm . . ."
>
> "Get up right now." Her eyes are scared and full of tears. "We have to go."

Now in this scene, I—the child, the central character through whose eyes the story is being told—am not interested in anything except the train. I'm having fun. On the other hand, I—the writer—am creating a scene in which Mama has received terrible news of some kind and is reacting to the news. As the writer, I am responsible for building the scene, which includes the concerns of all the characters as well as anything that may be going on in the background, such as the sound of the automobile driving off.

As you rewrite the second draft of your story, see if you can create a separation between the interests and concerns of the central character (you) and the other characters, making their wants and needs as clear and powerful as your own.

CHAPTER 5

Writing About
the Inner You

"You want me to read first—in public?" asks Rebecca, the slim, bright, hip star of my Sunday workshop. A bewildered look crosses her innocent features. "I thought you were my protector, my mentor. Now you want to throw me to the wolves?"

"Now, now, it's not that bad," I reassure her. Behind that look is a hint of anger mixed with fear.

Rebecca and I and several other members of the group are sitting in a booth at a 1950s cafe, Delores' Restaurant, discussing the upcoming public reading of our work. My friend and student, Mar Puatu, has created a new anthology of stories entitled *Sojourns* and has asked me to enlist Rebecca in kicking off the afternoon of storytelling that will publicize the book.

"No, no, not 'that bad.' Much worse, thank you. I thought you liked me." She picks up her water glass and stares into it. "Mirror, mirror on the wall," she murmurs, "why is Rebecca the shyest of all."

All of us who know Rebecca agree that she makes a terrific impression with her wit, looks, and graciousness. She loves being the center of attention, but she's not been ready for the next step—exploring her own work in public.

"Rebecca, Rebecca," I shake my head. "What am I to do with you?"

She chuckles, enjoying "Rebecca as victim, Bernard as tormentor." She says, "How about negotiating?"

"Your story is very funny, and you're so much better looking than the antique guys who've written the other stories."

She gives me another look, obviously not buying a thing I'm saying. "You want me to get up in front of a bunch of strangers *and* reveal the deepest part of myself. You want me to be that naked?"

"You didn't mind performing at the other public reading," I persist. "You told me how good it was for you."

"But I wasn't first," she squints at me. "I said it was good for *us*. Us in the general sense. I didn't say it was good for me. *You* said it was good for me. Remember how I hid behind all my hair. You could hardly see my face in the video."

Actually, I know very well what she means about feeling naked. When I read a story in front of people, even a happy story, I become very emotional. Tears usually fill my eyes and I do feel bare. *Why does that happen to me?* I wonder. I think back to a story I wrote about circling the Golden Gate Bridge in a single-engine airplane, the moonlight shining into the cockpit—my son, Jeff, and I flying—Christmas Eve—buddies. How much I love him and flying. I remember the tears when I read it in front of one of my classes. What is all this emotion about? Do I hate being a feeling person? Do I just not like people knowing that I have feelings?

"Well, OK," I sigh. "If you're not comfortable, we ought to go to plan B. We'll take the tarp off one of the antiques."

She smiles. "Ah, my mentor and my friend." There is a wicked glint in her eye, as if it's all just a game. "You're such a pushover." But I know her fear runs deep—and so does mine.

Composing

We will now discuss four additional ways of capturing feelings and getting them down on paper:

1. Use objects to convey emotion.
2. Use the five senses to convey your feelings.

3. Use inner monologue to convey your deepest thoughts and feelings.

4. Express inner emotion.

Use objects to convey emotion

One of the most powerful ways to convey emotion in our stories without using words is to use objects and invest them with great personal meaning. For example, if a man is thinking about the brother he recently lost through death, it would be appropriate for him to look at old photographs of his brother as a remembrance of better times.

When such an object is described effectively, it can have a strong emotional impact on the reader or listener. This concept is similar in many ways to one of the exercises used by actors trained in the Stanislavski system, called "circumstances surrounding an object." In this exercise, the actor builds a past life around an object so that, when it is used on stage or on film, the audience will see and feel the connections to the past—the happy, sad, poignant memories connected with the object.

To give an example from my own life, the interior of the car I own, a 1964 Volvo, has a wonderful smell to it. It is a distinctive smell, one that everyone who climbs into the car notices. But only I know that it is a smell almost identical to that of my father's Packard, a car I loved, a smell that reminds me of a happy time in my life when I was small and my father was alive and showing me things in and around Detroit, things I was seeing and experiencing for the first time.

The little story that opens this chapter uses this technique: Rebecca picks up the water glass, seeking to find in it a clue to the origins of her shyness. The next story employs this technique well.

Houses
by Eugene Mallory

The year is 1935. It is a bad year in Iowa. In 1933 the farm industry had no prices. Most commodities were not worth enough to pay the freight to market. Livestock, not worth the little it cost to feed them, roamed the country roads. In 1934 the drought came and very little grew. Prices went up but there was little to sell. Now in 1935 crops are fair but prices are falling like wounded ducks. The whole state, already drained of money, is thinking, "Here we go again."

The place is Lincoln Way, "fraternity row," Ames, Iowa. I have just stopped the car in a spray of flying sand at the curb. Something is wrong. The Chi Phi house, the house that was never dark, is now dark and stares blankly back at me.

Dorothy, my wife of two years, is with me. We are on our way to the house in Hampton where I grew up. We both know at once what must have happened, but neither wishes to say.

The Chi Phi house had been home to me during the years after my mother's death. My father had lain upstairs in the Hampton house, lost in the ruined corridors of his mind. What horrors he found there he could not, or would not say. One look into his eyes made the looker grateful for the silence. I had fled that house as soon as I could, and found refuge here, a second home. Now it, too, is gone.

The Chi Phi alumni had owned this house. A downtown bank had owned the mortgage. The bank had ended in that strange, sad holiday, the bank holiday of 1933. As long as the student residents could generate enough revenue for the alumni to keep up the interest and taxes, the house went on. The alumni had made up shortages before, but were too hard-pressed themselves to do so again. The bank liquidators had no choice either. The word was "foreclose." How many dreams and plans and lives, too, had been foreclosed in those bitter years! The word hovers, a chilling presence in the air between us, but we do not speak. I think I can make out the Chi Phi name plate beside the door and say, "I think I can see the name still there. I am going to look." I leave, before a woman's realism can end the faint and futile hope.

Halfway up the wall I am sure the bronze is there. CHI PHI. We did not flash our Greek around. The Greek was reserved for the plain red and gold badge. "Badge, not pin, you clod." I touch the name plate to be sure. The door is locked. It should not be, but unless repaired, the back door cannot be locked.

I go across the lawn and down the steep rutted drive. The flat unpaved lot holds no cars, or does it? There is something at the back. I have a little feeble light. A flash and I recognize the hulk. Stu's ancient and decrepit Auburn Speedster. It had brought him from Chicago in style, but once down the drive it never had the strength to bring itself back up. I turn away, leaving the carcass in its trap.

I head for the kitchen door, pushing aside almost tangible memories. Freddy Wilson's new hat, the endless verses of "God, but it's cold in Iowa." The door yields as I knew it would. The outside air is sharp with cold. Inside, the air is colder still, and lifeless and heavy in the chest. What was in this house? I had met death in that other house, on the days when caskets banked in flowers had stood before the curved glass of the parlor windows and old Mr. Beebe came to leave his card and pay his respects to those whose lives had worn away. That was a house where death had come. What went with death, death and desolation? Desolation has come here.

A verse from scripture I had learned in this house comes slowly back to mind. The Chi Phi founding fathers had used it in the ritual they wrote a hundred years ago. It was natural, since six of the twelve had Reverend before their names: ". . . the flower of the field flourisheth. The wind passeth over it. The place thereof knows it no more." Indeed, some ancient seed has passed and here it will be no more.

I suddenly realize that, lost in thought, I am wasting my feeble light. Do I need a light to think? I snap it off and soon find that in this place, in this darkness, I do not think so well. The light comes back a little stronger, and I decide to look into the dining room.

Something is crunching underfoot, the Chi Phi china smashed upon the floor. Vandals have been here, the tribe that ravaged Rome. Could they never die?

The huge oval table is still there but my light will hardly reach its length. It has been stripped and only rags of padding cover the naked lumber.

I call back the vision of the last formal dinner I saw here. The small town and country boys sweating in their stiff collars, hard shirt fronts and black bow ties. Our dandy, Meliher, at ease and resplendent in white tie and tails. The girls, bare arms and shoulders gleaming in the candle light. The strapless ones a bit uneasy as to just how much was gleaming.

All so young, rehearsing the glamour and sophistication of the lives they hoped to lead. The vision is hard to hold. The malignant gloom devours the candlelight. My little light is fading too, its battery sucked dry by the darkness and the cold. It is time to go.

When I reach the car, I tell the news, "I got in all right, but they are gone, and the place was vandalized."

Dorothy puts her arms about me and says, "You're shivering, Gene. Let's go home."

That car is new and fast. No killing wind can pass over us this night. The Hampton house is home again.

The next time I was on fraternity row, the Chi Phi house was gone and the basement yawned, an open grave. The details of the break-up, I never knew. No one was ever hopeful enough even to write and ask for money.

Money and hope were both in short supply in the Iowa of 1935.

• • •

You will notice that each object mentioned in this story has an enormous past that produces a strong emotional impact on the reader.

RE-CREATE EMOTIONS BY EXPLORING THE FIVE SENSES

In an earlier chapter, we identified certain emotions that we were able to put into a story. We added, for example, such phrases as "I am happy," "I am sad," and "I am nervous."

Now we can take our exploration of feelings to another level, incorporating the five senses into each moment of a story. Instead of writing "I am nervous," we can write "My hands are shaking," "My mouth is dry," and "My heart pounds in my chest." Use this technique whenever emotions are high, particularly as you approach the climax of a story.

CREATE INNER MONOLOGUES TO CONVEY EMOTION

One of the great advantages of the autobiographical story as a form is that the audience expects the author to write from his own point of view—"I" the storyteller. As part of this form, the author is expected to tell us his innermost thoughts and feelings.

For example, if a writer is frustrated with his marriage, he may pick a fight with his wife: "I don't want to go to the movies tonight. Why do we have to go out all the time? Can't we just stay in sometimes?"

This dialogue can be followed up with a more revealing thought or feeling: *Why do I (you) keep picking at her? She loves me (you) so much and I (you) just keep finding fault. What's the matter with me (you)?*

When writing inner monologue, we usually set it off from other text and dialogue by putting it in italics. If you are writing on a typewriter or a word processor that cannot set text in italics, you can enclose inner monologue in single quotes to distinguish it from regular dialogue. Another common method is to use context—the way we phrase things—to alert the reader to the fact that we are writing inner monologue.

Questions are a very effective form of monologue because they bring the reader deeply into the writer's struggle to become aware of what is happening. *Why am I . . . ? When will I . . . ? What is happening . . . ?*

I am often asked whether it is OK to invent inner monologue. The answer is, of course, yes. We do not ever want to violate the facts of a story, but there are no writing police around to say, "That inner monologue is not true!" So dig deep and invent.

Express inner emotion

In some stories, an event in the outside world triggers a flood of inner feelings, often conflicting ones. As with nonobjective paintings, such as those of Wassily Kandinsky and Jackson Pollock, the emotions may become detached from the object that inspired them. Or there may continue to be some reference to the object. In the late paintings of artists such as J. M. W. Turner (*The Fighting Téméraire, The Morning After the Deluge*) and Claude Monet (*Water Lilies*), there is always a hint of the object in the abstract swirls of emotion on the canvas.

Occasionally, the emotions of the inner world rise to the surface and appear as part of the outer world in a surprising and revealing portrait of the writer's own emotional landscape. Please read Stephanie Bernardi's story "My Mother's Death" (see page 276) or Bill Peterson's story "Bittersweet Remembering" (see page 264), which are fine examples of a strong awareness of emotions being part of the subject of the narrative.

To review, here are the steps to follow when "writing from within."

- Follow all the steps we have already discussed to set clearly in your mind a story or incident that you would like to narrate.

- Review the story or incident that is in your mind, recollecting how you felt with each turn of events during the story.

- Recall not only your emotions and those of any other central characters, but also how other, specific people around you responded to the situation.

- Allow yourself to make your emotions—your sadness, pain, awe, amusement, fascination, and so on—the subject of certain episodes.

The following are some inner emotions that deserve attention:

- Aloneness, as when my parents left me

- Feeling naked, as when I did something very embarrassing

- Exhilaration, as when I did something unique

- Sadness, as when someone dear to me left, never to return

- Frustration, as when something I tried and tried to do continued to be impossible to accomplish

- Peace, as when some lengthy struggle finally came to a satisfying conclusion

- Yearning, as when something I wanted very much became even more desirable than before

- Awe, as when something I participated in took on a life of its own

- Anger, as when forces beyond my control shaped the lives of those around me

— • • • —

*Now it is time for me to explore some events that hold some of my deepest feelings and emotions . . . I am traveling back over my sea of memories . . . I am beginning to see the moment . . . it is time to write . . . **now**.*

Reviewing

In reviewing your story at this point, you may find that you have more information to add to the story, information that the central character/narrator would not know. You can add such information at the end of the story in a P.S.

A P.S. is a postscript to your story. In it, you can add information that did not fit into the story, but is relevant, if only to the family—such as names, dates, places, or anything else you would like to add.

Particularly effective in the P.S. is information you wish the reader to know about the experience's effect on the rest of your life. If you detested spinach in the story and you never again ate spinach, the reader will probably enjoy knowing about this.

Conclusion

You now have the techniques you need to write your life stories, to express your inner feelings, as well as to describe people and events in the outside world. In your subsequent stories, try to achieve an effective balance of narration, dialogue, and inner monologue. Not every story requires such a balance, but most stories will be enhanced by it. And remember to use your inner thoughts and feelings, to "write from within."

Here is an updated version of the checklist introduced in Chapter 4.

LIFE WRITING CHECKLIST

1. Is my story written in the first person and in the present tense?
2. Have I stripped the story of adult, intellectual language?
3. Are my feelings in the story?
4. Do the details and actions make the story clearer and more interesting?
5. Does the dialogue help tell the story and make the characters more interesting?
6. Have I kept to one well-focused incident at a time?
7. Are the characters interesting, perhaps unforgettable? Are their qualities evident?
8. Are my feelings about the events clearly expressed?
9. Have I created monologues to convey inner thoughts and feelings?
10. Have I improvised the facts where my memory has failed?

Exercise

WRITING ABOUT THE INNER YOU

STEP 1: Begin by taking yourself back to an event that holds within it some of your deepest feelings and emotions. When you have finished writing about the event, check your work to see that you have written in the *present tense,* added your *feelings,* and written some *dialogue.* If not, go ahead and do these things. Try to include inner *monologues* as well.

STEP 2: Now it is time to write your feelings in an even more interesting and vivid way. Up to this point, you have been encouraged to add your feelings at each point in the story. "I am angry," "I am sad," "I am puzzled," and "I feel excited" are some of the phrases you may have used. These are good and helpful statements, and we will continue to use them.

However, there is a way of making such moments even more vivid for the reader, and that is to locate the feeling in parts of the body. Instead of saying "I feel angry," you can explore *where in the body that anger is felt.* For example, "I feel angry" becomes "My heart begins to pound," "My throat goes dry," "I clench my teeth," "My eyes burn." Heart, throat, teeth, eyes.

Here is another feeling: "I feel happy." To express this you may wish to explore other areas of your body, such as your legs, stomach, or toes. "My legs feel light," "My toes tingle," "The ache in my stomach has gone away." Explore what goes on in the various parts of your body when a feeling occurs.

Now, add these feelings to the rewrite of your story.

STEP 3: When you have finished your rewrite you can begin to *edit* your story. That means checking *spelling, grammar,* and *punctuation.* You can use any kind of language you want in your dialogue, but you do want to spell and punctuate it correctly.

CHAPTER 6

Cracking Open the Door to Your Past

"So many of my childhood memories seem to have disappeared," laments Arnold, a new student in my Musicians Union class. "I wonder what to do."

"Your past is like a refrigerator," I tell him. "Once the door is open, memories that are directly in front of you, the most vivid ones, will press themselves upon you. When you've finished writing about those, others in the back will come forward."

"Suppose I can't get the door open," he questions.

"There are more keys to unlocking that door than you can imagine," I say. "One such key is to concentrate on a place where vital, unforgettable things happened."

Composing

DESCRIBE A PLACE MEMORY

Here is a process that may help you pry open the door to your past. First, imagine yourself floating over that place of significance. Next, ask yourself, "What sorts of things did I do there?" Try answering your question with *-ing* words, action words. "I found myself *exploring* the house . . . *wandering* the woods." Finally, write down the *-ing* words that surface, and allow them to help you find specific, vivid moments about which to write.

Try to find memories from your childhood first. You can begin by describing a place that generated experiences affecting you or members of your family.

One such vital and unforgettable place for me is the farmhouse my sister and I have up in Maine. My father bought it for my mother during the Depression, and restoring it was their life's project. I spent almost every summer there from the time I was six months old until I was eighteen. Even now I return almost every summer.

As I imagine floating over the house, a flood of memories comes back to me: *watching* Abner haying with his two-horse team, *reading* by a kerosene lamp at night, *exploring* our pre–Revolutionary War farmhouse, *celebrating* V-J Day near a lake where the ties of a forgotten railroad lay underfoot, *forming* my first band to play at church suppers, *holding* hands for the first time in the picture show, *seeing* Mom and Dad happy together in a way they never were in Florida, *taking* my wife and infant son to Maine and *creating* our second child on the dock at Songo Pond, *filming* my sons exploring the old railroad, *working* side by side with the boys for more than ten summers to clear the brush that had overgrown the meadows during my neglectful years.

Here are some places that may contain significant, vivid memories:

- Places where I lived as a child

- Places where I played as a child

- Places where I did something I shouldn't have done

- Places where I learned a lesson I have never forgotten

- Places where I saw or experienced things that changed my life

- The place where Dad did his work

- The place where Mom did her work

- The place where Grandpa or Grandma lived when I was small

- The place where I experienced my first kiss

- The place where I worked for the first time

As we wander back through the years remembering the things we have done, particular moments from our past begin to reappear. The door of the refrigerator has swung open, and we see that the top shelf is full.

"But maybe I don't want to remember," you say. "My past was full of pain and I only want to get to the happy things."

The more deeply we write from within ourselves, the more fully we can capture an experience that may have been haunting us, find its meaning, and let go of it. This clears such memories, both positive and negative, from the front of our minds and allows us to explore previously hidden, but no less intriguing and vivid, memories.

— • • • —

*I'm getting ready to write what happened to me in a place of importance. I'm not going to get bogged down in details of the place . . . I'm ready to go back . . . way back . . . I'm going back to a vivid event in a special place . . . I'm going to begin writing . . . **now**.*

Reviewing

As we come to the reviewing phase of our work, we will add two other elements to our checklist:

- improvising with the facts when memory fails

- having concern for form and structure: finding the spine of the story

IMPROVISE: FILL IN THE GAPS WHERE MEMORY FAILS

As you continually unearth and confront your memories, you may begin to feel like something of an archaeologist. The brain is a magnificent and fascinating organ, fascinating because it often yields what it wishes to give us, not what we think it ought to be giving us. Within its rich bank of memories you have undoubtedly discovered several fragments of recollections that seem to form a whole, but somehow you cannot complete it—the names, places, and times that are the links between the fragments appear to be lost. As a result, you may feel stuck and unable to write or complete a memoir.

The experienced archaeologist not only knows where to dig for arti-facts of the past, but, when they are in hand, knows how to put them to-gether in such a way that he can make educated guesses about ancient habits, customs, and beliefs. The past becomes clearer.

So, what does one do if one simply doesn't have enough evidence to create the links to complete the story that is lurking inside one's brain? Frustrating, isn't it? A paradox—to know that one's most interesting memory is the story one doesn't remember.

This is where we must operate not as a scientist but as an artist, not as an archaeologist but as a lover—in fact, as more than a lover.

Picasso once said, "Art is a lie that tells us the truth," and this is the sense in which we must become artist, lover, seducer, and Casanova. As a lure to bring out the truth we must be willing to invent, to lie a little. Oh, not to ourselves, or even to our readers, but to our brain. Invention is a creative right-brain strategy that we sometimes need to sneak past the guard of our critical left brain, which, for reasons of its own, is try-ing to hide the past.

So, as you move from the terra firma of one clear-as-a-bell memory to another equally well-grounded memory, if you suddenly find yourself sinking into the quicksand of no memory, you can regain your footing by simply inventing parts of an episode until the clear memory appears.

Perhaps you don't like the idea of lying; perhaps this suggestion arouses in you the same enthusiasm that you had for castor oil as a child and curfews as a teenager. "I'm not a person who invents," a student will often protest. "If I wanted to write fiction, I would write fiction. I'm here to write my life's stories." This is all quite true. But we are not dropping invented artifacts into archaeological digs and trying to pretend they are real—a Piltdown Man approach to life story writing. Not at all.

Our purpose is to entice the brain into yielding the truth. So, once we have invented part of the story, we must rely on our intuition to let us know when something feels false, and then rewrite it, moving toward the truth as best we can.

Occasionally, the brain does not yield what we hope it will. In that case, simply preface the passage with a phrase such as "As well as I can remember . . . " or "My memory is a bit blank here, but I think the next part of the story goes something like this. . . ." A disclaimer like that is all you need. No one can then hold you to the facts; you are off the hook. If a question you cannot answer arises in your mind, by all means deal with the question by responding "I don't remember" or "I don't know." Such a question is integral to the story and must be answered, even if the answer is simply "I don't remember." This way the reader will not continue to puzzle over the question and be distracted from the rest of the story.

Here are some simple guidelines for improvising.

First, when facts are available, stick to the facts. Do not invent facts just to make a better-sounding story. If you do, people will come to mistrust you and will cease believing your stories.

Second, allow yourself to re-create and improvise your own feelings. The reader wants to know what is going on inside you. Do not suppose what others' feelings are unless you can read the expressions on their faces, hear what they are saying, or read their body language. If you try to tell the reader what other people are feeling, your reader will not believe you.

Third, allow yourself to re-create dialogue using the truth of your intuition and feelings as a guide to what is believable. Readers crave dialogue as an alternative to narrative and inner thoughts and feelings.

And finally, if the facts as you remember them simply do not feel real somehow, write what does feel real and add a postscript explaining the difference.

FORM AND STRUCTURE (1): FIND THE SPINE OF THE STORY

Form is a tricky thing to talk about with writers. It is one of those things that all writers and writing teachers love to discuss. Knowledge of form is what makes a writer an expert, just as being able to fill cavities is what makes a dentist an expert. Or at least that is what writers like to believe.

Essentially, form gives one's work some definable shape, so that the readers or listeners know where they are going and can enjoy where they have been. A story about a duck needs to be about a duck. A story about an abortion needs to be about an abortion. A story about an uncle needs to be about an uncle. As a writer, this involves giving the reader or listener little clues about what to look for or listen for, a coherent thread, or even a running gag.

Sometimes a mood or an atmosphere running through a story can provide form. Stories can hang heavy with memory and emotion. This, too, is form.

Each story has its own emotional logic, its own concerns, and the line of that logic is the "spine." Anything else should be left aside or saved for another story. Since the mind can hold just so many things in it at one time, we have to limit the mind's attention to those things that are related to the spine.

Let's suppose, for example, the beginning of our first draft is about taking a trip from Russia to the United States; the middle is about finding a house to settle in so that Mom, who is sick, can get better; and the end is about Mom's death and how everyone felt.

From the ending, we get a clue to the spine and the structure. In fact, the middle—Mom's getting sick—is also a clue. The beginning needs to relate to the end, so the beginning of the story needs to be about Mom's health or well-being. The trip from Russia is clearly a separate story.

Rewriting

For those of you who are continually working on rewriting your stories to make them more interesting and readable, other ways your stories can be rewritten to make them tighter and more effective are as follows:

- finding the beginning of your story

- creating a visual "look" to your story

- expanding the climax of your story

FORM AND STRUCTURE (2): FIND THE BEGINNING OF THE STORY

Here are a few simple steps to follow to find the beginning of your story.

First, ask yourself, "What is the most powerful moment of this vivid memory of mine? What is the moment I remember most clearly?" Then ask yourself, "Can I start my story *just before* this vivid moment begins?" Usually, as writers, we give much more introductory information than the reader needs, information that can be left out or rearranged.

After you have finished your first draft, look over your story right away. Find that first line of dialogue or action. Often, the closer we get to the more vividly recalled moments in the story, the more dialogue we will naturally write. That first line of dialogue may be a clue to the beginning of the story—and to the spine of the story as well.

Don't worry about starting off the story with a perfect opening when you are writing your first draft. *Finding the beginning is strictly a rewriting task.*

Remember, writers have to warm up, and that's what the first few paragraphs of each draft are—a warm-up, until you rewrite them. The first line of dialogue or action is where you begin to hit your stride. By that time, you are in the story—and so are we, your readers.

The story that follows is an example of rewriting by locating the first line of dialogue and rearranging other paragraphs. Notice how sections 1, 2, and 3 are rearranged in the second version for a better effect on the reader.

The Goose Story ——— FIRST DRAFT ———
by Vera Mellus

1

It was autumn. The leaves were turning red and yellow and it was a perfect day to take two little boys to the Los Angeles Zoo. I'm not familiar with the Zoo now, but then there was a barnyard where little children could pet goats and ponies, feed chickens, ducks and geese. They could also see a cow being milked.

My daughter and I packed a picnic basket and set off with two eager little boys. We strolled by the bears, tigers and other animals, but it wasn't till we got to the barnyard that the boys really became interested and had fun. Here they could come in close contact with the animals.

It was a perfect place to take pictures. How great to snap the children feeding chickens and to get those happy smiles on their faces.

2

I was so busy taking pictures I didn't notice a big, fat goose following me around.

I suddenly felt a hurtful pull and looked to see the goose had a tight grip on my big toe. He had braced his feet, stretched his neck to the last inch, and was hanging on.}

3

"I can't believe this," I yelled. "Look, Dede."

"Mother, give him a kick," I heard her yell, as she was having a fit of laughter.

"I can't. He won't let go."

"I'll get a stick," I heard my grandson say.

By this time we were all laughing so hard watching this silly goose.

A few days prior I had fallen in the shower and had broken the toes on my left foot. They were so swollen I couldn't wear a shoe and so was wearing sandals; one toe was so swollen it was white, and to a goose it must have looked like a fat, juicy grub. He finally gave up seeing whether it was going to come off and I went home with all toes intact.

● ● ●

Class members suggested Vera look at the first line of dialogue or action to see whether that was where the spine of the story began. Here is her second version.

The Goose Story ——— SECOND DRAFT ———

3 "Oh, no. I can't believe this," I yell, shaking my foot, trying to discourage a big fat goose from trying to eat one of my toes. "Get away."

1, 2 My daughter, her two sons, and I are in the barnyard of the Los Angeles Zoo. The boys are feeding the ducks and chickens and having a great time. I've been so busy trying to get those happy smiles with my camera that I haven't noticed this goose.

"Get away. Shoo," I yell.

"Mother, kick him," I hear my daughter say, having a fit of laughter.

"I can't. He won't let go."

"I'll get a stick," my grandson says. "I'll make him let go."

By this time we are all laughing so hard to see this silly goose back up, brace himself, stretch his neck to the last inch and hang on.

I had fallen in the shower and the toes on my left foot are broken. I cannot wear a shoe and so I'm wearing sandals—and one toe is so swollen it is white and must look like a fat, juicy grub.

VERA MELLUS Vera was in her nineties when she wrote "The Goose Story." She was born and raised in North Dakota during the wild years at the turn of the century. After the death of her father when she was very young, she recalls her mother running a tent hotel in Marmar. When her mother could not care for all the children, Vera crossed the country in a stagecoach and grew up in Glendale, Arizona, under the care of an aunt. She appeared in the first western movie shot in Glendale, in 1917, was educated in Los Angeles, married and raised two daughters. Bright, elegant, and wise, Vera came to the class "to leave something to my grandchildren." She died in 1989.

I brace myself and pull hard. He lets go. I limp away, then turn around. I'll never forget the look on his face. He stared at me—a look of triumph all over his face.

My two grandsons had a great day, but what really made the day was the goose.

— • • • —

Notice that the spine of the story is now very apparent: the goose's attack on Vera and the comedy that ensues. In the first draft, we had no idea what the story was about until we got to section 2. In the second draft, Vera drops much of section 1 and combines sections 2 and 3—the dialogue and the spine begin together. Notice also that she has changed past tense verbs into present tense verbs.

Sometimes I am asked, "If you are writing in the present tense in one part of your story, how do you make the leap to the next part if it begins, say, a month later?"

You can leap ahead to the new time by explicitly writing "Now it is a month (week, day, hour) later, and I am waiting . . ." or some similar phrase. You may also wish to give the reader a little second-paragraph backstory of what happened between the time the first part ended and the next began.

CREATE A VISUAL LOOK TO THE STORY

From the warm-up, we have created a wealth of material. From this material, we have found a first line of action or dialogue with which to begin the story. From the rest of this material we have constructed a second-paragraph backstory that tells us what has gone on in the past that is important to understanding the story.

At the same time, we want to be sure the audience can see the moment as if it were the opening of a movie: people acting within a setting of some kind, a distinct place where something is happening.

Here is an example from George Small's story "A Day at the Races." (See page 286 for the complete story.)

I'm sitting in the Hollywood Race Track dining room on the second floor. In front of me is a small TV screen showing the horses outside. It is a miserable day. Sheets of rain are pouring down on L.A. The bitter wind is cold and blows through the grandstands, forcing the bettors inside to the dining room.

In this example, George gives us a strong sense of the place and the present circumstances. From the very first line we can see him in the story and what he is doing, "I am sitting . . ."

There are a number of techniques we can borrow from the painters and sculptors of the past to make our stories more visual. We can use color, perspective, texture, and space—but most of all we can use light, especially the interplay of light and dark.

The film noir movies starring James Cagney, Humphrey Bogart, and George Raft from the late 1930s and early 1940s were immensely popular, thanks in part to the wonderful black-and-white cinematography. The superb camera work and astute direction allowed characters to emerge from the darkness halfway into the light like primordial reptiles half in and half out of the slime of creation (which is how Orson Welles' sheriff dies in *Touch of Evil*). These characters are often seen in silhouette or as shadows on a wall (as in Carol Reed's *The Third Man*) or with the shadow of a Venetian blind playing across their faces.

Much of the technique of such dramatic lighting can also be seen in the films and paintings of the early German expressionists. For example, Robert Wiene's 1919 film *The Cabinet of Dr. Caligari* showed us how an impression of macabre horror can be created if a face is lit from below, casting great shadows around the eyes.

Three centuries before, the Italian painter Caravaggio demonstrated the powerful impact of faces and figures emerging from darkness into light. Before him came such Renaissance masters as Leonardo da Vinci in the late fifteenth century and Masaccio in the early fifteenth century. In da Vinci's paintings, however, the play of light and dark is less for dramatic purpose than for illuminating the expressiveness of the body and face. For example, in the *Virgin and St. Anne,* the crosshatching of lines (especially evident in his sketches) gives each face and figure a depth and dimension never before seen in Western art, so that light and dark illuminate each person's feelings or state of mind.

We can do the very same thing in our writing, harnessing the drama of light and dark, as seen in the following excerpt.

Cricket   ——EXCERPT——
by Dirk Tousely

"Evening, Mr. Hattey," I muster, still unable to see him through the screen though I do detect the odor of his cheap cigar.

"I brought you a Dutch Master," I say as I open the screen door and enter the porch. I can barely make him out in the dusk as he swings slowly back and forth in his porch swing.

"Trying to suck in with me, huh?"

I ignore the son-of-a-bitch's remark, hand him the Dutch Master and ask, "Is Cricket ready yet?"

He rolls the cigar between thumb and forefinger, testing its quality, before saying, "Why the hell you call her Cricket? Her name's Josephine. If I wanted her to be Cricket, I'd uh named her Cricket."

"Harry leave that boy alone," comes Mrs. Hattey's voice from the darkest side of the porch.

"Oh, hello, ma'am. I didn't see you," I say, grateful for a champion in my corner.

"Well, I'm here. Don't pay no attention to him," she says as she rises and gropes her way through the gathering darkness to the living room door. "Gettin' kind of chilly for me," she adds on her way to the living room. But I know she's not chilly. It's hotter than hell. She doesn't want to listen to his badgering me again tonight, that's all.

A lamp in the living room goes on and casts its warm glow onto the porch through an open window. Now I can see Mr. Hattey clearly.

There's no change from a few nights ago. Same white undershirt with shoulder straps. Same woolly chest hair peeking out. Same khaki pants.

Same high-top work shoes. Same bottle of Hamm's beer. Same crappy cigar. Same three-day beard. Same long black hair streaked with gray and combed back over the ears ending in a duck tail at the back of his head. Same suspicious look. I feel I'm dealing with a muscular forty-five-year-old man powered by the brain of a fifteen-year-old medieval peasant. How could God have presented this churlish man and his doltish wife with a cute, lively kid like Cricket whose only fault is saying "you was" rather than "you were?"

DIRK TOUSELY Dirk makes his living writing books and newsletters on chiropractic matters. He yearned to be a writer from the time he was a teenager, when he traveled to Mexico, spending his time in bars until it was time to return to the United States. Now, some fifty years later, he has returned to his first love—writing.

• • •

Notice how effectively Dirk uses light and dark to capture the mood on this porch: "'Harry leave that boy alone,' comes Mrs. Hattey's voice from the darkest side of the porch," and "she rises and gropes her way through the gathering darkness to the living room door," and finally "a lamp in the living room goes on and casts its warm glow onto the porch through an open window. Now I can see Mr. Hattey clearly. There's no change from a few nights ago. Same white undershirt with shoulder straps. . . ."

In our writing, we have to be very careful about spending time describing a place or a setting so that it does not distract from or slow down the story. And making a story as visual as possible is especially effective at the beginning and during the climax.

FORM AND STRUCTURE (3): EXPAND THE CLIMAX OF THE STORY

"I wanted to know more of what was happening at the climax of your story," listeners often say to a writer. "It was so interesting, I just wanted more."

When you hear this kind of comment, I suggest you expand the dramatic moment when everything is coming to a head.

In films, for example, a dramatic moment of action or feeling may actually be done in slow motion or repeated in slow motion, from several angles. In one of the more memorable scenes from the film *A Man and a Woman* by Claude Lelouch, the camera circles the two lovers as they fall into each other's arms at the train station, as if spinning a web around them, sealing them off from the world outside, slowing down everything so it seems these passionate moments exist out of time. Such cinematic techniques allow the viewer/reader/listener to understand and savor every fraction of a moment of such a wonderful experience. Similarly, baseball players, when they are hot, describe the ball coming to the plate as "large as a basketball and moving slowly . . . easy to hit." Everything is slowed down, and the moment when bat strikes ball is expanded.

This is not to say that you, as writer, are trying to slow down the action. Including more dialogue, more reactions from the minor characters, and more of a sense of changes taking place around the action has the effect of speeding up the action because the story becomes fuller, more complete.

Expanding the climax of a story is a subject that deserves considerable attention—attention that will be given it in Chapter 8.

Following is an updated version of the checklist.

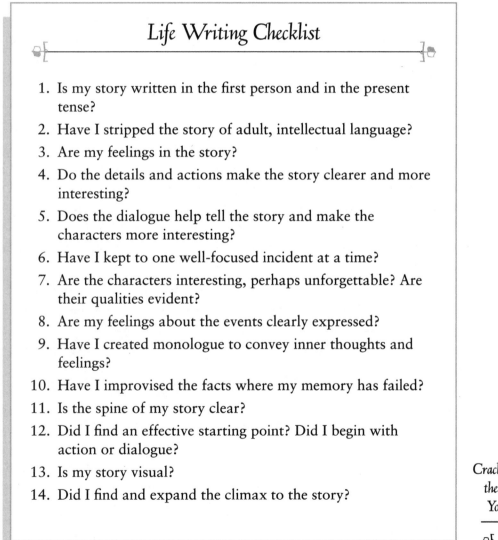

Life Writing Checklist

1. Is my story written in the first person and in the present tense?

2. Have I stripped the story of adult, intellectual language?

3. Are my feelings in the story?

4. Do the details and actions make the story clearer and more interesting?

5. Does the dialogue help tell the story and make the characters more interesting?

6. Have I kept to one well-focused incident at a time?

7. Are the characters interesting, perhaps unforgettable? Are their qualities evident?

8. Are my feelings about the events clearly expressed?

9. Have I created monologue to convey inner thoughts and feelings?

10. Have I improvised the facts where my memory has failed?

11. Is the spine of my story clear?

12. Did I find an effective starting point? Did I begin with action or dialogue?

13. Is my story visual?

14. Did I find and expand the climax to the story?

Exercise

Now that you have written your memory of what happened to you in a place of importance, see whether you have included your feelings, have written in the present tense, and have used some dialogue and inner monologue.

STEP 1. Now let's look at another step in the process, *finding the beginning*. Very often you can create a story by figuring out the climax to the story first. The climax of a story is the point toward which all the interest and emotion build. It is the point of greatest tension and greatest interest. It is probably what you remember most vividly. What is the climax to your story?

STEP 2. The next step is to begin the story just before the climax, looking for the beginning by locating the first line of action or dialogue that directly relates to the climax. In other words, when you first start a story, you may give a lot of description of where it's taking place and why you are there. This is just a warm-up for your mind to get ready for the real incident. Don't include this in your revised beginning.

Locate the beginning by finding the first line of *action* or *dialogue* that leads directly to the climax. Below is an example.

> It's a real hot day and I been up late with my buddy Mauricio here in Houston, Texas, so I'm not with my friends this morning. I am fifteen years old.
>
> I'm tired so I'm going to go back to sleep. We were partying all night.
>
> "Don't wake me up if anyone comes to look for me, OK?" I tell my sister.
>
> A little while later she wakes me up and says, "Your friend's been killed."

Looking back at this piece, the writer searches for the first line of dialogue, "Don't wake me up," and makes it the first sentence of the story. He also drops the phrase, "so I'm not with my friends." Here's his next draft:

"Don't wake me up if anyone comes to look for me, OK?" I tell my sister.

It's a real hot day here in Houston, Texas, and Mauricio and I been up late. I am fifteen years old. I am tired so I'm going to go back to sleep. We were partying all night.

A little while later she wakes me up and says, "Your friend's been killed."

This draft now has a better and more interesting beginning, doesn't it?

STEP 3. This is where you will be *setting the stage*. You may bring in factual information later in the first, or even the second, paragraph, after beginning your story with action or dialogue.

Notice that in the revised example above, the stage is being set in the second paragraph: *It's a real hot day here in Houston, Texas, and Mauricio and I been up late. I am fifteen years old. I am tired so I'm going to go back to sleep. We were up late partying.* Notice also that we might take the sentence *We were up late partying* and add it to the earlier sentence to tighten the story: *Mauricio and I been up late partying.*

Go ahead and rewrite, or better still, rearrange your first few paragraphs to find the beginning of your story and to set the stage.

CHAPTER 7

Developing a Writing Strategy and Choosing Writing Exercises

"What should I write about now?" asks a young student when we return from lunch. "Should I begin writing in chronological order? I've already outlined over thirty memories."

I smile at her. "Always go with the memories that are the most vivid. You don't have to write anything in chronological order." Then I add, "But it is a good idea to write a vivid memory from each decade of your life, just to give you a sense of the arc of your life."

Developing a Writing Strategy

Once we have written and rewritten the first few exercises and have written a number of vivid childhood memories, I suggest we all record a series of the most vivid moments of our lives, one for each decade. One way to do this is to note in a word or two, using index cards, the vivid moments in each decade of our life. Reviewing our cards, we will gain a powerful sense of what each moment is like without having to write the stories that come to mind. These are the *guide stories* through which the larger pattern of our lives will emerge.

Once we have recorded our decade memories, we can write three or four more vivid memories to fill in each decade. The most important decades to work on are the first two, from birth to twenty years. Later, after we have written each story, we can assess their impact on our lives, if we chose to do so, in a P.S. (see Chapter 5).

Please note that when I say "write a memory," I mean a *vivid* memory—not an ordinary, dull, repetitive memory. It is important that we seek out our vivid memories first, as well as the memories hiding behind the vivid memories. Like tenpins lined up in a bowling alley, there is only room for a few in the first rows, but when we have knocked those down, we have a chance to see what is left standing in the back and at the corners. These are the hidden memories, which we will work with in Chapters 8 and 9.

Nancy, a woman whose beloved husband had died earlier in the year, came to one of my workshops intent on dealing with her grief. But for many months she found herself writing about her childhood and the pain and the pleasure of growing up, never once writing about her husband and their life together. She felt guilty for some time, but I assured her that she was handling the process the right way. Eventually, she said she was ready and asked what to do first.

"Should I write about his death?" she asked. The fear and pain in her eyes was evident.

"No," I said, "write about the wonderful times between you."

Little by little the richness of their life unfolded. After several months, she felt cleansed: their happiness had been celebrated and now it was time for her to write about the end. At first she wrote in a clinical way, pushing away the pain and sadness. Her writing group quickly pointed out to her what was happening, and she began to tell us the story in a simpler, more vivid way.

"At last," she said, "I feel free."

We explore the memories we need to relive and put them to rest by fully experiencing everything that was in them to experience, including ways in which they remind us of old patterns from childhood, patterns that may or may not have served us well.

Choosing Writing Exercises That Meet Your Needs

You can easily tailor writing exercises to your own needs. You may wish to write more memories to see a shape to your life based on the memories you have been bringing to the surface. You may have a desire to develop your writing skill. Or you may want to write about your memories as an avenue to exploring your emotions.

The following series of writing activities will help you explore any or all of the above. They may be approached in any order, although I suggest you begin by writing one memory from each decade of your life and, if time permits, write at least half a dozen stories of memories from early childhood.

Exercise

PART 1: WRITE VIVID MEMORIES OF EACH DECADE

Working from the index cards on which you recorded a word or two to remind you of a vivid memory from each decade, now turn your decade memories into stories. As a collection, these *guide stories* will help you see some of the patterns that weave through your life, shaping who you are.

PART 2: HONE YOUR WRITING SKILLS

STEP 1. Write a vivid memory to develop your ability to use dialogue. In this memory, let your characters interrupt one another. Also explore unusual speaking qualities, such as a Jamaican patois or a southern drawl; Latino, Yiddish, or black-vernacular phrases; and slang. Such language adds richness to stories and builds strong characters.

STEP 2. Write a vivid memory in which each new, important character is introduced with a thumbnail description. For example, consider this thumbnail sketch of a newly introduced character:

> Uncle Eli walks in the door. Short, dapper, and quite small, he wears a faded dark suit and a sad smile on his face. There is a worn and yellowed handkerchief tucked neatly into his breast pocket.

This description tells us a lot about Uncle Eli—that he is a bit out of the mainstream, bent on keeping up appearances, but that life weighs heavily on his shoulders. It also tells us a lot about the writer—that she is observant and watchful.

> The guy runs by me. He is wearing something blue, a coat or a
> sweater. He's kind of youngish, maybe thirty. There is a sort of a smile
> on his face. It's kind of a scary, evil smile.

This thumbnail sketch works because it is fairly imprecise. It is believable as the point of view of someone who suddenly turns around and catches something out of the corner of his eye.

Now, try writing thumbnail sketches for your own characters.

PART 3: EXPLORE YOUR EMOTIONS

STEP 1. Write a vivid memory in which you allow the central character to hold two differing emotions at the same time, such as happiness and confusion, love and disappointment, or anger and awe. Remember to use all five sense to convey these emotions.

STEP 2. Write a vivid memory in which you turn inner thoughts and feelings told to the audience—*I wish he would be more truthful. It makes me angry when he lies like this*—to inner thoughts and feelings told directly to another character—*"George, stop lying to me!" I scream at him inside my head.*

This kind of direct but inner confrontation is even more effective when we allow the dialogue that comes from our mouths to be quite different from our normal speaking tone, which is often toned down. Consider another example:

> "I'll be back by six o'clock to pick you up," my son says to me. *I
> know he has no intention of being here by six o'clock or seven or eight.
> I won't see him for a long time. Why can't he just tell the truth?*
> "Okay," I say, my voice coming from a long way off. "Okay."

This passage can be revised by focusing the inner dialogue directly at the other character:

> "I'll be back by six o'clock to pick you up," my son says to me.
> *"Bullshit," I scream at him inside my head. "You're not going to be*

Developing a
Writing
Strategy and
Choosing
Writing
Exercises

◦⟨ 99 ⟩◦

here, are you? You're gonna disappear just like you did yesterday and the day before." My heart is pounding and my head aches. *I'm so tired of this . . . so tired.*

"Okay," I say, my voice coming from a long way off. "Okay." I sit down, rubbing my forehead as he walks out the door.

Now, try this technique with a memory of your own.

CHAPTER 8

Expanding the Climax
of the Story

During an advanced workshop, I welcome several faces from past workshops. Stephanie, a red-haired mother, for one, as well as Tamara, a whimsical young mother of two.

"Welcome to the second day of the workshop," I say. "It's good to see you all again."

"I'm glad I'm taking this workshop," Tamara says with a laugh. "It forces me to write. Otherwise, I just focus on my problems at home." The others nod their heads.

"It's not easy to tear myself away from small kids and a tired husband," says Stephanie, her broad smile and copper-colored hair lighting up the room. "I worked hard on this story."

I give her an encouraging smile, as I suspect she is about to dive into something important. "In this workshop, we are going to look at an important memory and see if there are places in each story, particularly in the climax, that can be opened up to reveal more of what happened than we remembered at first."

Each of the eight people in the workshop takes out the story he or she had written for the first night's work. One by one, they read and we make comments. Finally we get to Stephanie's story.

My Mother's Death   —FIRST DRAFT: EXPERT—
by Stephanie Bernardi

My mother is dying. Cancer has eaten away at her once lush full figure. Today she weighs sixty-eight pounds. This has only added emphasis to her pale clear blue eyes. The eyes that always knew everything. She stares transfixed on the painting in the corner. His picture hangs over her chest of drawers. In every house, it always has. The icy blue eyes peering out from eternity and always calling to us, "I still am."

The thick knife strokes of paint fill in his cherub cheeks, rosy as that of all healthy blonde and fair three-year-olds. Forever three. My brother. The one I never knew.

His presence, though, in our family is as definite as any of the other seven siblings. It is just that we don't speak of him. Somehow, this has only added emphasis to his memory. Losing him into that cold silent death of drowning is still painful to speak of, even now thirty-five years later.

"What do you see, Mom? Is someone there?" I ask her.

"Yes," she says, "Gary." I don't doubt this. I just want to know more. She has not spoken for weeks. She drifts in and out. Occasionally she babbles. My father says it's from senility, from the cancer in her brain. I don't believe him. Something more is going on.

• • •

"This is a very beautiful story, Stephanie," says one of the group members. "But I wonder if I could be brought into it a little more." Several others echo her thoughts. Stephanie looks a bit puzzled.

"Some of the language keeps us at arm's length, Stephanie," I say. "I suggest you take as much of your present, adult, reflective self out of the story as you can."

"Really?" she says. "I thought I had."

"Let's look at the first paragraph," I suggest. She rereads:

> My mother is dying. Cancer has eaten away at her once lush full fig-
> ure. Today she weighs sixty-eight pounds. This has only added emphasis
> to her pale clear blue eyes. The eyes that always knew everything. She

STEPHANIE BERNARDI   A mother of two small children, Stephanie assists her husband in his business and writes to keep her mind active.

stares transfixed on the painting in the corner. His picture hangs over her chest of drawers. In every house it always has. The icy blue eyes peering out from eternity and always calling to us, "I still am."

"Some of that language, while wonderful, is a little difficult to believe. I sense you could carve some of it away and get more of a hard, gemlike self to emerge."

"Really?" asked Stephanie, shrugging her shoulders unconvinced. "Well, I'll give it a try."

The next Sunday, the small group of writers reconvenes. Everyone is eager to hear what Stephanie has done. She takes out the story. "I don't think it's very good," she says. "I think I've pared it down too much."

My Mother's Death   —SECOND DRAFT: EXCERPT—

My mother is dying. Cancer has eaten away at her. Today she weighs sixty-eight pounds.

As I sit and watch her, she stares off, fixed on the painting hanging in the corner. His picture hangs over her chest of drawers. It always has. His blue eyes catch me as they call out, "I still am."

The thick knife strokes of paint add depth to his three-year-old cheeks. He is rosy and animated and forever three.

My brother. The one I never knew. Thirty-five years ago he drowned. He is never spoken of. This has only added emphasis to his missing place in our large family.

"What do you see, Mom? Is someone there?" I ask her. There is no response, just that quiet. "Mom, is someone there?" I repeat.

"Yes," she says. "Mama is here."

I don't doubt this. I just want to hear more. She has not spoken for weeks. She drifts in and out. Occasionally she babbles. My father says it's from senility, from the cancer in her brain. I don't believe him. Something more is going on. In the hospital last week, when I sat with her, it seemed she was talking to someone, but when I asked her about it, I could get no response.

"That's wonderful Mom. Is anyone else there?" I ask.

"Yes . . . Gary . . . and Helen." I am not surprised about Gary. But who's Helen? Helen . . . Helen? I think Grandma had a sister named Helen, I don't remember any special relationship though . . . at least she's never mentioned it. Maybe a childhood friend named Helen?

"What do they want, Mom?" I ask.

Of course, I know what they want. Here she lies in her suffering, shriveled up to nothing more than a faded memory of the mom she was. Her gestures are infantlike now. The fingers curled. And the hands. The part of her body that hasn't changed. I used to hate those hands. They were wrinkled beyond her age. My hands are the same. Now they are the only familiar part of her. I reach for them. Somehow, when I touch them and close my eyes for a moment, it is all forgotten: the feeding tubes up her nose, the diapers, the look of childlike innocence on her face that is pathetic from her. My once elegant mother even picks her nose and scratches herself.

(The complete second draft appears on page 276.)

• • •

"So you think this is an inferior draft, huh?" I ask. Stephanie nods. I laugh. The others do too. "Just goes to show what our self-critic knows."

Stephanie looks around. "You mean the rewrite is better?"

One woman in the group reaches over and touches Stephanie's arm. "It was one of the most powerful experiences I've ever had listening to a story. I cried all the way through." The others in the group echo her comments.

Stephanie is silent for a moment, then speaks. "Well, I'm glad I followed your advice, even if I didn't know it was working so well. But I see what you mean. Are there any other places?"

I have her read another passage from her first draft—

His presence, though, in our family is as definite as any of the other seven siblings. It is just that we don't speak of him. Somehow this has only added emphasis to his memory. Losing him into that cold silent death of drowning is still painful to speak of, even now thirty-five years later.

—and I point out how effectively she has reworked it.

Thirty-five years ago he drowned. He is never spoken of. This has only added emphasis to his missing place in our large family.

"Here you give us the action, the drowning first, then you tell us the impact on the family while getting rid of the purely intellectual concept: *His presence . . . is as definite as any of the . . . siblings.* This concept is one we as readers want to conclude for ourselves, and we do so by the end of the second rewrite."

"I see," muses Stephanie. "I guess it does work."

"But what's really impressive is the part that starts the climax, 'Mom, do you want to go with him?' Go ahead and read both versions."

Stephanie reads on.

My Mother's Death —FIRST DRAFT: EXCERPT—

"Mom, do you want to go with him?" I ask.

A long pause. I know what her answer will be. I don't blame her. This is not a life. But I need to hear it from her.

"Yes," she whispers.

Her eyes remain transfixed on the painting. She appears to be listening to something. To what? I tell myself not to judge this moment and just be with her. I know he is here.

Now she reads the second version.

My Mother's Death —SECOND DRAFT: EXCERPT—

"Mom, do you want to go with them?" I ask. I know what the answer is. I don't blame them. This is not a life. But I still need to hear it.

"Yes, but they do not want . . . to steal the family," she tells me. This shocks me. But I don't know why it should. I mean, I clearly understand this. My mom is the center of this family and with her gone who knows what will happen . . . maybe we'll all drown.

Already my father and I are not speaking. He hates me. I do not agree with him. And he does not like that. I try to understand him but I am angry that he does not treat her with respect. He lifts her roughly to put medicine on her bedsores. He talks in front of her as if she is not there. And worse, being a radiologist himself, he won't stop radiating this dying woman.

He says it's to keep her from pain, but the only pain I see is from the side effects. I just learned a new word today, "fistula." That is the hole that was just burned through her rectum into her vagina. Yes, I hate him too. Why won't he let this poor woman die? Forty-five years of marriage and he does not see what he is doing.

He is crazy with grief. Because I speak up, he has shut me out. He ignores me when I come to visit. I help take care of her in the day while he is working. I know she will not last much longer so I refuse to let him push me away. Last week I left him a birthday present hoping to make peace. It still sits in the entry unopened. He refuses to accept it. So there it sits for everyone to see his rejection of me. But I know she knows what's going on here and so do they.

"Mom, they're not stealing the family. Because of you, we're strong. We'll get through this. Your love will live on in all of us. We're all just scared right now but it will be OK," I lie to her.

"We must transcend this," she says.

Transcend? This is not my mother's type of word. I have never heard her use this expression.

— • • • —

I look around the room. "What is so stirring, perhaps mystical, even possibly mythical about this moment is not that she remembered more of the moment and wrote it in a simpler, more vivid way. What is remarkable is that she began to remember the whole story differently. At first she remembered her mother talking to her dead brother. But upon further probing she recollected that she had heard her mother doing something far more mysterious—talking to people on the other side—people whom Stephanie could barely picture—and Stephanie recognized that her mother was using the language of transformation, all difficult for someone steeped in religion to accept. But Stephanie's subconscious was beginning to let this information into her consciousness. This is remarkable writing and remarkable self-probing."

For the purpose of our self-discovery, it is important that every significant voice or person in a vivid moment be present, so we want to expand our climax wherever possible.

The truth of the event will gradually yield itself to the "path of the pen" as we rewrite the story. From time to time, as we reach the end of a story, we suddenly realize that our pen is telling us a different story from the one we had been writing. When this happens, we need to follow the path of the pen.

Stephanie's experience is a powerful example of this. Her mother was dying of cancer; Stephanie stayed with her mother most of that time. Where others shied away from intimacy, Stephanie drew closer.

The experience was extraordinary but puzzling to her, though she didn't know quite why.

In the rewrite, we find that the climatic moment has been expanded. In the expanding, Stephanie began recollecting that the event actually happened a bit differently than she first remembered: her mother was in the presence of a number of people she loved, not just Gary, her brother.

And a little later, as she continues to work her way through the climax, Stephanie opens it up even wider, giving us more of her feelings and her mother's feelings, and more of the mystery and the wonder of the death experience.

Expanding the climax of the story does three important things:

1. A fully fleshed-out climax creates intense interest in the reader. If the reader is ever to feel a bond with you and your story, it will come about through an intimate and vivid unfolding of the climax.

2. A better, more balanced story will appear. Most stories as they are first written tend to be heavy in the beginning—too wordy, too detailed—and too light in the climax. Stephanie's story is no exception. Better balance means that in rewriting, you may drop some things from the beginning while expanding your climax.

3. In locating the climax and fleshing it out, you may find that the story is actually about something other than what you thought it was about when you began.

While opening up the climax, Stephanie discovered that her story was really about the gift her terminally ill mother was giving her: a glimpse into the other side. Originally she thought the story was about her mother and her brother, which turned out to be the path into the story. The joy for us, the reader, is feeling each feeling, savoring each moment of this powerful episode in Stephanie's life: her mother's aiding Stephanie's transformation in becoming a more spiritual person.

Conclusion

As my students finish reading their stories and most of their questions have been answered, I commend them for their honesty, for the quality of their writing and their insights, and for their contributions to the co-hesiveness of the group.

"Where do we go from here, Bernard?" asks Tamara. "This feels like just the beginning." I look around the room. Most of them are intent on my answer.

"Tamara's right," I reply. "Now that we know how to write in a powerful, vigorous style that is our own, we can explore a deeper, per-haps more shadowy, even more expressive side of ourselves, plunging into hidden memories and hidden meanings still to be unearthed. This is the ground we will cover in the next workshop."

Tamara nods her head in approval as do most of the people in the room, including Stephanie. As we shake hands and exchange hugs at the door, I feel like the pastor of some very unusual church. "Hmm," I smile to myself. "That's okay." I watch as the two of them walk out together. I wonder what stories will emerge next.

The last to leave is Arthur. "I've enjoyed this workshop, Bernard. I really have. I think I will wait before I take the next workshop. I need to just write for a while, see if I can use what you've been teaching. It is very interesting."

"That's as it should be, Arthur. Each of us has to go at this material at his own pace. Some of us need to do a lot of writing and re-experiencing before we plunge into the more soul-searching parts of the experience."

Arthur shrugs his shoulders and nods his head, still a bit mystified. He turns to leave, then turns back. "Is it because I am a man that I am having such difficulties getting back into my past as if I were a child?"

I put my arm around his shoulders. "It's not easy for us to be men and express ourselves openly, with feeling. Most of our stories are about actions because that is how we experience life. We have to work hard to know what we feel between our moments of action." He nods his head. "We have to have two sets of eyes: one that looks outward and partici-pates in the actions of the world, the other that knows what we are feel-ing inside, physically and emotionally, each moment of our lives. It is not easy for us, as men, to do this. But we are making progress."

Arthur shakes my hand. "Thank you, Bernard."

"Hold on a second, Arthur," I say. "Come with me." We walk to my car and I rummage through my back seat, which is piled high with books and manuscripts. I take out a manuscript and look for a section called "Stories."

"These are good examples of men writing about their childhood with feeling, as well as action and dialogue. Read the stories of George Small and Eddie White. You'll see what I am talking about."

As I watch Arthur, I notice a sadness . . . and a hopefulness. Of all the people who will move on to the next phase of the writing process, I think Arthur is the one who needs it the most. Arthur, who still dwells unseen in the shadows of the closet, pushed there by three older, louder brothers who crave the spotlight in their family and get it. Will Arthur take the next step and step out onto center stage in his own life? I smile to myself as I see him lean against the car, already reading the first of the stories.

Exercise

HIGHLIGHTING VIVID MOMENTS

Locate the climax of one of your stories and expand it by doing any or all of the following:

- Add more dialogue, particularly if it is poignant, intense, and revealing.

- Expand and note a character's actions that reveal his or her qualities.

- Record more of your, the narrator's, feelings about the event.

- Add intense color or use dramatic lighting to intensify emotions.

The more of this you do, the more quickly the action will move and the more it will seem to suspend the reader in the middle of it, as happens in the famous sequence (if memory serves correctly) from Claude Lelouch's film *A Man and a Woman* in which Jean-Louis Trintignant hops off the train and sweeps up Anouk Aimée in his arms, the lovers rotate clockwise, while the camera circles them counterclockwise in slow motion, creating a web of intimacy and hunger sealed off from the outside world. Once you have expanded the climax of your story, note any ways in which it changes the story's meaning.

CHAPTER 9

From Rewrite to Insight: Uncovering Hidden Memories

In the middle of an in-service training I am giving at a Kaiser Permanente Chemical Dependency Unit, I suggest that the group begin the second assignment, writing a vivid memory from birth to twelve years of age. In the back of the room, I hear a mumble of some kind.

"I'm sorry, I didn't hear that," I say.

The person I thought had spoken looks embarrassed, as though I have caught him talking in school. "I said, 'How can I do that?'" he replies. "I was so drugged out, I didn't know who or where I was the first twenty-five years of my life.'"

Good point. If we don't remember who, where, and how we were, how can we take stock of our lives?

Like objects encrusted by coral far beneath the ocean's surface, our memories often lie hidden away. We have to pry off what surrounds them to uncover what lies beneath. Once that is done, we can begin to assess our lives. We must ask ourselves, *What is it that I know, that feels better remaining unknown?* How do we find the answer to this question?

The first step is to explore what we *do* remember. That is, if we remember nothing before twenty-five, we write a story about what we recollect at twenty-five.

Unearthing hidden memories is a bit like digging a mine. We sink a shaft where there is something we can dig into. Little by little, if we are willing to write as vividly as we can about the earliest things we remember, the memory will open up. If we are diligent, we will discover that somewhere in that memory is a clue to other memories.

There are any number of other techniques we can also try, such as writing with our nondominant hand, automatic writing, and hypnotherapy, to uncover hidden memories. I encourage exploring them all. These alternate approaches work well because each in its own way gets past the self-critic that keeps so much of our thoughts, memories, and yearnings tightly in its grasp. This is especially true if you are right-handed because the right hand is closely connected to the analytical, problem-solving, left side of the brain. The nondominant hand in a right-handed person—the left hand—is much more creative and less apt to be governed by the shoulds and shouldn'ts of the left-brain right hand.

The truth of this came to me very strongly some years ago. For a long time, I tried writing creatively, but without much success. Then along came the computer. At the keyboard I could type with both hands, correcting and moving things around almost as quickly as I could think. Sometime after that my sister asked, "Did you know you were left-handed as a child?" I reacted with surprise. "Dad didn't think it would be good for you to be left-handed," she continued, "so he had you changed."

As our memory begins to unfold, we need to keep writing stories that reach back farther and farther, to earlier and earlier times. The roots of the patterns of behavior we want to change lie in these early memories. At some point we may be able to see our behavior patterns, but until we see what they are rooted in, we will probably continue fighting with them, perhaps forever.

In a workshop I gave for the Los Angeles Actors Theater in the late 1980s, composed of the nine writers who gathered each Saturday for six weeks, one woman's stories showed remarkable changes from one week to the next. A trim, attractive, long-distance runner who was raised in convent schools as a young child, Lettie held us in shocked silence as we experienced her ever-changing story. As I listened, I noticed how powerful an experience it is for us as listeners to hear earlier drafts incorporated into the fabric of the storytelling experience.

Leaving the Farm   ——— FIRST DRAFT ———
by *Lettie Watkins*

As we stepped out the door to the waiting car in the driveway, my mother turns to my brother and me and says, "Take a last look. We will never come back."

What does she mean? Never smell the sweetness of the alfalfa fields again? Never pick wildflowers again? Never roam the fields again on bare horseback? Never be lulled to sleep by the wind singing through the pine trees outside my bedroom window? Never see the countryside bathed in moonlight?

I accepted what my mother said, because I loved her. She would never, never do anything to hurt me, but a small part of me still rebelled. A large part of me hurt.

As my mother slid into the driver's seat I scooted over so that I could be close to her.

We backed out the driveway and she suddenly stopped the car. She looked like she wanted to say something. My brother and I sit dumbly staring at her face waiting for a sign of what to do.

Mother slowly took off her dark glasses she had been wearing. Her eyes were swollen shut. The swollen area is angry with red, blue, green and yellow bruises around them. I sit horrified. The only sound is the car motor and the drone of small insects. I look straight ahead at the dusty road which leads from our house to the highway. I can't bear to look at her again.

I heard her voice say quietly, "Your father did this to me. That's why we must leave." Something inside my head says, "No, no, no."

● ● ●

After writing her memory down on paper, Lettie began to realize that certain parts of it were inaccurate. As she went over the memory again, she realized that she had not first seen her mother's beaten face in the car, but earlier and somewhere else. Rewriting *in the present tense* helped her recall the truth of what had happened.

LETTIE WATKINS   Lettie is a grandmother whose great passion in life is long-distance running. She writes in order to leave a legacy to her children.

Leaving the Farm ——— SECOND DRAFT———

Something woke me up. I turned and saw my mother standing in the doorway of the bedroom. She had on what she called a "house dress" with pretty little flowers all over it. Mother always looked pretty and neat even when she was alone. She said to me many times, "We must always be ready for company. Be proud of ourselves and what belongs to us."

This morning she did not look very proud. Strange that she did not come in and sit on my bed as she usually did to give me my good morning kiss. I could feel her reaching out to me although she hadn't moved. I didn't know what to do so I said, "Good morning."

She still didn't move. I sat up so it would be easier for her to kiss me. She finally left the doorway and walked toward me. The one board creaking as I knew it would. The board was left that way on purpose. At certain times, it was a signal to anyone in the basement tending the still that he should stay there and be quiet.

As my mother got closer I saw her face more clearly. I thought I was dreaming. Her beautiful blue eyes, which she was so proud of, were slits. Her whole face looked like a stranger's. It was covered with ugly bruises—purple, yellow, green. Her lips were puffy and cut with little bits of dried blood on them. The thought went through my mind, "Oh, I hope she doesn't kiss me." I felt bad for having that thought because I loved her so much.

When she finally spoke, her voice sounded hard. "Your father did this to me and we are going to have to move, so he won't have a chance to do this again." I just stared at her. I could not think. I felt numb.

My whole world fell apart at that moment.

• • •

Why did Lettie's mind play tricks on her, putting the incident in the car rather than in the bedroom? Perhaps placing the event some distance from where it actually happened made it less painful.

After hearing Lettie's second draft, the other members of the workshop sensed there was still more to be told. We all wanted to know more about how she felt as the episode was unfolding and more about her father's character—anything that would help her understand such a temper. In particular, we wanted to know what "my world fell apart at that moment" meant. We wanted to *see* it.

From Rewrite to Insight

⊶ 113 ⊷

So, in the third draft, Lettie changes the verbs from past to present tense so that the incident unfolds in front of her and the reader, a process that also helps her remember the incident more clearly. In this third draft, the new material is shown in italics.

Leaving the Farm ———THIRD DRAFT———

Something wakes me up. I turn and see my mother standing in the doorway of the bedroom. She has on what she calls a "house dress" with pretty little flowers all over it. Mother always looks pretty and neat even when she is alone. She has said to me many times, "We must always be ready for company. Be proud of ourselves and what belongs to us."

This morning she does not look very proud. Strange that she does not come in and sit on my bed as she usually does to give me my good morning kiss. I don't know what to do so I say, "Good morning," *as though things are normal. She still does not speak or move. I suddenly feel cold. Something is not right. Maybe if I sit up it will be easier for her to kiss me.*

I wait. She finally moves from the doorway and walks toward me, one board creaking as I knew it would. The board is left that way on purpose. At certain times, it is a signal to anyone in the basement tending the still that he should stay there and be quiet. *My daddy is what is called a Bootlegger. That means that he makes whisky and sells it to other people. This is against the law. I wish he would not do it.*

I hate making trips to the city with my mother driving the car, the rear seat filled with big cans of the awful-smelling alcohol. A big Indian blanket always covers the cans. Once a policeman stopped us and my mother thought for sure we would be caught. But we weren't, we just got a ticket.

As my mother gets closer I see her face more clearly. I must be dreaming. Her beautiful blue eyes, which she is so proud of, are slits. *She looks Japanese.* This is a stranger's face, the skin, the ugly colors—purple, yellow, green. Her lips are big with little bits of dried blood on them. I think, "Oh, I hope she doesn't kiss me." I feel bad for having that thought because I love her so much.

When she finally speaks, her voice sounds hard. "Your father did this to me and we are going to have to move, so he won't have a chance to do this again. *You and your brother will be living with Nona until I can find work. I promise we will be together again."*

Her chin moves in a way which tells me she is going to cry. Sure enough the tears roll down her cheeks and are allowed to drop on her breasts. Outside the sun dims.

Inside the air is chilled. The silence is heavy—broken only by the quiet scratching of the horn toads in their sandbox. I want to squash them. The movie star pictures are crooked. I want to tear them off the wall. The buzzing of the bees gets on my nerves. I want to cry but I don't.

I just remain silent. But inside I am screaming, 'I don't care what the reason is! I don't want to leave. This is my home!!'

We move to the city. There is a divorce.

• • •

In the new draft of her story, Lettie has substantially expanded the last line, "My world fell apart." Her memory has yielded more dialogue: "You and your brother will be living with Nona." It also yielded vivid details of tears, sun, air, sounds, and her experience of feeling unable to handle any more stress. In Lettie's search for the truth of what happened, her story became much more artistically powerful.

Most of all, Lettie's story reminds us that the search for truth can go on within all of us if we encourage it—that the deepest layers of our inner selves can be reached if we make the effort. The process of writing draft after draft, uncovering bits of the truth each time, is our ally. Once our subconscious releases a bit of the truth to the paper (or computer) before us, it is free of that piece and will relinquish another to see if we can handle that information, too.

It is as if the memory has a mind of its own: if we handle what it reveals to us with reasonable skepticism and an honest desire for more, it *will* yield more.

For other examples of memories yielding hidden truths in rewrites, please review the changes that took place between the first and second drafts of Stephanie Bernardi's story "My Mother's Death" (see pages 102–107) and between the first and second drafts of my story "Dad's Death" (see pages 65–68).

Exercise

Peeling the Skin from Our Memories

Following Lettie's example, try now to rewrite one of your stories to see if any hidden moments emerge, moments you could not have predicted but that speak to you from deep within.

If you are not sure where to begin, ask yourself these questions: "What else would someone want to know about this incident?" "Is there anything important that I have left out of or censored from the story?" Pay attention to the gnawing feelings in the pit of your stomach, feelings that say "it didn't happen this way." If you know there is more but don't recall it, try improvising to see whether you can create something to which your subconscious will react—probably by revealing the truth of what happened.

You see, the subconscious *does* want you to know the truth but, since it is charged with keeping you on an even keel emotionally, it will reveal what is there *only* if it is sure you are ready to see, hear, and feel it.

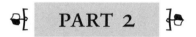

PART 2

Building a Library
of Significant Moments

Introduction

You now have a wealth of writing techniques at your fingertips and, after several weeks, perhaps months, of working on your memoirs, have probably recorded quite a few memories from your childhood.

In fact, you probably have as much technique as you will ever need. Your style will improve as you learn to edit your work more carefully, and your dialogue will become sharper as you listen closely to the conversations of those around you. But, all in all, you have the basic techniques you need.

You are now ready to take on more complicated experiences. The memories of childhood are often distinct and powerful, so they form wonderful stories almost by themselves. Adult life, on the other hand, is rather like a vast sea. A few things really stand out, but, mostly, our life is a series of larger and smaller ripples that spread out around us as we move in various directions.

For most of us, revisiting these memories may be painful as well as joyous. But remember that revisiting a painful past may be one of the most therapeutic things we can do for ourselves. By putting the experience on paper, reading it aloud, and hearing our words, we can begin to let go of it. Or perhaps we could say that it lets go of us.

At the same time, the incidents may show themselves to be part of a larger narrative, and they will take on a different meaning for us. We will begin to see patterns in our lives.

Perhaps we view our lives as failures. We may find that an accurate retelling of the first episode of this "failure" could lead to a reconciliation with relatives and friends we long ago alienated in some way. Or perhaps we were headed in a dull, ordinary, or pedestrian direction when one of the "firsts" in our lives occurred, redirecting our lives, and now we understand the meaning and value of the experience.

Virtually every religion on this earth has, at its center, a person who has undergone a journey of some kind, who has been through a number of trials and emerged on the other side in some way transformed or reborn. That heroic journey, so well chronicled by mythologist Joseph Campbell, is not the sole province of great or important men and women. In one way or another we are all embarked on our life's journey, are tested by life, and have the opportunity to be reborn. Some of us will experience this rebirth in the process of writing our life's stories, because only then will our lives make sense.

Two important areas of experience we will need to review are our relationships with our parents as we get older, and with our children. These relationships have often not been entirely happy and, particularly in the case of our children, the process may not feel complete. Nevertheless, we need to address these experiences as directly as possible. We have related many experiences from childhood in earlier stories; now, it is time to speak to our parents directly. Experience has shown that once we say what we need to say to our parents, we can then say what we need to say to our children. This is not easy, but the rewards are immense.

All of this is preparation for growing older. Most of us are fearful about this. We envision a state in which our faculties have diminished with age, our loved ones may be gone, and we are alone. But that is only one way of viewing aging. There are other ways, and we will discuss them in a later chapter.

When you feel you are ready for this voyage, step down into this little boat of creativity and journey into the vast sea of memory that awaits you.

CHAPTER 10

Love, Adulthood, and Family

Love

What makes most stories of love unusual is the sense that, although there is an objective world out there, when love enters—or leaves—the scene, everything, including the self and perhaps the world, is transformed by a new chemistry, a heightened awareness, as though one has taken a drug of some kind.

Love often places demands not only on the person in love but on everyone else around. When writing the story of your own first love, see whether you can recollect what effect the turmoil in your life and heart had on those around you. Since most of us have already experienced first love, we can only hope that those who come after us will have a grandmother as understanding as the one in this next story.

Advice to a Foolish Virgin
by Bess Shapiro

I'm deeply in love with Bill. I'm also deeply in lust with Bill. I have just reached my twentieth birthday. My heart is ready, and my body is clamoring for that mysterious consummation that will bind us together forever.

But where can that magic take place?

I share a bedroom with Grandma. I complain to her, after assuring her that she's the dearest roommate a girl could have.

"Dammit, Grandma! I don't have any privacy. What if I want to make a baby with Bill?"

Grandma gives me a sly smile. "Foolish little girl! Just say to me, 'Grandma, take a walk!' How long does it take to make a baby? Five minutes."

— • • • —

Perhaps you too feel it is time for you to return to your place of memory. Find your comfortable spot, close your eyes, recollect your earliest love, and write . . . __now__.

Adulthood

Young adulthood is a time when the dependent years of childhood have ended. The first significant phase of education is complete. For some, it means a high school diploma; for others who have worked from an early age, it means some skills have been acquired. It is the first time in our lives we are able to say, "I want to do such and such," and can expect to be free to pursue our goals and desires despite any lingering strictures of societal convention, self-expectation, or parental authority.

For some people it is a time of frustration, of decisions made unconsciously and later regretted: a college chosen hastily, a marriage and a family formed unwisely.

This stage of life is also a time when we acquire new responsibilities, a time when work begins to have real significance for us. Education and training may be behind us; enterprise, dedication, and accomplishment

BESS SHAPIRO   Bess was born in New York of a Russian immigrant mother who had at one time acted in the Moscow Art Theater of Chekhov and Stanislavski. In the United States, her mother acted in the Yiddish theater, where she met and married a young actor/director. The family moved to Salt Lake City, where Bess was raised to be a pianist. Bess came to class to write stories for her grandchildren, primarily stories of her wise and beloved grandmother, who appears in "Advice to a Foolish Virgin."

are before us. We may take on these responsibilities with some sense of awe at what we have chosen to do. The following is one young man's story of confronting his newly won responsibilities.

Field Trip
by Edward Ash

Ten o'clock Wednesday morning, November 17, 1957. For a change the kids in my sixth grade class at Terra Bella Elementary School in Pacoima are quiet. It is one of those infrequent moments when a teacher can sense that most kids are really learning . . . even if most of them are slow, academically. One group of students is reading from a fifth-grade book with me, and another group wrestles with review work I just assigned. The rest of the class is "free reading" from magazines or books I've checked out of the library. In about thirty minutes each group will switch activities. It's taken me all semester so far, to get them to this point. Feels pretty good.

That, of course, is just the moment the principal, bursting with power, walks in with two policemen. Without saying a word, she stalks over to Jesse Barrios, motions him up and out. Barrios is dwarfed by cops and outweighed three to one by her. Jesus H. Christ, no one even says "boo" to me or tells me a goddam thing.

I walk out on the tiny porch of my wooden bungalow, ready to spit nails. "What the hell do you mean by disrupting my class, and grabbing this kid right out of his seat in front of all the others?" I say this to the two big policemen crowding us there and think, are you crazy talking to cops this way?

"Go back inside," one of them says. "Unless you want to come down to the station along with the kid."

"What did he do? Damn it, he's just twelve, twelve and a half years old," I say.

"He's old enough to go to jail for stealing," one cop says.

Jesse doesn't say a word. But the principal pipes up, looking at Jesse as if he has just thrown up on her. "Can we finish this in the

EDWARD ASH   Ed is a retired school teacher who served in the army during World War II. Some of his most vivid memories are of his childhood when he was placed in an orphanage.

office? Mr. Ash, teachers may never leave the students alone! We should be in our room at all times. If you need to converse with the police, you may now be excused to my office. I'll take your class for a few minutes."

Inside, I say to the police, "Why are you trying to scare him? Jail? For a kid his age?"

"Never mind his age. Are you the guy who took the class to the museum?" the short one says.

"Yes. About a week ago. First field trip some of them ever had."

"Well, teach, you did a damned poor job supervising them."

"Hey, the kids were damned good. No fights, no one got sick, and they were pretty good on the bus," I tell him.

The tall one pipes up. "They were good at other things, too, like stealing."

"Stealing what?" I demand.

He takes a paper from a folder. "The guard swears he saw this kid take something from a display." He reads, "'Hacha . . . a carved figure of a head, black jade, six inches tall, believed to be Mayan, seventh to tenth century, on loan from the University of Vera Cruz, estimated value $6,000.00.'"

"And you think this kid, Jesse Barrios, stole it? Ridiculous!" I say, thinking, oh Jesus, he probably did.

"Well, if he doesn't tell us where it is or who he sold it to, then his little twelve-year-old ass will be studying in jail."

By now it is lunchtime, and the principal has returned to the office. "Don't you think it's time we called his parents?" I ask her. Then I remember: no mother and his father was usually drunk. His older sister was only home later in the day.

And the principal says, "Don't worry about him. I'll call Welfare. They'll have someone over at the station by now."

"Hey, let me talk to the kid alone."

"Are you a lawyer, too?" the short cop asks with a smile. "He talks to us before he talks to you."

"Jesse," I plead, "tell them you didn't do it for God's sake. You want to spend time in jail? No school? No family? No friends?"

"I don't have no friends." True enough. "Besides, I did it."

"What?" I think I'm yelling.

"Ah, Mr. Rrrrash, I took it," he says as if I should have known better, which I did.

"That's enough," intones the larger cop. Turning to me, a sneer on his face, he says, "Talk to the Sergeant. Maybe you can visit him in jail. He'll be there for about twenty years."

They goose-step him outside. A couple of hundred kids watch as they put him in the back of the car and speed off, lights flashing. He is so small I can't even see him. He is lost in that back seat, lost in Pacoima.

The next day I go to see Jesse at the home where the Juvenile Department and Child Welfare places him.

"Hey, Mr. Rrrrash! They finally let you in. I knew they would." He looks as if yesterday never happened.

"Jesse, you are in one hell of a lot of trouble. I don't think you realize how bad it is going to be."

He looks at me, the smile gone, his eyes darker than ever before, his tone low as he speaks. "Mr. Rrrrash, this thing I have done?"

"Yes?"

"Is very bad?"

"Very bad, Jesse," I say.

He looks directly at me. "Well, is all your fault, you know," he says with a straight face.

I push up from my chair. I'm ready to haul off and hit him. Was this kid ever going to accept any responsibility for himself? I shout at him, "My fault! What the hell are you talking about, Jesse? You took the thing, not me. Don't blame me like you always blame others at school"

"I did it. But I would not do it if you did not tell me, tell the class, all those things."

"What the hell are you talking about, Jesse? Are you saying I told the class, told you, to steal things? No one ever had to tell you to steal, you little bastard, you've probably done it from the day you were born."

"Mr. Rrrrash, you remember we study social studies? History? And how you tell the class how most of the kids have fathers, mothers, who come from many different countries, how people live hundreds and hundreds of years ago?"

"I never told you to steal."

"No. But you tell class how people from Spain come and steal gold statues, gold plates, gold masks from ancestors of people in class. You remember you say this?"

"Yes, I said that . . . something like that."

"You take class to this museum to learn our history and make us proud. We find out that long time ago we make the science, we know the stars and weather, we change the crops, we make the medicine, we have the religion. You show we are not all 'dumb dirty Mex,' or 'beaners.' We come from great people."

"Great people do not steal things from other people!"

"Like the men from Spain who ride horses and steal from our fathers?"

I shut up. I never thought this kid learned anything in my class. Take the class on a field trip to a museum to see Aztec and Mayan art? Nothing but groans from the class. But I wanted them to know that their heritage might be memorable and exciting. Was this going to be one of the more memorable and exciting mistakes of my life?

"All right, Jesse, so it's my fault. That's over with. Now tell me, what the hell did you do with the mask?"

He is very thoughtful. "I show you where it is. But no one else. Then you do what you want with it."

I go out, call the police, the Department of Child Welfare, the social worker, the principal. Finally after talking to a dozen different offices and signing a dozen sets of paper, they release Jesse in my custody.

I'm pretty weary of all this. I go back to see Jesse. "We're out for two hours, so where are we going?"

"You have your car?" he asks.

"Sure. Outside." I say.

"No one is going to follow?"

"So they say. Where to?"

"To get the thing. Come on." He walks out the door and I follow, dumb as a mule.

I don't have a key to my classroom; they are always kept in the main office. Apparently he doesn't need one, opening it faster without one than I ever did with one. Inside, he invites me to sit at his desk. I am really exasperated, fed up. Sitting at the small desk and taking orders from Jesse doesn't help my disposition at all.

He walks over to my locked closet, opens that without my knowing how, leans in, bends down, takes out a package, brings it to the desk. He holds it tentatively, thinking about what he is going to say. "Mr. Rrrrrash, this belongs to my people; it belongs to me."

"Just because you steal it, doesn't mean it is yours."

The twelve-year-old kid suddenly appears a lot older. His black eyes flash, the skin tightens on his dried, smooth-leather face. He takes a deep breath. "First, I show you something." He puts the package down, his look daring me to take it. Then, reaching inside his desk, he pulls out a small, flat envelope. "I never show this to nobody before." He opens the envelope and takes out an old picture, faded, bent and crinkled, showing a man's face in profile. It is the exact image of Jesse; the nose is more prominent and curved, but the resemblance is perfect. "My real father," he boasts. He puts the picture down, takes the unwrapped package, opens that and shows me what he had stolen.

The basalt "Hacha," the ax, dark and speckled, glistens with power and glory in the dusk. Slowly he raises it along the side of his face. Slowly, I feel myself move back in the chair, astonished. His hand is shaking, his breath pained and strained. He places the carved face close to the photo. Every characteristic on his father's face, on his face, is the face on the ax. They might all have been cast from the same ancient mold. The lineage is uncanny and striking. The patina and age of the piece only emphasizes how minute the facial changes are and how direct the line is.

I look at him for a moment. I had never seen Jesse show a tear. But I do now. I look away, damn it, or I would be bawling, too. I think of the cardinal rule they stress to any male school teacher . . . never touch a kid, no matter what. To hell with that. I put my arms around him and hold him tight until he stops.

"Oh, Mr. Ash, Mr. Ash, what am I going to do? You think I go to jail forever, the way the cops say?" Jesus, has he really, finally, stopped using those damned rolling "r's"?

"You won't go to jail, Jesse. First, I need to talk to a lot of people. Pack that thing carefully. It goes back to the museum. Lots of people, kids and adults need to see this."

I get to a phone, make an hour's worth of calls and arrange to take Jesse to his home.

Tired and worn out, anxious to get to my apartment, I drop him off and start my car. A shout from Jesse who turns just before he goes into the old shack. "Hey, Mr. Rrrrrash! Is this yours?" and with his wicked, shining smile he throws something to me and then vanishes inside. My wallet! When did that little bastard swipe that from me? I head for home, a stupid grin on my face.

At the end of the semester Jesse will finally go to Junior High School. Academically he's only a C student. Otherwise, straight A.

Ten years later, a police car pulls me over and I wonder what the hell I've done this time. In the mirror, I see him get out of the car, and swagger over. I roll the window down as he bends toward me. "Hey, Mr. Rrrrash!" I hear a loud voice say. "Guess who?"

———•••———

Now it is your turn. Roll back the pages of the past to the time when you stood on the brink of young adulthood about to be thrust out into a wider world than you had known before. Sit back in that easy chair, perhaps thumb through some old photo albums or newspapers from the time when you were in your late teens. When you are ready, close your eyes, recollect your past, and write.

The Love of Your Life

As we look into our past, a light illuminates many events we have experienced, and bathes the face and figure of the person who has been the "significant other" in our life, the person destined to be the love of our life. As we gaze at this light, we see that it emanates from a certain place. If we study that place, we see that it is the place and time we first met this beloved person. Now is the time for us to describe our meeting with this one who has brought so much illumination into our life.

This may sound unrealistic if your marriage(s) or relationships have not been happy. But this is the time to put aside old and new wounds, a time to return to that point in life where the light of love was clear, where hope, beauty, and awe were evident, and when a path into the future began to open up.

*Find that most comfortable of places for yourself, perhaps get out that photo album, put one of your favorite "oldies" on the record player, and re-create that first meeting with the person who has meant so much to you. Write it . . . **now**.*

Once you have written about your first meeting, you may wish to continue with other stories and incidents that tell of the ups and downs of your relationship with this very special person.

If the relationship ultimately ended, such as through divorce or death, you may wish to link the various episodes together so that the character and qualities that made this person so fascinating to you are traced from the beginning to the end of your relationship. You may even show how these qualities may have been responsible for its termination. Please read Rebecca Harmon's story "The End" as an example (see page 271).

Recollecting the very best in those whom we have loved is important to our later lives. In my own case, my former wife, the mother of my two children, and I have kept alive an affection for each other and have allowed a firm friendship to grow out of the ashes of our failed marriage. Part of it is her willingness to recollect for herself and the kids the whimsical way we romanced, reminding them of the good times we had, planting in them the idea that they are the children of parents who have cared about and enjoyed each other throughout life, divorced or not.

If you have had several marriages or relationships, each important relationship deserves to be treated in a new story, as if you two were meeting for the first time.

Honest observation is essential for writing stories of life with your beloved. No matter how the story ends, the stresses and strains of a continuing relationship deserve an honest portrayal. When we explore trauma in Chapter 12, we will deal more deeply with the need for honest observation.

Viewing your relationships from the perspective of your first meetings may help you to recapture the bright light of idealized love as you first experienced it. You may find that you have reached a fuller, deeper level of feeling, or that you have reached a place of boredom and stagnation. Perhaps the retelling will open up some possibilities for a better relationship. Perhaps you have reached a point of agonizing and bitter cynicism about the future of this relationship and all others. Whatever your situation, it deserves to be recorded unclouded by your changing feelings about that person. Each phase of life deserves to be seen accurately for what was or is there at a certain time.

If you are ready, go ahead and write about those other significant moments in this relationship. Be honest, fair, and open. That is all you, your audience, or your loved ones can ask of you. He or she would want you to open up. No loyalties are being violated; most of the people who will read or hear what you are composing have had similar experiences. Sharing those experiences will help others release, relieve, and unburden themselves.

Children—and Parents Too

Of all the writing tasks my students have undertaken, writing about one's children seems to be the most difficult. "Why is this so?" I ask. They answer that for the most part their relationships with their children are unresolved and therefore very difficult to put into words. As we continue to discuss the issue of parent/child relationships, however, another explanation begins to surface.

Many of my older adult students feel that their children do not know who they are. "My children see me as a parent," says Bess Shapiro. "Or as a person who was defined and labeled long ago," adds Gina.

My sons and I have discussed this, and my younger son agrees he has been inclined to see me as the father he knew when he was about twelve—quick-tempered, insistent, invasive of privacy. Hopefully, I'm not so much this way now—many years later.

However, for children who leave home at eighteen for college and careers and are no longer around much, it is hard to see changes. It is even harder to call a halt to defining those whom one has known a lifetime and ask, "Who is this person I have known so long?"

My older adult students are divided about whether or not this circumstance ought to be changed. Many feel it is easier to allow their children to see and remember them as the children wish; others feel they want very much for their children to know them as they really are now.

There are two things to consider when listening to the echoes of our children's voices. First, we will want to recollect the significant moments in our children's lives and the feelings we experienced then. Our children, in all likelihood, will have different feelings and recollections, and they may even wish to record their own versions of the events.

The second thing we may wish to do is describe the way in which we, as parents, related to our children and grandchildren—what we hoped to accomplish and what we did accomplish in having and raising our offspring. We may also wish to talk about the characters and qualities we see in our children and grandchildren, and relate these qualities to those of their parents and grandparents. This is important because at one time or another in our lives we are searching for our identity. To find certain traits in ourselves and see how they relate to our ancestors can be quite helpful.

After describing some of these, we may wish to go deeper, to reflect upon moments when our relationships changed, for better or worse. Maybe we as parents made a decision that had a significant positive result, or maybe we failed to make an important sacrifice at an equally critical moment. If we were responsible for a failure, now is the time to own up to it. Our children may not have forgiven us, but forgiveness may be closer than we think. Or our children may have done something that hurt us, and now is a good time to bring it out in the open. Not as a complaint, but as an honest story.

Writing about our children aids in the process of helping them to know who we are. Having them read our efforts to record and define our relationships to them often stimulates a great deal of discussion, some of it painful. It will probably help if we make it clear to them that there are no immutable truths to be found in our stories about them, that our writing is only our version of the truth, and that we welcome their version as well.

For one example of a parent struggling with his relationship to his children, please read Max Levin's story "Anya" (see page 195).

One caution: There is a special trap in describing one's children. It is called sentimentality, which is waxing ecstatic about how wonderful they are long before the reader or listener has a chance to know them as people. It is better to be as objective as possible, letting various situations and the way the children dealt with them delineate their characters. Then it is appropriate to write about how you felt after the event. Of course, if the event is one in which your feelings changed progressively, from concern to fear to terror, or from amusement to laughter to hysteria, it is appropriate to write about how you felt as the event was unfolding.

●　●　●

Now sit back in your easy chair, and go back to where the stories of your children all began, perhaps where conception actually took place. . . .

CHAPTER 11

"Right You Are
If You Think You Are"

Differing Points of View

"OK," I say to the ten people gathered around me. "Let's write about an experience we have in common and see how our perceptions compare." Most of the five couples smiling at me have been married to each other for fifty years or more and are here for a little renewal.

"That should be fun," says Ruth, a woman in her early seventies. "I know exactly what we will write about."

"You want me to put on paper how I ran across the pavilion and slid at your feet, just to ask you to dance," laughs her husband Jerry. Ruth smiles at the thought.

We are gathered together on the second evening of this weekend workshop in beautiful, rustic Carmel Valley, California. The feelings among the couples are, for the most part, warm and filled with loving memories.

The next morning, however, one couple, Jeff and Mary, takes me aside. Younger than the other couples, in their late forties, they are perplexed. "We can't agree on what to write about," says Mary, a wry, thoughtful woman. "When I suggest one thing, Jeff says no."

"Yeah, and everything I think we could write about, Mary doesn't want to expose," chuckles Jeff, her handsome, boyish husband. "She even suggested we write about not being able to agree on something to write about."

"Well, why not write about that—the experience of not being able to agree?" I laugh.

The two of them look at each other. "Hmm, why not," laughs Mary. "We will write about last night."

So off they go to write about not being able to agree on anything to write about.

Their situation is not unusual. Oftentimes, particularly within families, we will disagree with one another about what took place. Our memories of the same event just don't correspond.

In fact, few events are ever experienced or remembered the same way by two people. Most of us argue incessantly that "our" version is more accurate than "their" version is. Some of us, in writing our life's stories, actually modify our own remembrances by including facts and the memories of others with whom we shared the experience. "There must be one version of what has happened that is correct," we suppose. Someone has to be right and someone has to be wrong.

One of the more interesting challenges of the modern age has been to come to grips with the idea that there is no one universal, immutable truth that exists outside our own perceptions. There are only points of view about what exists. If many of those points of view agree, we conclude that those agreeing points of view constitute a truth, at least for the time being. Differing points of view might arise later on, but this does not make them wrong or false or unreal. There are only differing truths, particularly where it concerns our memories.

In drama, this was articulated most forcefully in the early years of the twentieth century by Luigi Pirandello. His plays *Six Characters in Search of an Author, Tonight We Improvise,* and *Right You Are If You Think You Are* provide us with unusual points of view, each argued powerfully, leaving the playgoers to decide whose version is correct.

If we also approach the writing of our life's stories from the position that there are no "truths," only versions of the truth, then we can respect, admire, even enjoy someone else's version of events or experiences that seem very different to us.

For this exercise, find an event or experience that left a strong impression on you, one that you are certain a close relative or friend of yours viewed quite differently. Correspond with your relative or friend, reaching some agreement about the event you are recollecting. Then each of you write about it. Exchange versions, compare them, and then write a commentary about the similarities and differences. My guess is that this task will result in a lot of laughs or lead to a great deal more understanding between you.

Below are Jeff's and Mary's stories of the experience of not being able to agree on what to write about.

The Undecided Story
by Jeff Thompson

Mary and I are each lying down on our own bed, across from one another on each side of the room.

She says to me "O.K., we need to decide on what we are going to write about, or would you prefer to write your own story?"

"No," I reply, "I would rather do a story together."

"All right then, what's our story going to be about," Mary asks.

Looking back at her I try to think of a good story for us. "Let's see, after all these years together we should be able to think of something," I said.

Pause . . . couple minutes goes by and finally Mary speaks out. . . .

"How about the time you sent me back to my parents in Michigan?"

I take a second looking back at her and then say . . . "Oh no, we can't write about that. Besides it gets way too involved and it really sounds negative, to me at least."

"No, it doesn't," says Mary. "That would make a good story."

Silence again. . . . Finally I speak up.

"We could write about the fun times we had remodeling a fixer-upper. Remember the insane times we had with the house in San Diego. We both nearly killed ourselves. I sanded the floorboards in the living room with an electric sander. A week later I ended up in the emergency room with severe pain in my side. It turned out to be a badly strained muscle. Man . . . did that hurt."

"Right You Are If You Think You Are"

JEFF THOMPSON   Jeff is a former banking executive who is exploring his creativity in midlife through computer-generated animation. He is a Vietnam veteran, and a number of his stories focus on his wartime experiences. He is married to Mary Molinar.

"Oh yeah," says Mary, "I sort of remember you being hurt, but we weren't living together then. Anyway, you living in LA kept me from knowing what was going on in your life at times."

Silence for a short while . . . We lay on our beds looking at each other and start laughing. . . .

"There's got to be something we can write," says Mary. "How about the Concord Apartments fire. Now that was scary."

"Yeah . . . you're right, it was. Let me think about that."

"It's getting late," Mary interjects, "and we need to decide on a story, or would you like to write something on your own? You know you could put together something about the time you picked up your dad from Ford Hospital in Detroit, do you remember?"

"Not really. My memory of that is not very clear," I say, "and it would take me some time to describe all the events leading up to that time."

Several minutes go by. . . .

"Here's a thought," says Mary laughingly. "Why don't we write about just not being able to agree on what to write about. What do you think? Anyway maybe by morning we'll know for sure."

We both roll over and fall sound asleep.

The Undecided Story
by Mary Molinar

We walk into the room together. It's been a long and fun day of writing and playing. "What do you think we should write about, Jeff? Do you have any ideas?" I say. Jeff lays himself out on the bed, resting his head on his arm. We're both silent. "I can't think of a thing," I think.

It's Saturday night of a two-and-a-half-day weekend writing workshop. Bernard has assigned all the couples present to write about the same event from their own perspective. It sounded easy and fun. After all, we've known each other 20-plus years. There should be plenty of events to write about. And Bernard always gives the caveat "or write anything you want" after he gives an assignment. The thing is, though, that he knows, secretly, that most of us

MARY MOLINAR   Mary is a businesswoman who is devoting more and more of her time to writing. Her ambition in life is to write a children's book.

won't feel free to choose that "out" of an assignment. I always take it up as "my next challenge."

"So Jeff, what ideas do you have?" A long silence. Damn, I'm always the one who comes up with the ideas, and then he feels trapped by ideas. I'll just wait for him. More silence. "Meow, meow," comes from outside. "Hey . . . the cat came to visit." I walk to the door to let her in. "Prrrr, Prrrr, Prrr," comes from this furry beast as she jumps on my bed. "Well, you could write about your side of the story of the dirt bike ride . . . you know . . . when I first realized I was physically attracted to you, but I don't have my story with me," I say. My mind drifts off to that memory and I'm lost in a time long ago, my body leaning into his. "Well, you don't have it with you, so we can't write that."

"How about when we decided to get married then?"

Jeff is very quiet. "I don't think I remember, so how could I write about that?"

"Oh, you know . . . it was 1984 in the fall . . . if I remember right I gave you an ultimatum." How dare he not remember such an important event, anyway. Damn, it must be an unpleasant memory he's blocked from his mind. Jeff rolls over on his back, staring up at the ceiling. "Well, I can think of some sexual escapades we've had, but that might be too X-rated for a writing group." I smile to myself and agree we don't want to tell that much of ourselves. "How about the night we first made love . . . not write about the actual 'doing it' but about that night then," I say. He rolls over and looks at me from across the room. "Now let's see, when was that . . . my mother's birthday, is that it? Mom and Bob were going out. That's why we were together that night, right?" "Yes, yes, that's right." "Well, I don't think that I can write that," Jeff responds.

The cat walks up to my face, purring loudly. "This is a very loud cat, who never stops purring." I pet her for a while as we drift off into our separate worlds, thinking of what to write. "Hey, how about when you kicked me out of the house," I say. "Now that's a story." No reply. Jeff sits up now as I roll over on my side. "No, no, Mary, no one would understand. Anyway, why would we want to write about such a negative event?" "But I don't think of it as negative because it was an event that forced me to look at myself and change." "Yeah, well, I don't think that's what he had in mind," Jeff says, turning toward me. "Anyway, it's much too complicated."

"Right You Are If You Think You Are"

I get up and go into the bathroom, needing to move around. Jeff rolls onto his back again, eyes closed now. "Hey, Mary . . . I know . . . let's write about the fire." I walk back into the room. "Hmmm, that's a story. Actually there have been two fires. Remember when I lived on Long Branch, and the guy with the ammunition in his garage." "Yeah, I was there, but the other time was more scary." I smile to myself. "Well, O.K., I guess we could write that." Jeff and I look at each other, sleepily smiling. "Maybe we should write about how we can't decide what to write." Jeff laughs. "Well, that's an idea." We're both quiet for a while, drifting off. "Let's sleep on it and see what ideas strike us in the morning, honey." "Yeah, I'm tired now from all this thinking. Let's go to bed, Mary."

———— • • • ————

In reflecting about the episode you wish to record, you may conclude that one of the stories you've already written would do just fine. If so, get in touch with the person in the story, who many have experienced the episode differently.

If you wish to begin a new story, remember that one of your objectives is to renew or revive an old relationship, so it is best to tread lightly if the subject is at all controversial or painful. But do not be reluctant to share your feelings as you remember them.

———— • • • ————

Let some vivid memories of incidents or experiences you've shared with others come to mind. Give the people involved a call; ask them to write out their version. Don't be daunted if someone says no. Find a person who says yes.

CHAPTER 12

Trauma and Crisis

"**B**ernard, I have something I want to write about," murmurs Diane, an attractive woman in her early fifties. "It's been on my mind a long time. But I'm uncomfortable with the idea of writing about it."

"What's bothering you, Diane?" I ask.

"Well, it was pretty traumatic," she replies. "I'm not sure I want to relive the pain."

"It may be painful, I know," I answer. "But my experience is that once I write about a painful experience, I feel cleaned out." Diane gazes into my eyes with a great deal of concern. "You have heard me talk about my father's ill health and my mother's mental and emotional problems," I continue.

"Yes, I know." Diane turns and stares out the window of our class-room, pondering.

"Writing about it has helped me clean things out," I say, "perhaps to forgive, in a way. Certainly to lighten the burden."

She remains silent for some time. Finally, a flicker of a smile crosses her face. "OK, I'll give it a try."

Traumas may be genuine tragedies, intensely experienced, perhaps even caused by ourselves. Now is the time for us to view them clear-sightedly. Sometimes, they are the untimely deaths of people we love. Often, they are shocking injuries to someone we love, or even to ourselves. When writing about these experiences, there are four things we must do.

First, we must prepare for reliving the experience and writing about it; just as an athlete goes into training, we must go into training. And just as a part of training and conditioning is mental—"psyching up" for the task, visualizing good things happening—so we must encourage ourselves by congratulating ourselves, telling ourselves what a good thing it is we are doing.

Second, we must finish the story once we have started it. Despite the tears and pain, we must keep writing.

Third, we need to maintain our objectivity. As the writer, our job is to make the reader see the truth, to describe to the reader what we see and experience and feel, so that the reader goes through that pain or feeling or experience.

Fourth, we need to resist the temptation to editorialize or moralize about what has happened. We are storytellers; we need to tell stories. Sometimes, at the end of a tragic or traumatic experience, we do come to certain conclusions about the way the universe operates. If this happens to us, it is appropriate to say something. And it is perfectly all right to express confusion and bewilderment at the nature and power of the Creator of us all. But keep it real. One honest observation is worth more than all the platitudes in the world.

These four points will help you through remembering and writing the painful episodes among your life's stories.

The following story describes such an experience. You may wish to examine it closely to see whether it implements the four suggestions above, and whether the story is helped by them.

Double Trouble
by Diane Hanson

"OK, Gene, tell me what you know," I say over the dinner table at the Wagon Wheel restaurant in Ventura. He and my husband, Jack, have been selling cars together for over a year. It is early 1965.

Last night, I had called Valley Dodge to talk to Jack, but Gene answered the phone. "Oh, hi, Diane, Jack's not here. Did he tell you he was working late again?" he had said with a smirk in his voice. That alone added to my suspicions.

"Gene," I had said, "what are you implying?"

"I really can't go into it here and now, but I think we should talk," he responded.

I hesitated. I didn't want to spend time with Gene, but I did want to know whatever he knew about Jack's affair. "OK," I said. "Where and when? Remember I still don't drive. I don't have a driver's license and we have no car. Also, Newbury Park is 40 miles from the dealership in Van Nuys."

"Hmm, let me think a minute. . . ." he said. "Why don't we go to dinner tomorrow. Jack has a dealer trade and will be out late—maybe all night," he adds with a sneer. "We need privacy to discuss this, so we shouldn't meet at your house with your kids around."

My curiosity was peaking. "Well, OK. Can you be here at 7:30 P.M.?"

"Sure, I'll see you then, I have to go now. We'll talk tomorrow night," he had said and then hung up.

"Well," he says now, playing with a spoon on the table, "I'm sure that you suspect that Jack is having an affair and want more details or you wouldn't be having dinner with me."

"Gene," I say, "I need specifics, something strong enough to confront him with, so that he can't lie his way out of it." I stare at Gene.

His eyes divert while he says, "I know that he is seeing some secretary, I think her name is Eileen, from one of the other Dodge dealerships. I'm not sure which one. It has been going on for several months. Other than that, I don't have any real details. He's been tight-lipped about it. I guess he thought since my family and I had visited you on a few occasions that I might say something. Therefore, he's been careful not to say too much around me. The other guys don't like him much, so he doesn't confide in them."

I sigh. This is not what I had hoped for. Now I feel like the whole evening was wasted. The information he has given me isn't enough to

DIANE HANSON   Diane was married young to a ministerial student with whom she had two children. Initially, she came to life story writing classes to write about the experience of living through the death of one of her sons due to cancer. She recently married a dentist.

confront my husband of six years with. I want stronger grounds for a divorce than "mental cruelty."

"Look," says Gene, "I know that you're disappointed and must be angry but surely you know that he's playing around on you. I understand this isn't the first time either."

I nod, "You're right. It's not the first time. The first time was when he was still in Bible School and I was pregnant with our second child. It probably won't be the last time either. The divorce will be easier and faster with evidence."

"Are you really going to divorce him?" he asks.

"Yes," I answer, "but his unfaithfulness isn't the complete reason. He's just a lousy father and husband. He's constantly criticizing and demeaning me, and now he has started to do it to the boys. He ignores the kids. He never takes me out. He's never home to spend time with us. When he is around, he just yells and complains. There seems to be a big emptiness inside him, which he tries to fill by having affairs. He can't provide for us financially. Last month, his commission was $7.00. We have nothing but bills that we can't pay. He spends his money on his girlfriends, on silk suits and Italian shoes so he will look successful to his clients. Meantime, his kids need clothes and new beds." I sigh. "I'm only 24, and I don't want any more of this."

There is a lot of anger in my voice. I look up at Gene, who is staring at me. He didn't know how I felt. But then, how could he? The only times we have been together was when he and his wife and three kids came to visit, or when he rode his motorcycle on his day off and stopped by our house. Jack always monopolizes the conversations. I never get to say much, much less what's on my mind.

"Look, Gene," I continue, "thanks for whatever you are trying to do, but I had better get home. I have to pay the baby sitter out of my grocery money, so I can't stay out with the meter running. Thanks for dinner. It's the first time I've been out in months."

"All right," he says as he reaches to pay the check.

Once in the car, Gene says, "Let's take a little drive. It's still early."

I just want to get home but I say, "OK, but not a long drive."

We head north. The ocean is on our left. The moon glistens on the water. It seems so peaceful, especially in comparison to my life. No matter what happens, the ocean continues its own pace unknowing or caring about a man or woman's troubles.

I feel the silence in the car, a growing uneasiness. I look over at Gene. He is just driving. His prominent Italian profile and dark hair are outlined in the light of the oncoming cars.

"I need to get some gas," he says.

I feel tense and nervous. What? After a few minutes drive, we see a gas station and he pulls in. There is a telephone booth there. I sit in the car and watch as Gene talks to the attendant and then goes to the men's room. I feel so uncomfortable and I don't know why. I glance again at the phone booth. I have the strongest urge to call Beverly and tell her to come get me, but I'm not even sure where we are. "This is foolishness. What do you think will happen?" I can't answer myself, but my hands feel clammy and I want to run, but I don't know where. Gene returns to the car and we leave the station.

We continue the drive in silence. I want to talk to break this dreadfulness, but I feel so uneasy that my throat is closing up. My heart is beating fast. Gene is also quiet. "What is happening here? Why do I feel this way?" I ask myself again, and still get no response. Then Gene drives off the road. I can feel the tightness in my spine and my stomach jerks. We are on a dirt road near the oil wells in Ojai.

"Gene, where are we going?" I ask anxiously, but he doesn't answer. He drives over the bumpy road, passing a worker's shack, and then stops and turns off the car. It is dark, and I can't see anything.

"Gene, what are you doing?" I'm really scared now. "Gene, I have to get home!" I feel panic. My armpits are prickling.

Gene turns to me and says, "I'm going to rape you now." His voice is controlled and calm. I am stunned into silence. He begins to move towards me. He grabs me and starts to tear at my clothes. I begin to struggle with him. I have worn a white dress with pink polka dots and a jacket to match. Also a girdle with stockings and high heels. It was my Easter dress last year. I do not want him to tear my dress. I clutch at it and stare at him with terror in my eyes.

"If you don't help me, I will hurt you," he says in a firm, angry voice. I go numb. I do not believe what is happening.

"Gene, why are you doing this?" I plead with him. He slaps me and pushes me down on the seat. Maybe I should kick him in the groin. There isn't much room in here to get at him or away from him. Could I overpower him? If I could, what would I do then? I don't drive. I don't know how to handle the car. If I got out of the car,

Trauma and Crisis

141

where would I go? We are in the middle of a dark oil field! In these heels, I could never run fast enough to get away. The buildings I noticed on our way in appear to be empty, but if they have men in them would they help me, or would they rape me too? Gene is ripping off my stockings.

"Gene, please don't do this, please I beg of you." His mouth comes down on top of mine. I try to push him away. I want to bite him. What if I hurt him just enough to make him madder? What will he do then? The struggle is exhausting me. I lie still and try to catch my breath. I try to get my bearings, try to decide what to do. He is pulling on my girdle. "That should keep him busy for a while," I think.

"You had better help me or you'll be sorry." I hear the anger in his voice and feel his frantic hands tugging on my girdle. I become very calm, and my mind drifts. If I go along with him, it will be over in no time. I don't think he will beat me and leave me here. I decide to help him to take off my girdle. I feel a coolness come over me and a detachment from my body.

What is happening to me? It is like I am floating outside myself and I feel no pain or fear. This is nice. I like this floaty feeling. I do feel the pressure of Gene's body on mine, but it seems a far distance off, like my whole body is filled with Novocain. It sorta feels like when I gave birth to Jimmy and got a spinal. I was numb from the waist down. I could feel pressure but no pain. This is the same—kinda. This is really crazy, I think. Then I notice that Gene has stopped moving and is beginning to sit up.

"See, it's over," I tell myself. I sit up too. I stretch and begin to look for my clothes. Gene is leaning over the steering wheel. His head is resting on his hands. I get all my clothes back on and wait for him to say or do something. I must wait and see what his mood is so that I do not anger him.

He raises his head to look at me. "I feel so terrible. I don't know how I could have done that to you. You of all people," he says with a sob in his voice. His head is back on his arms.

I am shocked. What shall I do? What shall I say? "Oh, God, don't fail me now," I pray. "I know that you are there God. I know that you are always with me. I don't understand why this is happening to me. Please help me." I still feel unusually, unnaturally calm. "Gene, it's OK. Just take me home now. I must get home to my kids," I say calmly, like nothing happened.

"I feel so terrible." He begins to cry.

The panic is returning and I want to get out of here, but I need him to do that. "Gene, it will be all right. Please just take me home." I plead, while trying to keep the panic out of my voice. What will happen to my boys if something happens to me?

"Are you sure?" he asks. "I really care for you. Do you know that?" He stares deeply at me. "Do you think that I could see you again?" he asks.

I go rigid. Certainly, he is crazy. What will I do? How should I handle this? I wonder. "Gene," I say, "we both have had a rough night. Let's get home. Get a good night's sleep. Why don't you call me tomorrow and we'll talk?"

He brightens and visibly relaxes. I feel better. I have to get out of here before I lose it. I feel the panic rising from my stomach into my throat. My insides are trembling. I feel so close to screaming, but I can't. This man is on the edge, he could do something really crazy. I must remain very calm, very cool, very in control. "Do you think that it will be OK? I really want to see you again," he asks.

"Sure, Gene," I say in what I hope sounds like a cheerful voice.

"Good. I feel a little better now. You do forgive me, don't you?" he asks in a little boy voice.

"Sure, Gene, it'll be OK. You'll see . . . let's just get home now. After all, you have a long drive even after you drop me off." I force a smile at him and he starts the car. My heart leaps for joy along with the engine. I hold my breath, anxious for us to get closer to civilization. I can't wait until we are on the freeway so we can go faster. I want to get home to my kids, and I want to get there fast. We are off the dirt road and back on the paved street. I feel so much better. Gene glances over at me. I look at him. My face is stiff and a smile won't come. He drives on and reaches the blessed freeway. As he gets on it, my blood soars. "Faster, faster," I think. He is watching me again and I feel the tension returning in him.

"I can't face what I have done," he says as his voice grabs. "It would be better if we both die." I wait, I say nothing. What can I say? God, where are you? Tell me what to say! I have a crazy person here. My body is beginning to tremble. One minute I am calm, the next I begin to shake and shiver but I must hide it from Gene.

"I think that I will kill us," Gene says. Panic rushes through me and then the calmness again. I look at him. Still no words come. His face is stuck in a grim expression. "Do you know what I am going to do?" he says with the voice of a sleepwalker. My mind is blank. It is like I have no control and don't care. I am numb and cold. He looks at me, I look back at him. All is quiet, then he says, "I am going to get the car up to 120 miles, then I am going to drive it into the freeway overpass."

Everything seems to go gray but I am still silent. No words come to mind. He begins to accelerate. I watch the speedometer. It begins to climb. We are at 85 mph. I feel excited. The faster he goes, the faster I will get home. I just have to time this right. I watch the road quietly. Then I look at the dial again—we are going 100 mph. We are going very fast. I love it. I will be home soon. I want him to go faster. I must be getting crazy too.

"We are at 110," he announces. Then he says, "There is a freeway overpass coming up. That is the one I will drive into." I glance at the dial, we are almost to 120 mph. I look at the ramp coming closer. "There it is," he says again as he looks at me. "I am going to drive right into it. Do you want me to do that?"

I watch it coming closer and closer, my eyes are glued to it. I want to get home fast, so I want to go fast as long as possible. Slowly I move my eyes to look at him. "Shall I do that?" he asks.

"Gene, I don't think you really want to do that," I hear myself say. The voice is so calm, it doesn't seem to be mine. Our eyes meet and I do not blink. I slowly look back towards the road. We have passed the overhead ramp and Gene's foot is getting lighter on the pedal. I feel a long breath leave my body. The crisis is over . . . or almost.

We drive in silence. The silence makes me uneasy. I feel the panic beginning again. "How can I keep myself together until I get home?" I wonder. I must say something to him to keep his mind occupied, but what? Panic is in my mind and belly. Then I hear . . . "Gene, it would probably be best if you dropped me at the corner of my street. I don't want the sitter to see you," I say in a conspiratorial tone.

He smiles and says, "OK." He seems less tense. He drives to the Wendy Drive off-ramp for my house. I feel so relieved. I could hop out and run from him, but I don't think I will have to. He is going to behave. I can hold on—it won't be much longer. He stops at my corner. I grasp the door handle. I must not rush out, or he will get upset again. I must remain calm. I am almost home.

I must say something—what? "Gene, thanks for dinner. You will call me tomorrow, won't you?" I say with a smile like I had ended a date. That should keep him calm.

He smiles and says, "Sure, I'll call you. Early." I get out of the car, turn and wave. I even stand there awhile as he drives off.

On unsteady legs I turn and stiffly walk to my house. I am shaking so badly I can't get the key in the lock. As I fumble the sitter opens the door. She is just a kid from across the street. I cannot lose control yet. I do not want to upset her. I pay her quickly, thank her and watch her cross the street.

My house is quiet. I check on the kids. They are asleep and Jack may not be back from his "dealer trade" tonight, if in fact he really had one. I sink onto the couch, but my body won't relax I am so tight. All my muscles hurt. I ache everywhere and realize the tension I have been under. My neck and jaw are rigid. I push myself off the couch and, using the hall wall for support, slowly head for the bedroom. I struggle to remove my clothes. "I am going to burn that dress," I tell myself. I am so cold and shaking so much that I can hardly walk to the bathroom. I want to take a hot shower. I want to cleanse myself and warm myself. I run the water real hot and step inside. It feels good but I cannot stop the shakes. After a few minutes of standing under the hot water, I know I will not get warm, so I get out. I reach for the towel and rub myself. The shaking is worse so I head into the bedroom to sit down on the bed. My head drops into my lap and I begin to rock myself back and forth.

"What's wrong with you?" I hear a voice say.

I look up and Jack is standing in the doorway. I try to say "nothing," but my teeth are chattering and no words will come.

He walks over to me. "What has happened?" he asks.

A million things flash through my mind. Should I tell him? He is my husband; he should comfort me. If I tell him, he will know I was trying to get information about his affair. He has the affairs and I go for one dinner and I get raped!! I don't understand this. He touches my shoulder and I recoil. The tears are stinging my throat. My stomach is so tight it is jerking. I feel like I am going to throw up.

"Jack . . . Jack," I sputter but nothing else comes out. He sits next to me on the bed. I am rocking faster. "Jack . . . Gene raped me." I spit out the words.

"What?!!!? What were you doing with him??" he demands, leaping up from the bed.

I am numb and feel pain all at the same time. This is not the comfort I was hoping for, but knowing Jack how could I expect anything else. My teeth are chattering and I cannot explain any further. My head feels like it will snap off at my neck. I do not want to talk anymore. I know that, somehow, Jack will blame me for the whole episode.

He begins removing his clothes, getting ready for bed. I must get out of this wet towel, I think. Then try my best to stand up.

"I can't believe you were with Gene," says Jack. "You probably deserve what you got."

That shocks me, even coming from insensitive Jack. I go numb again, then the calmness returns. I really hate this man. I cannot live with him any longer. I can't get far enough away from him. A divorce would be an improvement.

I slide under the blankets and am so tense my body doesn't seem to touch the bed. Jack climbs in next to me. He lies still and is silent.

I do not think that I can be this close to him. He is so hateful. He is even worse than Gene. I hate him. I start to turn to leave the bed. His arm wraps over me.

"Jack, please. Just leave me alone." I try to twist away from him, but he holds me down. I cannot stand being held down. Not now. Not after what happened.

"Did he hurt you?" he asks. I hear no concern in his voice.

"I don't know. I'm too cold and tense to feel anything," I say in a dull, even tone of voice. "Please let me go. I can't sleep. I'm going to make myself some tea." But his arm stays tight around me. I freeze. I know what he wants. I panic. "No. No, not again, not tonight. No!! No!!" I say as we struggle. He pushes himself on me.

I do not struggle anymore. I have been through this once tonight and this is no different. It is all the same. Jack or Gene. Gene raped me tonight but Jack has been raping me for years. I hate him. This is the last time.

"I want you to know that it doesn't matter to me," Jack whispers in my ear.

'Well, it matters to me,' I think but say nothing. He never cares or waits to see how I feel about anything. I have nothing to say to him. He pushes himself into me. It hurts. I flinch.

"I thought you said he didn't hurt you," says Jack. I say nothing. It doesn't hurt now, not anymore. I feel nothing. I don't want to feel anything. I wait. Again it doesn't take long.

'Thank you God. Why did this happen to me?' I ask God, but get no answer. I release my grip on the bottom sheet. My hands and fingers ache from holding the sheet so tight. My whole body feels like it is two inches above the bed.

Jack turns over and falls into sleep. I lie in the dark and try to think. Jack knows I will not tolerate him any longer. I know that he will try to make life difficult for me even when we divorce, but I don't care. I just have to get away from him. I will not allow him to dump any more emotional or mental abuse on me or my kids. I will divorce him and make a new life. It will be just me and the kids, but that is how it always has been anyway. I take a deep breath and begin to relax. I cannot tolerate my life with Jack anymore. If anything good came out of this evening it is the final realization that I must divorce. I cannot sleep. I must plan my escape. I must get away.

P.S. I did get away. A few days later, Jack moved out. Soon afterward I filed for divorce claiming "mental cruelty." Jack began to tell everyone that I had committed adultery. He contested the divorce, saying he wanted the kids and the house. It took two years to get into court. On our court day Jack brought Gene to testify against me. This was totally unexpected and unnerving. So I settled out of court by waiving the two years of child support that Jack had not paid and I got the kids and the house.

Three years later, while driving home from work (I now could drive and had a car), I noticed a man walking along the sidewalk. I knew him from somewhere but couldn't place him. He looked at me. Before I realized it, my car was trying to run him down. In a flash, I knew it was Gene. When he saw me, he dashed into a store to hide. I never saw him again.

After finishing her story, Diane went more deeply into it by doing a self-assessment.

SELF-ASSESSMENT

What effect did this experience have on my life?

For a long time I was emotionally withdrawn and not trusting of men.

How did it feel writing this story and sharing it with others?

I was surprised at the depth of my emotions when writing and especially when reading the subject matter to the class. It brought back much of the feelings of the moment. My heart was racing and I felt fear. My hands were clammy and trembling. So much was still so real—even after 25-plus years.

How did the "child" in me handle this experience?

As a child, I had been taught not to cause a scene—especially in public. These teachings overrode my instincts that told me I was in danger.

Was there a part of me that was a victim in this experience? How did that part of me handle the experience?

I was definitely a victim of rape by both my husband and his friend, as well as the "old tapes" regarding appropriate behavior. I was also a victim of a society where women are not be believed when they cry rape.

Do I see a pattern emerging? What is it?

Trying too hard to please. Going along with the situation. Not speaking out about my feelings. Feeling wronged and victimized. Then getting angry. Releasing my anger in an unproductive way (screaming and yelling, becoming demanding, issuing ultimatums, feeling guilty and sulking).

What is the origin of this pattern?

I was told "Don't argue with your father. It doesn't pay. It just gets you more upset and him more angry."

So talking or arguing with a man has always been difficult. It has meant the loss of a close, emotional interchange with the men in my life. When there is strife, I close off. I don't share my inner feelings—especially if I think they will be perceived as negative. If I get angry, I take the risk of not being heard, not being understood, not being accepted. The other person will be even angrier and will reject me.

What patterns do you see emerging from this crisis moment in your life?

Certain patterns have revealed themselves to me over the past few years of my life (1987–92). It hasn't been until recently (early 1992), through the Life Writing Class and understanding that I have been "co-dependent" all my life, that I have been able to see the patterns.

These patterns have been in my personal relationships, especially with men, but also with women.

I will enter a relationship and at first the friendship grows and both of us are rather interdependent. The second step emerges when I convince myself the other person "needs me."

I like to be needed. They need me to "help them." This has usually been emotionally. I rarely have had enough money to help financially. A financial need would be more obvious to me that I was being used. Emotional giving was good to do.

Soon the other person would begin to "need" me and to "depend" on me. It would make me feel good to be needed and necessary to the other person.

I would give to the relationship until I became drained or exhausted. I would feel that I gave more than my share. That I was carrying more than half of the relationship.

Then I would get resentful and angry. I couldn't leave it, though, because the person still needed me and I enjoyed being needed. I also felt in control when the other person needed me versus me needing them. I just needed them to need me.

When it became too much for me, I would throw my hands up in disgust and run from the relationship.

Sometimes after a brief rest of a few weeks, or several months, I would feel guilty for having let my friend down. Most often I would relent and go back into the relationship and begin the cycle again.

When I finally gave up totally, I would become very independent. I would stay alone and begin to heal myself. I enjoyed the "being alone" and not having to worry about anyone else. I had a good job, a nice place to live, I paid my bills on time and always saved a little something. I felt emotionally relieved that I was not carrying around someone else's baggage, that I was not weighed down with another's problems. When I was alone, I had no real problems—at least none that I could not handle.

Then the loneliness and restlessness would set in. I would want another new relationship. One that would not end up like the last one. There was hope that it would be different next time.

Those were the patterns and the cause was co-dependency, which was caused by:

1. I was raised in a co-dependent household. My father was the demanding, critical, hostile, and judgmental person, while my mother played the victim role and was passive-aggressive.

2. I was the oldest of six children and had a lot of responsibility toward them. Especially the youngest three who were 11, 12, and 13 years younger than I. I was a surrogate mother. I felt the responsibility to care for them and to help fix their problems.

3. I was raised in a strict, traditional church that preached putting the other person first. Sacrificing myself to others' needs.

4. I married young (18) to a man who had the same traits as my father and felt called to be a minister. This reinforced all the above.

5. I had my first child two weeks before I turned 19. Too much responsibility too soon. I accepted the "victim" role that had been handed down to me by my mother.

6. I had my second child by age 22 and felt locked in and trapped, thereby repeating the pattern taught to me by my mother.

7. My marriage continued until even I saw that my husband was too much like my father. He was beginning to criticize and demand things of my children that they were too young to deliver. He became verbally more abusive. I didn't want my children to grow up under those conditions. When the situation between my husband and me grew even worse, I divorced him.

8. After six years of marriage I saw some light and decided to break the pattern. I divorced my husband. Not getting any counseling and not even having heard about co-dependency, I struggled along as before. I had no new tools with which to make the change. So the patterns repeated themselves.

Is there another, better way?

Facing problems is facing reality. As soon as a problem arises, I go into a headspin or shock. Then I regroup and reevaluate. I gather all the facts. I analyze the information and then, using my instincts and good judgment, I try to make an immediate decision. I decide on a plan of action and begin to implement it.

———— ••• ————

It is very important for us to face up to the traumas of our lives and write about them using all our skill and effort. As Diane's moving story shows us, getting them out of ourselves and into the open releases us from the burden of carrying around all the guilt and pain that has weighed upon us for so long. The more honestly we write about the event, the more fully we will release it.

Some of the very best work done in my classes has come from people who not only put their pain down on paper but put it down eloquently, not as a complaint but as an object for themselves and others to experience and contemplate.

By no means will the pain and anger of the past always result in painful, angry stories. Some of the funniest stories come from bottled-up anger: a few deft strokes of the pen, and a mean parent becomes a wonderfully absurd and short-sighted little person.

It also sometimes helps to work against the dominant side of oneself in writing. If we tend to be complainers about life in the present, it may help us to find the good and wonderful things that happened to us in the past. If we tend to be always rosy, it may be wise to look beneath the surface of our lives and confront some of the darker moments. Every life has them. We will find that the more of the one side we confront, the more of the other side will gradually emerge. The more the pain gets cleared away through writing, the more the pleasure of life will reappear. We will find that our memories will begin to return with surprising clarity.

But keep in mind that we don't want to *think* about writing. We want to write. Picking up the pen and simply writing, even if we have nothing specific in mind, is the strongest commitment we can make to getting our life down on paper. Once the pen moves, images will begin to come back. So keep the pen moving. Later we can find out where the actual story should start. When confronting trauma or any difficult episode, the best way to begin is to just begin. You can assess your own experiences by responding in writing to the questions in Diane's self-assessment.

— • • • —

Now it is time to relive once again some of the things you had hoped would remain hidden from view for the rest of your life. Congratulate yourself for your courage. You deserve it. Go ahead—jump in and start swimming. The results will amaze you. Believe me.

CHAPTER 13

Profound Experiences

Some years ago I gave a workshop devoted to exploring and writing our lives' most profound experiences. I was quite surprised by the kinds of stories that were read: a doctor who traveled to India to experience levitation; a woman able at last to enjoy the touch of a man just shaking hands with her; a peace corps volunteer who escaped a revolution in Africa; a participant in a shamanistic workshop who sees into another world.

A great many of us have had quite profound experiences during the course of our lives, experiences that cannot be easily defined or understood. With this chapter, I hope to encourage you to put down on paper some of the more unusual, hard-to-believe experiences that have occurred in your life.

Writing about profound experiences can be difficult for three reasons:

1. What happened is so out of the ordinary, it is difficult to describe.
2. Because the experience is unusual, we may be tempted to come out of the story and tell the audience what is so significant about it.

3. The event may be so unusual that we fear other people's judgment of us, as so often happens with people who tell of out-of-body experiences.

The best way to handle these concerns is to tell the story one moment at a time. Then, in a P.S. at the end, you can tell the audience what significance this moment has had for you. You may also wish to note your fears about telling the world of this experience. Writing about our fears is an effective way to dispel them.

One type of profound experience we may wish to write about is one or more "turning points" in our lives when things that had been going badly finally began to turn around. Again, the trap in writing such a moment is to talk about the story rather than to let the story tell itself. So, go ahead and tell the story, seeking out the climax in your mind. Begin just before the climax, and then write through to the end of the experience.

Whatever the antecedent reasons may be for having this experience, discuss them in a P.S. to the story.

The next story is a good example of a profound experience and the reflections that recalling such an experience can bring.

The Descent
by Willi Hill

Prologue

What profundity do I possibly have, for God's sake, I ask myself for the hundredth time. What is a *most profound* life experience?

It's Saturday afternoon, October 22, 1995. Time is getting short, and I'm desperate. I'm not even close to having my article written for tomorrow's writing workshop.

I go to the dictionary and look up the word *profound:* having intellectual depth; possessing knowledge and insight; going thoroughly and penetratingly into a problem. Characterized by intensity of emotion; deeply realized or felt; all-encompassing.

WILLI HILL   Willi is an Orange County businesswoman who devotes her free time to self-growth and personal development.

I've had many peak experiences, but could I characterize any of them as profound?

The Event

Boom. Boom. Boom.

"This is what it will sound like," intones Dr. Horner. "These drums will drive you on your journey."

It's summer, in the mid-1980s, Ojai, California. I'm trying to relax on my mat. On all sides of me are bodies, other people seeking enlightenment.

I feel apprehension and excitement: will I be able to do this? I feel so inadequate around these people. I'm sure they must have had more experience at this than I have. They all seem to know what they're doing. I just wanted to find out and experience what Shamanism is. I'm just following along and pretending I know what I'm doing. I'm fidgeting; I notice other people fidgeting.

Dr. Horner continues on with his instructions. "It's important to remember what happens on your journey so that when you get back you can report it. When I give the signal to come back, you will have fifteen minutes. Remember what I told you about the danger in staying. You must start back immediately."

Boom. Boom. Boom.

The drums have started. This is it. They're so loud, booming into my ear. How can I possibly relax with this booming sound in my ear.

Boom. Boom. Boom.

There's no time to think. I must hurry. My time is short. I go immediately to my preselected place to begin my journey of descent deep into the earth. I have picked out in advance the deep, deep spring of my childhood, where *National Geographic* once in an article said it was so deep that prehistoric blind fish lived at the bottom.

Boom. Boom. Boom.

I quickly go to my jumping-off place and dive down into the water. It's not cold, because I had planned for that in advance, and I can hold my breath as long as necessary. I propel myself farther and farther down until I find a cave. I swim in and find myself in a dry, warm tunnel. The tunnel leads downward. I continue down farther and farther into the tunnel. There is enough light to see, and the rocks don't bother me because I'm able to lightly skim over them.

Finally, after a long time of following this tunnel I come into a wide open space, like a huge room or hall. It's brightly lit, full of people who seem to be very busy, briskly going back and forth, doing whatever their job is or going wherever they're going. They don't pay particular attention to me, but they're friendly. As they pass, they nod or smile or say hello.

I continue on, then enter a smaller room, not quite as bright as the other area, a rose-colored room. The movement is somewhat slower but the people are still moving about their business. They're friendly. They nod to me and say hello. I say hello to them. They continue on.

I keep on going and I come to a smaller room. It's a yellow room. Much fewer people. They're moving in kind of a slow, almost floating manner.

I continue on and go into another room. This time it's a blue room, light blue. The air has kind of an electric feeling to it. There is very little movement. People are moving along the floor in a walking way but they're floating. They're aware of me as I'm aware of them.

I'm now in a pale white room. It seems to be a resting room. There are things that look like cots attached to the walls, and people seem to be sleeping in the cots and other pale white people, beings, or whatever they are, are attending those in the cots.

I go through a few more spaces or rooms, and then suddenly I find myself in a strange kind of chamber. It's like the inside of a circular cave, almost womblike, and it is inhabited by some beings who are seated behind a table, a circular table that curves with the room, kind of horseshoe shaped.

I'm standing at the entrance of the room and begin moving toward the center. I don't get a good look at the beings. They appear to be white forms, not clearly defined. I'm somewhat overwhelmed. The one at the very middle seems to be the leader. At first they don't notice me, and then suddenly their total attention is fixed on me. They begin communicating with me, not by words but by a thought process. They communicate with me as all in one.

Their first question is: *Who are you?*

I'm so stunned. At first I don't know how to answer. Then I'm able to communicate with them by the same type of thought process.

Thinking to gain some time, I say to them: *You tell me who I am.*

Then immediately they respond, all in one: *No, you have to tell us who you are. We don't tell you.* Then they repeat. *Who are you?*

Without thinking I respond immediately, *My name is Ginscnnt-teh.*

They say to me, *That's who you were before. Who are you now?*

And somehow I know they're absolutely right, that's who I was before. So I have to think for a second as to who I am now. I say to them, *I'm Willi.*

They say to me, *No, that's the name you're called. Who are you?*

I try to think and give them an answer.

Suddenly the drums stop and I hear a voice far away saying, "You have fifteen minutes." The chamber begins to dissolve. The beings have lost interest in me.

I don't want to go yet. There are so many questions I need to ask. But I can't be late. There are dangers in being late.

I begin to make my way out through the various rooms, out the main hallway, back up through the tunnel. Quickly I scramble up through the rocks, through the puddles of water. I make much better time coming out than I did going in. I have to. I don't want to be late. Quickly now I get to the beginning of the long tunnel and see the water, dive back into the water and start on my upward journey to the top of the spring.

I hear Dr. Horner's voice saying, "Now you're back." But I'm not back yet. I'm still in the water. Finally I reach the top, get to the edge and climb out.

I'm not ready to be back yet. I wish I could have stayed. But others are now stirring, getting up off their mats and moving themselves around.

My mind is clear, but I'm physically exhausted. I feel a pang of regret that I was so close to maybe discovering something important and had to leave.

But the session must go on. I have no time to linger on regret. We must now go about the business of reporting what happened to us.

Epilogue

Was that a profound event? Have I been given a glimpse of myself? If so, who do I see? I see someone who is actively seeking a new experience, someone who is willing to go to the depths of the earth in hopes of receiving some bit of information or wisdom, someone who wants to know who she is, someone who is most of all a seeker.

It's a new way of looking at myself. Instead of seeing myself as that strange and different person who's never satisfied with knowing, who always thinks of herself as being in the dark, always trying to read between the lines, I now see myself as a seeker of knowledge, of wisdom.

Maybe that is the profundity after all.

P.S. One other thing keeps tugging at me about the event, something my mind keeps rejecting. When the beings asked me the second time, quite insistently, *Who are you?* I replied immediately and without hesitation, "Ginscnntteh." It was an automatic and positive response. They said, *No, that's who you were before,* and I knew immediately that is who I was before.

Before what? At that moment I knew automatically it was in reference to a former life. But I've never brought that out in my writing or conversations on this event because I reject the idea of reincarnation. Logically it doesn't make sense.

But, on the other hand, much of life doesn't make sense.

———— • • • ————

Look back through your life. What experiences stand out as profound, as unusual, or as turning points in your life? As you write, focus on the experience rather than on how people might respond to your story. Tell the story one moment at a time. If you like, add a P.S. about the significance the experience had for you. You might refer back to Diane Hanson's self-assessment in Chapter 12, which is a useful technique for exploring significant events in our lives. Profound experiences are also good opportunities to look at ourselves more closely, as discussed in Chapter 18, Experiencing the Story as a Mirror of Ourselves.

CHAPTER 14

The Later Years

I n Chapter 10, "Love, Adulthood, and Family," we explored the first love we had when we were young and our feelings surged within us and we imagined the object of our affection to be one and the same as the fantasies we had of him or her.

We also looked at another kind of love, in which a person of significance entered our life and rocked our boat. Life changed because of him or her. We began to learn life's lessons while entering into a lengthy, enduring relationship with this significant person.

Now it is time to look at love of another kind—love in later life.

We are just beginning to recognize in our society that love of a very passionate kind is possible at any and every age. In my classes there are numerous people who have forty- and fifty-year relationships that are vigorous, growing, and evolving.

Here is a wonderful story of love later in life.

A Green-eyed Monster
by Lily Tokuda

"Get your hands off my husband!" I scream silently at Miiko as I stare at Tadd and Miiko walking ahead of me. Miiko-san drove us for miles from Hiroshima City looking for a restaurant she picked in the mountains of Yamaguchi Prefecture. This place is lit up like day and there is a complex of restaurants in the huge castle-like building with a tall white tower gleaming against the dark night.

I feel a fine mist. Though it's a lovely spring night, I feel cold. Miiko-san, a divorcee, is a daughter of our friend Izue-san. Now we are walking around smelling lovely smoky barbecued teriyaki meat and other exotic Japanese food from the various restaurants.

Miiko-san hangs onto Tadd's arm and Izue-san is holding onto mine. My stomach hurts, no, I guess it's really my heart that's aching. I try to act nonchalant. After all, Tadd and I have a wonderful marriage, all 46 years of it. Tadd loves me and he is good to me but I cannot help noticing many Japanese women, young and old, are fascinated by him. He is attractive, so different from the Japanese men who treat their women as their inferior. And they don't dress as sporty and smart as Tadd.

Tonight he is dressed in a pair of jeans and has a black windbreaker on over a light blue golf shirt. Izue-san is chattering and I can barely hear her because my ears are ringing—or is that my heart? I swallow. My mouth is dry. I need a drink of water or I need a stick of chewing gum. I need my Tadd. We go through a maze in search of a special restaurant. Miiko-san slows down. "This is the place." She stops. I don't care if this is the best or the worst place. I am not hungry.

"Ko, ko (here, here), Lili-san." Izue-san drags me by the arm to the entrance. We remove our shoes and get on the tatami floor. Tadd takes his shoes off and Miiko straightens them out. Damn it, that's my job.

I am consumed with jealousy.

LILY TOKUDA   Lily was born in the United States but accompanied her terminally ill father to Japan when he chose to die among his family. She was educated at Catholic schools in Japan through high school. She returned to the United States just before the bombing of Pearl Harbor. Reunited with her family, she was interned at Hart Mountain, Wyoming, where she met a young enlisted man visiting his relatives. They fell in love and within six months were married. She spent most of the war years on an army base. Her husband Tadd and his unit fought with bravery in Italy, with over half of the unit dying during the campaign. After the war, Tadd found it difficult to find work, and began working as a gardener. Lily and Tadd have three sons. She writes her stories so her grandchildren will know about their grandparents.

We find an empty table. Tadd pats a seat next to him for me to sit. We all sit on the floor on little blue cotton pillows. I don't feel good. My smile must look sickly but Tadd doesn't notice.

This place must be popular all right. The place is jammed with young people. In fact, we, Izue-san, Tadd and I are the only old ones. Miiko-san in her designer's outfit fits right in with them.

A waitress in a blue kimono brings us menus. "The barbecued chicken and veggie sounds good," I tell Tadd since he cannot read Japanese.

"Tadd-san, you should try their Kamam-meshi, it's their specialty," Miiko-san tells Tadd in her husky voice. She and her mother pull out cigarettes. If Tadd offers to light them, I will throw up.

I look at the menu. My chest feels so tight that I cannot breathe. My mouth is still dry. I drink a little cup of hot tea our waitress pours. It's hot and scorches my mouth but I welcome the tea.

Our food comes. I don't taste anything. Izue-san keeps up her chatter, damn, damn, just leave me alone, please. Soon we are through. Tadd gets up to pay. This is our last night with them and we want to treat them.

We find our shoes among the hundreds of pairs of shoes. As we leave, Miiko grabs Tadd and Izue-san gets hold of my arm. I look for a bathroom. I want to be by myself. I want to cry.

Back into the car. Tadd sits in front with Miiko-san and Izue-san and I climb into the back. I imagine their hands touching. My gosh I am getting paranoid. I must stop this. I must be sick in the head.

Finally, we are home. After our customary hot furo (bath), we bid our good night to Izue-san and Miiko-san. "Doh-mo arigato, it was lovely," I say.

We get into our futon. I feel cold in spite of the thick futon. I have to talk. I have to tell Tadd how I feel. "You know, darling, I felt real, real sad tonight." My voice sounds strange to my ears.

"How come?" Tadd gropes for me in the darkness.

"Because I wanted to walk with you instead of Miiko. I wanted to hold onto your arm."

"Hey, I'm old enough to be her father."

"Ha, I bet she doesn't feel that Tadd is old enough to be her father," I say to myself. I wonder when she lost her father.

"I love you, you know that." Tadd holds me tight and reassures me. I smell his clean soapy smell. I feel a little better. Not one hundred percent, but much better. Even at my age, that green-eyed monster can still get to me. Will I be like this even when I am in my 80s and 90s? I wonder.

● ● ●

Lily gives us a story dense with humor and feeling. It draws us into the experience from the very first line. In her well-balanced narrative, Lily reveals clearly the depth of her feelings. The story also puts to bed two stereotypes: that older adults don't have much sexuality, and that those whose emotions are hard to read, that is, "inscrutable" Asians, don't have emotions.

Stories such as these remind us that, for all of us, there are many un-expected twists and turns to our life's path and that we can best prepare for them by remaining optimistic about and open to whatever is coming next.

The next story is an example of the kind of love that supports many a long-term relationship because the relationship's sharp edges are ac-cepted with humor and private resolve.

Men, Women, and Jerry Brown
by Anne Freedman

"Anne," shouts my friend Lou as he storms into my house, "why don't you have the radio on? Jerry Brown is wonderful today. He's always good, but today is exceptional. How do you work this thing, anyway?" Lou fiddles with the radio as I gather up the papers in front of me. Lou continues. "You should keep it tuned to KPFK all day. All the programs are good."

Somehow being told what to do rankles. I tell Lou it is a relief to my ears to enjoy silence and I need to balance my checkbook and see how much money I have. I can't attend to two things at once.

Lou now has found the station and Jerry is blaring away. But Lou isn't deaf. I am.

The Later
Years

❧ 161 ❧

ANNE FREEDMAN   Anne was born into a "classically WASP family" in Washington, D.C., where her father was on the faculty of American University. Married at a young age to a liberal minister, she spent her early married life in Maine. Divorced, with a young child, she got into social work and moved to Los Angeles. She uses her stories as an op-portunity to review her life and to leave something of herself to succeeding generations.

"Do you need it that loud?" I ask, and add, "I don't."

Lou is 87 and I am 83. We've known each other for 48 years. His wife, Alice, was my best friend. It's silly to quarrel, but I do hate to be bossed around.

I recall the dramatic scene of last week, that first week of August 1996 which included the 50th anniversary of the bombing of Hiroshima.

Last week Lou burst into the house more forcefully than today, berating me for not listening to Jerry who had as his guest a retired general, now an anti-war activist.

Rick, a young man who works for me occasionally, was typing in the back room.

I had been sitting in the breakfast room with our friend Sam, discussing what to plant in the garden he has prepared for me. It is hard to transfer my thoughts from vegetables and herbs to politics.

"You must listen!" shouted Lou. "Everyone must listen! Go and get . . . Rick. I'll pay for his time." I made no move to summon Rick, and Lou was exasperated. "If you won't get him, I will," he declared, soon returning with the bewildered-looking Rick.

All four of us crowded into the little breakfast room just in time to hear the general take one last call from a listener. The talk show was over. We missed the important point.

Rick returned to his typing while Sam and I joined Lester in the living room to discuss politics. I was still fuming. What right did Lou have to order me around, I was thinking. And that's not all that's bothering me. I resented the implication that what Lou holds important is more so than what I value. Is that a gender difference? Are men's concerns to be loftier than women's?

What is it that holds me and Lou together? Apart, we spend our days quite differently. Together we play bridge; we attend the Unitarian Church; we sometimes go to movies or discuss psychoanalysis. My daughter Ceel and I shared a house with Lou and his family for three years, which gives us a feeling of comfortable familiarity. We are interested in each other's children and grandchildren. But what do we get out of the time we spend together?

Recently this has been more on my mind as I have seen two women I care about struggle with their relationships, trying to decide what they want out of life.

One has a husband wedded to his work. They love each other, but have no time together. She is frustrated and unfulfilled. What can she do?

The other is a serious graduate student preparing for a demanding profession. She met a man of similar ideals and interests only to discover that he was afraid to spend too much time with her. He is not ready to make that commitment. I am not sure what this phrase means these days, but I know that my young friend is unhappy and hurt. She is left wondering what is the ideal relationship between a man and a woman.

And then there is my dear granddaughter, Rebecca, who pictures her ideal future as making a home for a husband who returns her devotion and shares in bringing up the children. I wonder where she will find a man who shares this vision.

I return my thoughts to my situation with Lou. Do I have time for a man in my life? There is so much I want to do while I am still able. I need to find missing papers, label pictures, update my will, dispose of as much as I can that my children don't want. It will take a long time.

I'm not ready to give up my real pleasures: my writing class and my music. So where does Lou fit in, with his passion for politics?

We used to have a cocktail before dinner on bridge nights. For me this was a relaxing time, when Lou would read me the comic strip "Doonesbury" or a short story or a letter with difficult handwriting. Or we might just talk about the day's happenings. But Jerry Brown has come between us. Jerry's show finishes at five o'clock. If we wait till then for cocktails we'll either have no dinner or be late for bridge.

I'm glad to listen to Jerry in Lou's car or by myself, but he's not my idea of a good cocktail accompaniment. I'm sure that alcohol is bad for my health. If I'm going to drink to keep Lou company, I want Lou all to myself, not shared with Jerry, but I should feel guilty if I asked Lou not to listen. Oh Jerry, why couldn't you have a breakfast show?

As I consider my problems and Lou's I realize that I miss him when he isn't around. I love to hear his cheerful voice. I know I can depend on him. I often wish he were different. No doubt he feels the same about me. But, as my little granddaughter used to say, "Nobody's perfect," and at our age I'm afraid this is as perfect as it's likely to get.

———•••———

Sometimes writing about a person very close to us is difficult. First, the many years of living with him or her may have led us into a state of semiblindness in which we no longer really see the person. Second, lingering resentments may be coloring the way we look at him or her.

The solution is not to ignore the areas of conflict between the two of you but to step back a bit and see whether you can find some humor or irony in apparent "faults," such as leaving the refrigerator door open after a midnight snack. Looking at the incident with a kind of childlike awe and fascination does wonders for our relationships.

———•••———

*If this chapter on love in later life touches you in some way, reminds you of your experiences of those you love, write about the moments that come to you . . . **now**.*

CHAPTER 15

Writing Family Histories

Our efforts up to now have been directed toward creating writers where none existed before. Many peo-
ple, however, for a variety of reasons, do not want to write their own life
stories, yet they are interested in having their histories recorded or wish
to record someone else's story. The techniques of writing these kinds of
stories differ from those we have used and discussed previously.

There are essentially two ways of writing other people's life stories:

1. Writing down your experience of listening to your Mom or Dad,
   Grandma or Grandpa, or other family member telling stories of the
   past, while *capturing the relationship that existed between you and
   the storyteller at the time the story was told to you.* In our life
   story writing classes, we call these *family histories.*

2. Recording a person's life on tape; then, using the techniques
   described in Part 1, transforming the narrative into intense life
   stories using dialogue, narration, inner monologue, and so on.
   After writing each story creatively, the writer checks back with the
   storyteller to be sure that what is written is as close to what
   happened as possible.

Narrating Another Person's Story

Many of us who set out to write life stories are primarily interested in writing about the struggles and history of our parents and grandparents. "I want to tell my children about my parents and grandparents before it is too late," they say. Typically this kind of story is a simple narrative retelling of the past.

> My grandfather was born in the Ukraine. When he was 16 he was forced to serve in the Czar's army. After a year he escaped and made his way to America. . . .

While reading this sort of narrative, we, the readers, find ourselves asking a number of questions: How did the narrator hear about his grandfather? Who told him the story? How do we know it is true? How did the people involved (the grandfather and the narrator) feel about these events?

Out of a need to answer these questions, another, more authentic way of telling family histories has emerged, one in which the feelings of both the storyteller and the writer are evident while the story is unfolding.

"When writing this kind of family history," I tell my students, "let the reader know how you learned about the story." Were you sitting on Grandma's knee or taking a walk with Grandpa? Let the reader know what you remember Grandpa or Grandma doing or feeling while he or she is telling you the story. That way we get both the story and your relationship to the storyteller. We will believe it and feel it more fully. The next story is a good example of this kind of writing.

Family History
by Lucy MacDougall

My mother is dozing after lunch when I get to her room in the nursing home. Three nickels she won at bingo are still in her lap. She wakes right up at the prospect of an Eskimo Pie and her weekly copy of the *National Enquirer*, which she has told me at this point in her life she enjoys more than the Bible.

"How have you been?" I ask. "Fine," she says. At death's door, in the grip of gray depression or desperation, my mother always says fine.

I sit on the edge of her bed, scanning the state of her health in the wheelchair for myself as she bites into the chocolate covering. Will I be like that in 25 years, with occasional spurts of spirit and energy, living days the size and shape of postage stamps?

Her gaze, though, is intent still. She gobbles the Eskimo Pie while I stare at her. Now she is staring at me, impatient, ready to get on with it. I pick up my pencil and paper in a hurry.

"I was my father's favorite," she says right away.

My mother has been waiting patiently for days while I poke around in the past for her immediate ancestors. Now she is looking forward to being born and getting on with her own personal first-hand memories. Three other babies had to be born first. "Edward came first," she says, "then Albert and Percy, and I came next." Her mother named her Irene Jeannette Scherrer. 1883. The first girl.

Her face suddenly clouds. I know. It is going to be about Percy. It is always sad about Percy. Little Percy got sick with diphtheria and my grandmother and the housekeeper took care of him, but it was while Grandma was at work that he died. "Your grandma would never go back to work after that. She took care of us and did piece-work at home. Percy was her favorite," she explains.

"But I was my father's favorite," my mother says again, anxious to make herself once more the rightful star of her own story. "Much more than Roma."

Here comes Roma, upsetting the order of the years. Here she comes, pushy little sister, on the scene in my mother's memory when my mother's barely gotten herself born yet. "Just like her," my mother says when I mentioned it, the surface of her placidity shaken even after 80 years by the appearance in the family of Roma with her dark hair, dark eyes, rosy skin, her fresh, demanding, little-girl ways, not taking any time to be a baby in my mother's memory.

"Eddie would ask her for a glass of water," Mother says, "and she'd bring it to the table and spit in it before she gave it to him."

LUCY MACDOUGALL   Lucy was born in Brooklyn. She married a writer shortly before World War II and moved with him to Los Angeles when he was hired to write *Objective Burma*, starring Errol Flynn. Always interested in writing, she began working at *LA Magazine* after her divorce. Life story writing gives her the opportunity to force herself to remain creative. Once into the process, she began to see how it helped her review and understand her life's path.

Writing
Family
Histories

"Wait a minute. That's later, when Aunt Roma's a little girl. She's not born and you're not even five yet."

"I don't remember anything until then," insists my mother stubbornly. "That's the way Roma was. But my father liked me more because I took after the Scherrers. They were very well-bred people, I told you that, and I took after that side of the family."

So my mother didn't want to be like her mother any more than I wanted to be like mine, or my daughters want to be like me. She had great admiration for her mother's fine qualities, but also seemed to feel a little above her. I ask her about this. She stirs uncomfortably. It is too late in life to bother to lie. "Well, a little," she confesses.

But my mother absolutely hated Roma. Probably because she felt my grandma spoiled Roma. "She let her get away with anything," mother complains now for the thousandth time. Since my grandma was a gentle, quiet person, she must have had it hard to keep Roma in line. I ask about Roma's terrible sins. My mother's anger is good as new. "My shoes," she cried. "I was saving them for best and when I went to wear them, she'd worn them out. And borrowing my best kid gloves from my bureau drawer, without asking, of course, and she stretched them." Roma's real sin, though, I can see, was taking center stage, struggling to take over princess position in the family.

To get her mind off Roma, I tell her my memories of what she had told me in the past. The old joys soften her grievances. Wearing a mulberry satin hair ribbon on the braids of her fine hair, ruffles on the dresses her mother sewed for her, carrying her roller skates from the hard-packed dirt of Watts Street to another village street, Mulberry, I think, where a man with a store had put in a stretch of cement in front. Roller skating for hours.

"I didn't go to school until I was 7. Your grandma taught me at home," she says. When she finally went to school, they put her in third grade.

"I was very smart," she says pridefully. "My brother Eddie and I learned piano. The German teacher rapped our knuckles for any mistakes. Eddie would practice for hours, but the teacher said I had more talent, even though I didn't practice." Her face warms at the thought of being able to top the brother at something.

"Talent needs practice," I point out, becoming the mother. She doesn't agree. "Eddie got the bicycle just because he was a boy. He got the camera. He went on day trips with my father. He got it all, just because he was a boy." She still resents it. She has to have something more and better than he does, so she's kept the teacher's remark deep inside for years to balance the books.

She's kept everything deep inside, that's her style. She never told Eddie or Roma or anyone in the family how she felt. "It made me sick. Roma and Eddie fighting all the time over who got what. I couldn't stand it. I'd crawl under the dining room table and hide there until it was quiet and I could come out."

Harold was the change of life baby for my grandma, a blue baby, my mother says. I remember Harold was always dear to her. I liked him, too. An agreeable moon-faced man when I was a little kid. He was born to my grandma when my mother was 12. Harold Blessing Scherrer, named after some friends of Grandma's. Grandma liked to name her children after her friends to honor long associations.

"I brought him up," my mother says proudly. "I carried him around. I fed him and dressed him and changed his diapers." She'd told me that again and again, and what a help it was to Grandma, who hadn't counted on her last little blessing.

My mother gets a bit confused about this now. "I had this little son, Brian. He was my little boy."

"No, Mom," I say gently. "That is my son. He's your grandson."

"Oh. Yes. That's what I mean. It was Harold who was my son."

"No. He was like a son. Remember?" She shakes her head. She can't seem to get it right. "You were 12 or 13 and he was your mother's baby. You took such good care of him," I add.

She averted her face. "Of course," she says, but I can tell she is embarrassed that she hasn't got that stuff straight.

She is tired. The past is pictures in her head and in mine, but it's more than that. The pictures fill our whole bodies, take them over. We are both tired.

That is enough for today.

• • •

As Lucy records her mother's story, we have an opportunity to get to know several relationships: Lucy's to her mother and vice versa, her mother's to the past, and Lucy's own views of her mother's sisters and brothers. The assignment was made easier for Lucy because she had recorded and noted many conversations with her mother over the years.

Notice the way the frame Lucy creates—the mother speaking to Lucy the narrator—helps us see and feel the mother's struggle to get the facts straight, and feel Lucy's patient yet amused concern for her mother.

Because Lucy's mother speaks directly to Lucy, we, the readers, experience the story through Lucy's eyes. It is important for us as readers or listeners to know through whose eyes we are experiencing events at every turn in the story. It creates belief in the story. It also increases our interest because writer and teller have a relationship to share with us, in addition to the subject matter of the story itself.

A hundred years ago we would not have thought to ask, "From whose point of view are we seeing the story, and is it to be believed?" Until the middle of the nineteenth century, writers like Poe, Dana, Scott, Thackeray, Hardy, Melville, and many others told their stories from a godlike, or omniscient, narrative point of view, and we accepted this point of view as truthful. But in the writings of Stephen Crane, Henry James, and James Joyce, and in the dramas of Pirandello, readers became more aware of the person through whose eyes the story was being experienced and seen.

So, as contemporary readers, we no longer take for granted the truth of a story unless we know something about who is telling it. By recording the relationship of the storyteller to the writer, we get a more authentic and believable view of the family history that is being told.

Writing from Recorded Narratives

The second type of family history integrates "writing from within" techniques into an oral history narrative. The first step in this process is to record one's own story or that of a friend or relative on a tape recorder. Then, using the techniques described in Part 1, the oral narrative can be transformed into a series of separate stories that stand on their own.

An example of this second type of oral narrative is "Pool Hall," a story from the life of Ted Brown as told to and written by his former wife, Grace Holcomb. "It all started with those tapes," she says. "We got him a six pack, cracked it open, hit 'record,' and let Ted go. The story I wrote might have been just a few lines on tape. I just took it from there.

"Oftentimes," she says, "what I did creatively might not have been accurate, but it got him to remember what did happen." She adds fondly, "It's all up there in that thick skull of his somewhere. I just had to shake it loose." With his input, she made changes, then brought the story to class, listened to more comments, reworked it, showed it to Ted one last time, revised again, and finally had a story. Here is an excerpt from her story.

Pool Hall ——— EXCERPT ———

told by Ted Brown
written by Grace Holcomb

Our town, Collbran, Colorado, only had about 300 or so people in the 1930s while I was growing up, and we had the usual assortment of stores in town.

By and large, the very best place in town to kids was the one and only pool hall. We loved it. As pool halls go, it wasn't much. Just a large room with a couple of big windows, usually dirty, and an inside toilet, one of the few we had. There was a bar all along one side of the room and beer and whiskey were sold, but not too much whiskey. Mostly everybody was a beer drinker. But if you wanted to just nurse a bottle of whiskey in private there were five or six tables and chairs. Men would just sit with the whiskey and a shot glass; they always drank it neat, and everybody knew enough to leave them alone. If they wanted company they would sit at the bar. The tables were mostly used for playing cards. The men played pinochle and pitch during the day and poker at night.

The pool hall was where the cowboys headed when they got paid and were in town to tie one on. Those poor bastards worked like dogs and pretty much lived like dogs too. They only got to town once a month when they got paid.

TED BROWN AND GRACE HOLCOMB   Ted grew up on a sheep farm in Colorado during the Depression. The nearby town of Collbran was as rough and colorful as any western town of the 1880s. Part Native American, Ted spent a lot of time outdoors while growing up. He joined the army in 1940 and saw service in the Philippines as a point man on patrol. His unit was the first to liberate Manila, and he saw firsthand the infamous death camps in the Philippines. At the war's end he was hospitalized for jungle rot. Released from the army, he kicked around for some time, eventually heading west for the hardrock mining in Death Valley during the fifties. Eventually he met and married Grace Holcomb. They had one child and were divorced. Ted and Grace have remained close friends over the years, and Grace came to class "so that we would be able to tell the grandchildren about Ted's life."

But the pool hall meant more to us than cowboys. Old Dewey Fitzpatrick hung around there too. He was an old man, must have been 50 or so, and he would spin stories for us.

"Dewey, please tell us again about how you lost your fingers?" we'd plead. "Well," Dewey would say, "sure you boys can take a bloody tale?" "Oh, yes, sir," we would answer. "You ain't agonna tell your mammas I done gave you bad dreams, are you?" he asked. "Oh, no, sir," we answered in chorus.

He then proceeded to tell us how he was fighting bears and this one bear was extra special mean. Dewey beat off the bear, of course, but just for damned orneriness the bear jumped up and bit off the ends of two of his fingers. He would then hold them up for us to inspect.

That old dope would go on telling stories about skinning buffalo and fighting Indians. We figured some of his stories could be true, he sure was old enough.

He just did odd jobs around town, and was the town drunk if he could afford it, but he always had time to spin a tale or two for us, and they were never quite the same except for the bear and the fingers. He never changed that story. He'd tell us about being in the middle of a buffalo herd and a whole company of Indians came at him. "But, Dewey," we would protest, "last time it was only a few Indians." "Well, hell, boys, think that only happened once? This was a different time," he said. "Shut up now, and listen or I ain't gonna tell you no more." We would all be quiet because you never knew what he was going to say each time.

One time Dewey was in the pool hall, pretty drunk, and went into the toilet. Fred Wallace wanted to go in the toilet and old Dewey wouldn't get off the pot.

Fred was the son of Bill Wallace, one of the biggest and richest ranchers around that area, and Bill Wallace was one of the meanest sons-of-bitches we had. He was built and looked like a pit bull and his son Fred was just like him. Fred was about twenty when he was trying to get Dewey out of the toilet and it made him madder than hell. The other men heard the commotion in the toilet, but by that time it was too late.

Dewey was dead. Fred had dragged him off, then hit him so hard Dewey's head hit on the edge of the toilet bowl, killing him instantly.

Poppa was constable at that time, so he told us this story. Poppa came and told Fred to go on home—he would decide what was to be done later.

We had no courthouse or judge in Collbran, so Poppa and Fred drove into Grand Junction. Bill, Fred's father, was already in Grand Junction. Poppa came home the same day and so did Bill and Fred.

Poppa never did say what happened, and I never knew. All he would say was "Well, you know Bill Wallace has a lot of influence around here."

The town was pretty well divided over whether Fred should have gone to jail, but with time, it was forgotten. But the little boys of the town, of which I was one, never forgot it. We all wished we were bigger—we wanted to hang Fred ourselves. We all wanted to be the one to tie the noose. We missed old Dewey. He had been our friend. The pool hall was never quite the same with Dewey gone.

— • • • —

The beauty of this technique is that you, the writer, are not in the uncomfortable position of asking questions and having the subject answering them, as if in numerical order. What happens is that once you have asked a question or two—"What is your most vivid memory from your days in the army?" "What is your most vivid memory from your early twenties?"—and have gotten an answer, you then return to the person being interviewed with a printed copy of the story for him or her to read. Even better, you can read it aloud to him or her.

In listening to the story, the person will almost always remember more. He or she will begin to add greater detail. If not, you can probe a bit: "Do you remember anything else that happened about this time?" Little by little, the person's memory will loosen up and reveal more and more.

Recently, I used the techniques described above to help a man in his seventies to write his life story. The grandson of one of the last important mandarins of Vietnam and the son of a wealthy industrialist who was kidnapped by the Communists in 1946, Jean Jacques had been a police detective in Hanoi in 1940, a soldier for the French in 1944–45, and a diplomat for the French for forty years. On his own, he may never have written down his compelling tale.

PART 3

Expanding and Managing
Your Creativity

Introduction

Most of us would like to believe that we are at least somewhat creative. But we often suspect that we are not and that, in the great scheme of things, it truly does not matter whether we are or not. The truth is probably just the opposite. We are creative, all of us, and it matters very much.

Life, however, has a way of impinging on us, convincing us that its concerns are far more important than our real or imagined yearnings to create. To a greater or lesser degree we have to deal with life concerns, but we must also leave ourselves room and opportunity to create. A few years ago I was having lunch with a friend of mine, who had been a Hollywood production manager and line producer for more than twenty years. "Barry," I said, "how do you see yourself? What is it that you do, other than taking care of a multitude of nuts-and-bolts production problems? You've been at it a long time. You must get bored."

He grinned. "I do everything in my power to get things ready for the production—cameras in place, locations ready, cast and crew in position, sets dressed, lighting and sound all set for the flip of a switch—so that the director can do his creative best with cast and cameraman. Sometimes I get tired and frustrated, but not bored."

This is a great image for what we need to do for ourselves—*become powerful and effective production managers so that our director and creative team can do their best.* We need to surround ourselves with people who are supportive of our creativity, be our creative efforts artistic in the traditional sense or creative in some other way. Likewise, we need to give ourselves the time each week to create. Equally important, if we have emotional baggage that weighs us down and diverts us from creating (and many of us do), we must have the courage and intent to define that baggage, to find ways of letting it go, and to begin our creating and continue this creating. When we do this, we will find that many of life's cares become much less burdensome. Our lives have more focus and purpose. In this way, we can look forward to a path that is productive and fruitful until the day we pass from this earth.

After fifteen years in the film business, I made a short film of a Ray Bradbury story entitled "The Flying Machine." It turned out well. On a tiny budget it told a good story, was well acted, and transported people to a time in ancient China when a man who created—the flying man— had to face his most severe critic, the Emperor, who feared the consequences of this burst of creativity. Yet one more battle between critic and creator. It turned out to be an ironic exclamation point to yet another failed relationship—this time with a woman I loved very much. It was the beginning of another long and difficult time in which I began to see that exploring something in life besides filmmaking was necessary.

One of the areas of life I needed to explore was reexamining my relationship to my parents; another was the arena of autobiographical writing. When I began, I was not a writer. I was a teacher and a director who knew something about contacting the actor's imagination. In the years since, I have overcome many of my own fears of writing, and have been able to do as I tell my students to do—take risks, engage my self-critic, believe in myself, write every day, keep going.

Having listened to what I tell my students, I have come to enjoy putting myself on paper. It enables me to see my relationship to my parents in a unique way and to value myself as a child dealing with death and abandonment. It has helped me to develop the willingness, techniques, and peace of mind to tackle a large project—writing the life of a Renaissance prince, a seven-hundred-page novel I have had in mind since the age of twenty-two but never attempted because I didn't believe I would be able to devote years of my life to a single piece of work.

At the age of fifty-seven, I see myself as having cleared a path through much of the garbage, emotional and psychic, that overwhelmed me in my twenties and thirties. I went as far as I could as a filmmaker, but finally had to confront all the fears, anxieties, and craziness from the past, stuff I had avoided for most of my youth and young adulthood.

Whether my work is good or not is not the question. I would like it to be. I work hard for it to be so. But, more importantly, I have cleared a path so that I can create and help others create. The *Tao* is visible. I have become a satisfactory production manager for my own life. I have given the *creator* in me the opportunity to create.

To me, the most remarkable consequence of my search for my own *Tao* is the ironic fact that those who suffered most when I was lost in the "creative craziness" of my twenties and early thirties—my two ex-wives and my two children—are still close and wonderful parts of my life. My ex-wives are cheerful, wise, and supportive. My sons are boon companions—solid, insightful, purposeful, and humorous. Somehow, my suffering did not translate into lifelong suffering for them. For this, I am grateful.

The meaning I take from all this is that whatever our search may be, we can conduct it in our own way without being cut off from the love of others . . . and without their having to suffer forever just because we become unpredictable. There is plenty of room for quest and relationship. We must, therefore, *manage* our creativity.

CHAPTER 16

Embracing Your Self-Critic

"My life is a mess!" laments Rebecca, a member of my Sunday afternoon writing group. In her early thirties and with a writing talent that sparkles, Rebecca ought to be sitting on top of the world, but she seldom writes. (Her story "The End" appears on page 271.)

"Mine too," echoes Diane, a wise and insightful woman in her fifties whose self-deprecating writing style is hilarious to all but her. Like Rebecca, Diane can barely get herself to her computer to write once every two weeks—just in time for the workshop.

As I look around the room at the other eight members of this writing group, I see agreement reflected on the faces of several of the most talented—particularly Dirk and Jackie, as well as a new member, David. Others, like George, who runs an art school and has extensive experience as an actor and artist, and Mary, simply go about their work, writing a little each day without a lot of agonizing.

Why do some of them have their creativity so well in hand while others struggle? I ask myself. *What can I do to help?*

One afternoon as we are reading our stories, Diane talks about how her self-critic is having a wonderful time dynamiting all her efforts. "'Diane, you're such a stupid idiot,' it says to me, 'thinking that anyone will want to read your writing.'"

"I would like to hear that voice in your story," says Mary. "It really is a very funny voice."

"Not funny to me," Diane grimaces.

"Maybe you need to put it down on paper so that you can hear and see the voice of your critic, rather than simply running from it," I suggest. "Let your critic have its own voice. And answer it with *your* voice."

Diane shrugs with indifference, but the next week she returns with the following story.

Them Boots Is Made for Walkin'
by Diane Flor

I drag myself upstairs to my bedroom, carrying the bags of clothes it took me three hours to accumulate. God, what a chore shopping is, getting dressed, undressed. There must be an easier way. Like have someone put the outfit together, bring the clothes to your house and try them on for you. Yes, that's what I'll do someday when I'm rich, have somebody else do the shopping and trying on.

I'm anxious to see if the skirt I got goes with those multicolored boots that I haven't had much to wear with, so once again I get undressed and slip the skirt on. I swear, those mirrors at the store are rigged, I know my butt didn't look this big when I tried on the skirt there. Damn, no wonder I hate shopping. Oh, well, let's get the boots and see if they match.

That's funny, now where are those boots? Why aren't they here with my other boots? Let's see, maybe they're over here with my shoes, no . . . hmmmm, now that's really strange, what the heck did I do with them? This is really crazy.

No, you are really crazy, look at you looking on the shelf with the sweaters, like they would be sitting on top of a bunch of sweaters. Oh, yeah, that's good, why don't you look under those tennis shoes on the floor a few more times, or maybe move those slippers again, you never know . . . you might not have seen them hiding under those slippers. Or, wait, wait, maybe under the sandals, maybe you're looking right at them.

DIANE FLOR   Diane is the mother of two children and a former hairdresser. She came to life writing to recover memories of her childhood.

Right, or maybe you're losing your f_____ mind! How the hell could you lose a pair of boots that you wore three times!

O.K., let's regroup. Where did I wear them last? Did I take them to Vegas when we went in January? Maybe I left them in the hotel room? Let's see, what clothes did I take to Vegas to wear? S___! If you can't remember what you did with the boots, how in the hell do you think you're going to remember what you took to wear?

Yeah, well, maybe I took them down to San Diego when Rick got married. Maybe I left them in the hotel room there, what with all the commotion that was going on. I wonder if I called them if they would know. Or if I did leave them there, would they still have them?

Oh, my God, I can't believe you said that! Are you nuts? What do you think, they're going to hold a pair of boots for six months, till some fruitcake like you remembers they forgot them?

O.K. Wait a minute, this is an easy one. I have pictures to help me out on this one. Now where are those pictures I took when we were down there? That will tell me if I had them there or not. Ahhh, here they are.

Well, that was good. At least you remembered where the pictures were. Oh, could you just shut the f___ up for a minute.

O.K. So, that settles that. We didn't take them to San Diego. Oh God, how the hell could I forget what I did with a lousy f___ing pair of boots.

Now I'm really getting mad, but I don't think that's what's making my heart race.

What's making my heart race is fear. Is this how Alzheimer's starts? Oh, I may joke about it a lot, but this isn't funny anymore. How could I not remember what I did with those boots? It's not like they were in my closet a hundred years, like some of the s___ I can't seem to throw out. I just got them six or seven months ago, for God's sake! So it's not like I just forgot that I gave them away three years ago, or something.

God, this is so scary I can't even believe it. Am I suddenly just going to forget where I put things? This is only a pair of boots, but what if it's something really important, and I don't have a clue?

O.K., now calm down. It isn't like I haven't remembered where I put something before, so why am I panicking? I've forgotten plenty of times where I've put things, and I eventually find them. Don't I?

But a pair of boots, how in the hell many places can you put a pair of boots?

It's not like a little piece of paper you've written a phone number on and stuck someplace. A little itsy-bitsy piece of scrap paper that you could have stashed anywhere. It's like a big thing! Not something you stuff in a drawer or mix in with some papers. I just can't believe I can't find them. I must be losing my mind, there is no other explanation.

The ringing of the phone startles me, making me jump. The pictures on my lap scatter to the floor.

"Hellooo. . . ." comes my daughter's voice in a teasing tone. "Does there seem to be a problem?"

"What?" I say, thinking how incredible it is that we are so connected that she would just sense that I was having a problem.

"You called?" she laughs.

I called? Oh my God! I'd completely forgotten that somewhere in between looking on my sweater shelf and under the tennis shoes I had left her a message.

See what I mean, I can't even remember what I did ten minutes ago!

"Tami . . ." I say, trying to hide my panic, "you know those brown suede boots I got that matched that purse with the different colored patches on it? Did I loan them to you, 'cause I can't find them anywhere. . . ."

"No," she says, "just that black one the time I had the cast on. Remember, I was going to wear it on my good foot. . . ." Her voice trails off in the distance, as I stand in the doorway of my closet staring at the plain brown suede boots that have been sitting there all along. I had even taken them out and tried them on earlier, while I was looking for the multicolored ones.

Suddenly a light goes on in my head, both exciting and scaring me at the time. "Wait a minute," I say, cutting her off in mid-sentence. "Maybe it was only the purse that had the patches on it. Maybe these plain boots are the ones I got to match the purse."

"Yeah, Mom, the boots didn't have different colors on them. They just matched one of the colors on the purse."

"Oh my God, Tami, I can't believe what I just put myself through," I say as I tell her the story. "I swear to God, I really think I'm getting Alzheimer's. Either that, or I'm going crazy. I'm serious," I say laughing hysterically. "I mean I don't know if I'm relieved that the boots were here all along or not. What's the difference if I thought I lost them or I just forgot what they looked like?"

We hang up and I glance around the room. Let's see now, where did I put that article about the herb that improves your memory? Was it in the paper, or did I see it in a magazine? Did I cut it out, or did I throw it away by accident?

Or did I . . . wait a minute, hold on just one darn minute. I'm in no mood to go through that shit again in one night. I'll just have to figure this one out tomorrow.

That is if I still remember tomorrow what it is I wanted to figure out.

• • •

From this burst of writing, it is apparent that Diane's sense of humor is intimately connected to her self-critic, which is also strongly connected to her deepest feelings: her uncertainty about the world, her vulnerability, and her ironic appreciation of life.

As I reflect on Diane's story, I am reminded that this powerful force, our self-critic—while so often turning us away from enjoying and pursuing our creativity—can become one of the most dynamic sources of our creativity.

I sometimes see that my students are annoyed with me for pushing them to confront their creativity. They often hold back these feelings, but every now and then they come out. Once they allow themselves to put this annoyance on paper—really an irritation with the raging internal battle between self-critic and creator—the creativity flows nicely.

Exercise

WRITING A DIALOG BETWEEN YOUR CREATOR AND CRITIC

If you are intent on creating, but feel that you have apparently ground to a halt, write down all the hostile, angry dialogue going on in your head, dialogue that says, *You can't create, you don't want to, to hell with anyone who says you should create.* Sit quietly, and listen to how your inner dialogue responds when you think about creating. Write down whatever you hear, without judging it. When you are finished, read over what you have written, and see where it leads you—you may be surprised.

Then take a step backward and look at it again. All that negative stuff that has come rushing through can seem pretty funny when you gain some perspective. In fact, setting up a dialogue between your optimistic, creative side and your critical side can be quite humorous, even if it does not seem particularly funny when you are writing. So read your work to your writing group or friends. You may discover how humorous it really is—as Diane, Rebecca, George, and Mary from my Sunday writing group have all found out.

CHAPTER 17

Handling Creativity
and Depression

We will now look at another source for our creativity grinding to a halt: the relationship between creativity and depression. There is a great deal of literature circulating in the larger world that says something like "creativity and depression go hand in hand" and that they are "unavoidable." In a recent documentary about creativity and depression that glanced at the life and work of Anne Sexton, the academic narrator seemed intent on linking suicide and creativity as though they were partners for life. This is nonsense. The relationship between creativity and depression is active and alive, not inexorable and all-encompassing.

As a young filmmaker some thirty years ago, I created a documentary about life in the barrios of East Los Angeles. Although technically not of very high quality, it was raw, truthful, and compassionate. I was proud of my work. Soon a number of people in the film business and the Latino community were saying the same thing, including such documentary filmmakers as Haskel Wexler, whom I respected very much.

A few awards came my way, and I began to feel excited about my prospects as a filmmaker. "You are terrific!" I told myself. "Probably the next great documentary filmmaker." If I hadn't been arrogant enough already, I soon became impossible. I gave myself over to imagined press conferences, award ceremonies, and contracts for ambitious, well-financed projects. I imagined the film having a wonderful impact on the world around me—teachers, police officers, and social workers all changing their attitudes because of it. "Ah, you have opened my eyes," I could hear them saying.

I avoided work in the industry as a cameraman or editor for fear I would not be available when "the industry" came calling. Nor would I take any full-time teaching jobs lest I became "distracted" or unavailable for the next great documentary, which eager producers would be offering—soon, no doubt. My wife became impatient and bewildered by my Olympian attitudes.

Harsh reality soon began to take over. No fat contracts. No overnight success. No Academy Awards. If the film had a bit of impact, it was because I worked very hard to get people interested in it. I took it around to police organizations, teacher/parent groups, and community gatherings.

Waiting for something to happen, I fell into a void. For days at a time I felt depressed . . . empty . . . uncreative . . . listless . . . hardly alive. All this talent and nowhere to take it. Somehow, I thought, the world owed me recognition—and a living.

The listlessness into which I was falling was all the more scary because it reminded me of the pictures I held in my mind from childhood—pictures of my mother lying on her bed day after day, month after month. Pictures of her manic breaks—taking me and my sister out of school and leaving us with her brother while she disappeared—haunted me. "Is this what I am falling into?" I wondered.

As I searched East Los Angeles for another film to do, attending various functions and community events, I met an attractive young woman, a dancer, and began an affair. Never mind that I was married with children to care for. Never mind that she was as confused about her life as I was about mine. Somehow, I thought she was certain to be an avenue to greater creativity. The affair was soon over. My wife, Gail, was baffled by my behavior, but probably not as bewildered as I was.

"I have to get out of this depressing, constricting, middle-class life we are living," I declared.

"I'm not leaving my house," she answered. That and the kids were as much certainty as she had in her life. Fortunately, in the four years and two children of our marriage, she had been solid and focused—graduating from UCLA, returning for a master's degree, and now teaching. So we parted. Now I had to deal with divorce and separation from my kids, as well as depression and an unfocused career.

In fact, I went on to make more films and to experience many more of the ups and downs of being a creative person in an unpredictable business. I lost another marriage, never made any money to speak of— and also did a few shorts that pleased me, had some wonderful moments, and learned a great deal about life, creating . . . and myself.

The arc I have described here is not unusual for creative people. A great number of the people I have talked to who are or have been in the film business have gone through the ecstasy of creating and then the postpartum depression of finishing a project and seeing no material rewards.

One of the things I have learned over a long period of time is that, whatever one's strengths and weaknesses may be, the film business will highlight each . . . and propel us into no end of heartaches until we have examined these attributes and made changes where necessary. To be able to make such changes, it would be helpful to understand the relationship between creativity and depression, for it is intimate and profound.

The Triangle of Creativity and the Shadow Triangle of Depression

"I'm going to stop writing, just for now, while I get through my depression," says one of my students. Over the years, I have grown used to hearing this from some of the most creative people in my workshops.

Discovering that you are creative is an exhilarating and unsettling experience. For the most part you probably never knew you were in the creative cycle, except that in many ways you are unlike the people around you: you see the world quite differently from the way your friends see it, you have different goals, your learning process is different, your moods are different. Other than that you are quite normal, right?

Think about this next question, and write down your responses to it:
In what ways would you say you are different from most of the people you know?

When I was in college, I read the *Tao* of Lao Tze. For me, the most telling passage in this small book was an enigmatic poem, "The Tao" (The Path), which said something like, "when you are on the Tao, you will know it, and when you are not on it, you will not know it." That one line has kept me on track most of my life and has proven to be profoundly true.

As a creative person, your unusual searching process, whether mental or emotional, is not easily defined by others. But by the end of it, your process is what allows you to feel as if you have found the path that Lao Tze speaks of. Accompanying that sense of finding the path is an exhilaration that can be very seductive—and perhaps short-lived.

Now, think about this next question and, if you wish, write a story about what you discover:
Are you aware of a path—a creative process of uncovering and discovering—in your life? When did you first become aware of it?

Depression creeps quite easily into the lives of creative people early in their development because they have little or no control over when, where, and how they can regain the path when they lose it.

Scientists in the field of human behavior describe depression in a number of ways, including the following:

1. anger that wells up and is unexpressed
2. an event that goes badly, connected to other events that go badly, leading to the inner conclusion that *all* will go badly
3. a deep and prolonged anxiety about the future and one's ability to survive in it

Whatever definition we use, one thing stands out for us: when we are on the path, our mode of searching pays off; things unfold out of us without difficulty, and often the world responds well to what is coming out. Usually we are elated. The opposite of this experience is depression.

There are a number of things we can do to make the path more evident and our depression less cosmic. The Triangle of Creativity shown below may help you find and maintain the path more and more often.

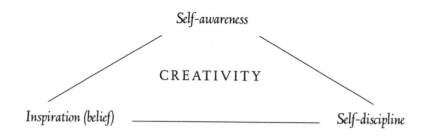

Self-awareness

CREATIVITY

Inspiration (belief) ———————————— *Self-discipline*

When we are off the path for a long time and the path seems most re-mote, the Triangle of Depression captures the spirit of what usually emerges.

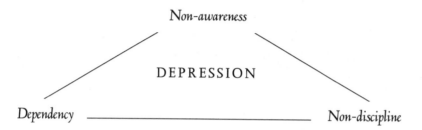

Non-awareness

DEPRESSION

Dependency ———————————— *Non-discipline*

Where does one enter the Triangle of Creativity? you may ask. At the lower left-hand corner, at *inspiration*.

For the creative person, inspiration is a most misunderstood experi-ence. "I am waiting to be inspired" is a phrase we often hear from artis-tic people. Linguistically, the word *inspire* means to *breathe in*. Well, breathe in what? Breathe in what is around us, that is, put ourselves in situations where we allow others to *inspire* us and to be *inspired* by us.

As a former college, USAF, and tournament circuit tennis player, I have always played the game at a highly competitive level. As I grow older, the great pleasure in playing tennis on a high level is that anyone on the court who is having a really good day inspires the others to play better and better, opponent and partner alike.

Behind the fact of letting others *in* (inspiring them, breathing them in) is our deep need as a creative person: to be able to believe that the world in which we find ourselves makes sense. True, the world is full of catastrophes of one kind or another—personal and cosmic. But what we as creative people (and I define *creative* as making something out of nothing) seek is an avenue into its "inner" order, an order that is there, but that each person must find for himself or herself. It is not available through the communal efforts of others, such as consciousness-raising groups, or even the solitary experience of meditation. It is available only through the actual manipulation of the materials through which we express our creativity—armies, if one is a general; babies, if one is a parent; students, if one is a teacher; pen and computer, if one is a writer.

With belief and a willingness to inspire and be inspired, we can begin to seek self-understanding, provided we are willing to do so in a self-disciplined way. This means that we contract with ourselves to manipulate the materials of our area of creativity, for a certain number of days a week, a certain length of time, *without fail*. What we accomplish is less important than our giving our creativity a chance to express itself.

Self-awareness means we have an understanding of the emotional baggage we bring to the table and a willingness to do everything possible to eliminate that baggage. It also means that we accept the limits of being a creative person.

A job is only a means of surviving and is not an end in itself. Our goal is to find high-paying work that affords us the opportunity to explore our areas of creativity with as much time to ourselves as possible. We must specify to ourselves the amount of money we can live on (minimally) each week and work toward achieving that level of income with the least expenditure of time and effort (without relying on others to do it for us and without depriving our children of the opportunities they deserve).

During my formative years at the University of Michigan, a cousin of mine, Bob Culver, was a powerful influence on my life. A watercolorist of great talent, he understood the relationship between work and career. When I met him, he was in his fifties, the father of two, and a draftsman at General Motors. Each year for the previous thirty years he had worked six months at GM, and then, with a little money in the bank, he would take off for northern Michigan and paint for six months. Each year he became a little more successful than the last, and he amassed a huge collection of work. In my sophomore year in college, a gallery showing in Detroit brought him prominence and financial independence, enabling him to quit GM and work part-time as a teacher at Cranbrook Academy. From him I learned that I could live normally—have a family and work—while following my singular, creative path.

In our lives there are people who inspire us, are inspired by us, or are a part of our process of self-awareness, self-discipline, and creativity. *Everyone* in our lives must become a part of this process: children, spouses, parents, business partners, and so on. And they can. James Joyce is known to have created numerous events in his life just so he could try out an experience before he wrote about it.

By allowing people who are not part of the Triangle of Creativity into our lives, we set up ourselves to enter and reenter the Triangle of Depression. It is as simple—and as challenging—as that.

Exercise

FINDING YOUR WAY

If you find yourself and your creativity, both actualized and potential, subject to bouts of depression, I suggest you try this exercise. When you feel depressed, find a quiet place to think about and write answers to the following questions.

1. Would you describe your personal life as a *mess*? If so, what is making it a mess?

2. Are you a creative person? What do you do that is creative?

3. What do you do that is both creative and artistic?

4. What would you like to do that is creative, artistic, or both?

5. What voice tells you not to do the creative-artistic thing you would like to do—that says you can't, or don't bother, or similar things?

6. As you think about doing the creative-artistic thing you would like to do, what does this voice say? What is the dialogue in your head?

7. What could you do right now to pursue the thing you would like to do? (For example, my friend Marianne, after having been terrified to sing in public since childhood, signed up for a voice workshop.)

8. Write a story in which the voices in your head—the doubting, undermining, self-critical voices—become part of a humorous dialogue with other positive or practical voices. (For an example,

see Diane Flor's story "Them Boots Is Made for Walkin'" on page 180).

9. Do you find yourself sinking into a depression when you think about creating or when you *finish* creating? Describe what happens.

10. What do you do to combat this depression?

11. Where do you enter the Triangle of Depression? What do you think this reveals?

12. What steps can you take to move from the Triangle of Depression to the Triangle of Creativity?

13. Are the people in your life inspiring and supporting your process of self-awareness, self-discipline, and creativity? Who is supporting it, and how do they do it?

    Who is not supporting it, and in what ways do they not inspire and support you?

    If you are not being inspired and supported, what steps must you take to insure that you are surrounded by people who *will* do these things for you—no matter whether your creativity is expressed in artistic terms or in your professional or personal life?

14. Do you believe that creativity is important in your life? If so, how is it important?

    How well do you manage your creativity?

    What steps can you take to manage your creativity more effectively?

15. After you have explored your self-critic in several creative stories, have begun to move from the Triangle of Depression into the Triangle of Creativity, and have started to manage your creativity more effectively, write a story of how life feels under these conditions. Add a P.S. to your story in which you reflect on what the story says about you.

—— • • • ——

If the story and the P.S. have given you helpful insights into yourself and have helped you define your tao of creativity, refer back to this section of your writing if you sink into the more negative side of exploring and managing your creativity.

CHAPTER 18

Experiencing the Story
as a Mirror of Ourselves

U p to now we have reviewed our stories by adding a
P.S. at the end and by expanding it in a full-fledged
assessment, as in the story by Diane Hanson. Now, we come upon yet
another way of looking at ourselves, one that is highly imaginative and
fits into our new, more creative view of ourselves: experiencing the story
as a mirror of ourselves.

As I have guided my students through the writing process, I have noticed that their stories often contain truly magical insights about the writers. Sometimes the writers grasped these insights, sometimes not. Looking
closely at the stories, I saw the process happening in several ways.

First, I could see that the "writing from within" techniques, particularly writing in the present tense, gave each writer a sense of innocence
and freedom from criticism. The stories reflected this freedom, often
yielding experiences on paper different from the ones the writers had
carried around in their heads for most of their lives.

I noticed that the process of sharing a story often pointed the writer
in the direction of moments in the story that needed to be expanded. In
digging into the climax of the story, expanding and opening it up during
the rewrite, the writer often uncovered a very different story. One such
example is Stephanie Bernardi's story "My Mother's Death," which tells

the writer something quite different about the experience as she expands certain moments (see pages 102–107).

In some instances, the rewriting process led to a completely different version of the story from what the writer thought he or she was writing, revealing what I call "hidden moments." For instance, in "Leaving the Farm" by Lettie Watkins, the first version yields to a second version that is much more complete and in which the truth of what happened is much less hidden. The third version reveals even more of the truth, a truth Lettie had kept hidden from herself for many, many years (see pages 112–115).

I also began seeing wonderful insights about the writers of some of these fine stories, even though the writers themselves were not yet seeing what the stories were telling them. When I asked the writers how they saw themselves, they often appeared inarticulate, confused, and off-the-mark in their answers. How could I help them to see what their stories were so clearly telling them about themselves?

My first breakthrough came when I realized that most people are reluctant to take center stage in their own lives. Having been told that writing in the first person is self-centered and offensive, they are inclined to leave themselves out of the story by using "we" instead of "I" or by focusing on what others are doing. This is an effective way of not looking at one's own behavior. The "writing from within" process could and did bring out the behavior in a clear and truthful way, but it would still take some doing for the writer to see himself or herself with clarity and detachment.

I began my search by listening for stories in which the writer was in pain about some past or present event, but was writing with honesty and feeling about that event. I noticed that the event often revolved around the actions of parents, children, or a divorced spouse, and that the writer was feeling victimized and blamed the other for all that happened. When this occurred, I guided the writers back through the story, helping them to see how the characters were telling each other a truth that may not have been seen.

"Ask yourself, 'Who am I in the story?'" I suggested. "Use the story as a mirror of yourself. When we are in pain, we often cannot see ourselves very clearly. But a story is a mirror and it will tell us the truth, if we allow it to."

A few days after the Southern California earthquake of 1994, I was sitting among a group of older writers who had been meeting every

Monday for five years. Everyone had been telling or reading stories about his or her experiences of the earthquake, such as stories about relatives and friends calling to inquire about the person's safety. When it came time for a good-natured, seventy-year-old German-Jewish refugee to read, the room grew quiet. Max Levin had been in considerable pain over the way he was being treated by his children. We wondered whether this story would be about that concern. He began to read in his soft, slightly accented voice.

Anya
by Max Levin

The phone rings. I pick it up. "Hello?" I say. "Are you OK, Papa?" I hear a voice say. "Anya, where are you?" I ask my daughter. "In Paris," she replies. "Paris??" I protest. "Your mother said you were in California." I hear silence from the other end. Then the phone clicks off. I am very unhappy. I have not heard from either Anya or my son in over a year. Their mother is turning them against me. I wait a few minutes then I call their mother's number. It rings and rings.

Finally, Anya answers. "Anya," I say, "why are you doing this to me? It has been a whole year since you and I spoke . . . what have I done that has. . . ." "Papa, I am sick and tired of your negativity, always playing the part of the victim, the Jewish refugee from the holocaust. I'm tired of it." She slams the phone down. I feel crushed.

* * *

Max looks up at the group. Everyone is moved by the piece. (For an earlier story concerning Max's relationships, see the second edition of *Writing from Within*.) The feedback from the group is that the story is honest and moving. Several listeners who have similar relationships with their children mention them to Max.

Max is tormented by the distance between himself and his grown children. What can he do to win them back, he wonders aloud. It occurs

MAX LEVIN   Max became a child actor and appeared in several films. In the mid-1930s, his parents saw the need to get out of Germany and did so. Eventually, Max landed in Hollywood where he appeared in small roles in a number of films. During these years, he became interested in the restaurant business, owning and managing several well-known eateries, including Barney's Beanery where he met Anya's mother.

to me that by holding this story up to Max as a mirror, some answers may unfold.

"Max," I say, "what would you see if you held the story up as a kind of mirror of yourself?" Not quite sure what I mean, he doesn't answer. "Let's suppose," I continue, "that your daughter is telling you something she wants you to hear, and that you've done a very good job of getting what she says onto paper. Her words have a great impact on us. We feel them. So do you. Now, let's suppose she is speaking the truth. Is there a place in your life where you are behaving like a victim?"

"Well," he says, "my ex-wife is keeping them from me. She is poisoning them against me." Max looks hurt and sad.

"What I mean is, can you find a place in the *story* where you are behaving like a victim?" He looks at me with a blank stare. "Let's read the first couple of lines again."

> The phone rings. I pick it up. "Hello?" I say. "Are you OK, Papa?" I hear a voice say. "Anya, where are you?" I ask my daughter. "In Paris," she replies. "Paris??" I protest. "Your mother said you were in California." I hear silence from the other end. Then the phone clicks off. I am very unhappy. I have not heard from either Anya or my son in over a year.

Max looks up, not quite sure what the words mean.

"Max," I say. "What voice is that saying *'Where are you?'* and *'Paris? Your mother said you were in California'*?"

Max's head begins to nod. "Yes, I see. It is the voice of the victim. Poor me. Right there in the story."

"That's the truthfulness of the story. But there is more."

He smiles. "Yes?"

"While you were writing those lines, do you remember any other voice wanting to be heard as you talked to Anya?"

Max leans back and laughs. "Yes, I wanted to say *'Comment ça va?'*—how are you? in French."

The whole class laughs, realizing that he had almost chosen a light, pleasant retort to his daughter but instead chose the response that had so often been his.

"What is really interesting, Max, is that you almost wrote those inner thoughts, but didn't. You almost let yourself see that there was another, higher response in you, but you didn't quite let it out. But you did entertain it. It is pretty clear that everything you need to know about yourself and about why your daughter has been keeping her distance is there to see, in the mirror of the story." I stop to let the words sink in.

A slow smile comes over his face. "I understand better." He looks around the room. "Thank you. I will rewrite the story."

"We can see in this experience," I say to the group, "that everything Max needed to know is in his story. The thing he left out was the thing he needed to discover about himself, the playful, nonjudging voice that will help him establish a new kind of relationship with his daughter, one that has no burden of guilt behind it. But the voice was there all the time. It just needed to be brought out."

Writing Mirror Stories

We can see that the stories we have written may well turn out to be very helpful mirrors for us to see the things about ourselves we need to know, but that are normally hidden from us. Most of the time, our self-protective, critical mind keeps these insights safely from our view. But when the story is well and honestly told, it can become a prism through which the truth about ourselves passes into our consciousness without being filtered by our critic.

I wondered whether I could create an exercise using guided imagery to move some of my more advanced, searching students into a focused, meditative place. That way, they might begin to see themselves differently—not as they want to see themselves, or as they fear seeing themselves, or as others see them—but simply as they *are* in the story.

I ponder this as a student, Tamara Randall, reads her story "The Beach." (The story appears on page 281.)

When she finishes reading, I look around the semicircle of students. Everyone seems eager for more. "Now is the time to improvise, Bernard," I say to myself. "Go ahead, take a risk." I want to do some guided imagery work, but am uncomfortable. This is not how I usually conduct my workshops. But I know it is what I must do.

"I would like you all to close your eyes," I say. "I am going to take you through a visualization that will help you see yourself more clearly in the mirror of your story. Wherever it takes you, you will then go ahead and write about that experience."

Once the students are comfortable, I begin the visualization prompt.

"I am imagining that I am in a desert. There are flames all around me. Ahead of me, I see a white light. I begin moving along a path that opens up through the flames, until I reach the white light. In the light, I see a mirror appearing. In the mirror, I see the story I have just written. As I look into the mirror, I begin to see a picture of myself in that story I have just written. Who is the person staring back at me from the mirror of the story I have just written? What do I see about myself that I didn't see before? As I see myself appearing in the mirror of this story, I will write about that person I see . . . *now*."

As soon as I am finished, my students begin writing. Tamara asks to read her self-assessment first.

The Beach: My Self in the Mirror
Tamara J. Randall

I am a young girl and I am in my element, free, playful, giggling, laughing. I glisten and shine. I love the world. I love unconditionally. I am innocent, pure light and energy. I hold the world in my heart. I am sensuous, succulent, smooth, sharp, hard, soft, real, dreamy. Imaginary worlds are mine.

In the mirror I see many women old and young. I pick the one on the beach that day. She is precious to me. I love her and I want to keep her here with me always. She is pure sunshine, pure energy, pure love, pure freedom, pure child.

• • •

When she finishes reading her mirror story, she wipes away some tears. "My marriage is in terrible shape," she whispers. "My husband is so critical. He sees nothing about me and the way I live my life that is of any value. He thinks I am just a child. I have a lot to give him, but he won't see it and won't accept it." She picks up a tissue. "This mirror or whatever you call it helps me . . . so much. I realize I am special." Again she wipes away tears. "I have a lot to give. It hurts so much that he can't see it."

TAMARA J. RANDALL   Tamara's mother, a 1960s hippie, took her very young children to Mexico, where they lived hand-to-mouth for fifteen years. Tamara's stories are filled with the mystery of native religion and folkways of Mexico. She is the mother of two children.

Tamara wrote "The Beach" at a time when her marriage was at an end, when her highly critical husband could see nothing valuable about her and the way she lived her life. Resurrecting this memory and seeing herself in the mirror of that story has done a great deal to remind her of her essential worth.

Exercise

You are now ready to look into the mirror of your own story. The best way to begin is to review any one of the stories you have written, and then ask yourself the following questions:

1. Who am I in this story? (Describe your qualities—courageous, vulnerable, broadminded, teasing, crowd-following, and so on.)
2. What do I see about myself in this story that I didn't know before?
3. What impact did this moment have on my life?
4. Along with the other stories I have written, what am I learning about myself in this story?
5. What are my feelings toward those close to me as revealed in this story?

These few questions, and our answers to them, will be important to us as we review our life's path. They will encourage the process of self-discovery. To ask them of ourselves is not to judge ourselves in any way. Our intent is simply to calm the waters of experience for a time so that we can see and savor who we were in those long-ago moments.

If it is difficult to get the self in the mirror into focus, use the visualization prompt to which Tamara and her writing group responded. Repeat it aloud to yourself, have someone else read it to you, or record your own voice and play it back just before you begin to write.

Now, write an assessment of yourself based on the person you see staring out at you from the mirror of one (or more) of your stories.

CHAPTER 19

The Benefits of Writing from Within

Writing from within ourselves, going beyond the facts and into the moment-to-moment feelings of our lives, can be scary but also deeply liberating. Done honestly and diligently it can help clarify our lives, allowing us to value our strengths, forgive ourselves and others for real or imagined hurts, and release events or people who have confused, angered, or weighed upon us. We can then embrace more fully those who have given us love, support, and guidance, and can look forward to that which is ahead of us.

How can we get the most from the "writing from within" that we have done? One way is to ask at the end of each story, "What did I learn from this experience back then? What am I learning from the experience now? What am I holding back that I could express?"

Healing from Within: Handling Loss Creatively

At a certain point in our lives, people we care about deeply begin to fail. Perhaps they are still living but need care we cannot provide and must be placed in an appropriate facility. Perhaps they hardly recognize us. This can make us feel very alone. Our sense of loss affects us deeply, and our self-esteem is often badly shaken. Our resolve to write, our discipline, may also be shaken: we don't want to write; we dwell on the object of our loss, excluding all else.

Writing about that special person may be difficult, but it is necessary for us and for them. Writing of the sweet, happy times is good. Writing of the struggles is good, too, as is writing about the absurdities and ironies of our relationship. And sometimes the results are quite surprising.

A student of mine had been having a hard time writing during the first few months of class. Her stories were short, factual, and very limited in what they revealed. When I asked her what was happening, she replied, "My husband is in the hospital with Alzheimer's disease. It's very hard to think of anything else." She was trying to avoid thinking about him by writing stories that had little to do with their relationship or the human or humorous side of the man. He had been a prominent physician, and she couldn't help but see the difference between the way he had been and the way he was when she visited him. "He's only conscious five minutes out of the hour," she said. "Even then, just barely."

I suggested she do the difficult thing—take the bull by the horns and write about their relationship. She was younger than he, a devoted wife, awed by his place in the profession, content to write about the trips they had taken around the world traveling from one professional meeting to another.

"Write the stories of your life together," I suggested. "The growing-up years, the struggles, how absurd he could be."

She laughed. "Oh, he could be. Maybe I should write about the time he was drunk in Paris and got propositioned right in front of my eyes." The class laughed and began clapping, wanting this stuffed shirt unstuffed.

An Evening in Paris
by Helen Winer

"Show me the way to go home.
   I'm tired and I want to go to bed . . ."
   Lou is singing as we walk along the boulevard in Paris in June of 1954. He had lectured at the university that afternoon on his specialty, dermatology, and we had stopped to have some wine after his talk.

"... oh, I had a little drink about an hour ago
and it went right to my head ..."

Barbara, our college-age daughter, has been getting more and more disgusted with her father and so she steps back to join me and her sister, Marylee, who is 14. Lou keeps on singing.

Just then a very pretty floozy walks up to Lou and says, "You want to come home with me?"

"No," says Lou, waving his hand toward us. "I've got my wife and daughters with me here and I'm just singing. Say," he says, looking at her face, which is very close to his, "I'm going to send you to the best dermatologist in Paris. Tell him to treat you. You've got some bad-looking moles on your face. You don't want to have your pretty face spoiled by these moles, do you?" She looks at him in complete surprise. "Say Helen," he turns to me, "Do you have Jean Civatte's card in your purse? Give it to this girl." I give the card to her. "Now run along kid." He turns to me. "Come, walk with me instead of with the girls." He smiles and begins singing. . . .

"Wherever I may roam, on land or sea or foam
You can always hear me singing this song . . ."

Barbara and Marylee and I join in as we walk down the street.

"... show me the way to go home."

* * *

The class was delighted to see a different, informal, human side of their relationship. They were pleased that Helen could look at this dying man, the man she loved and adored, and see his imperfections and absurdities and laugh at them even as he lay dying a few miles away.

"Take this story and read it to him," I suggested.

She looked at me as if I were an idiot. "He's not conscious," she said, perplexed. "He can't even speak and he can't hear anything." She shook her head, almost in tears.

"Whether he seems conscious or not, read it to him," I insisted. "Believe me, he'll hear it. And he'll love it. Just hold his hand. Whether he

HELEN WINER   Helen grew up in Minnesota where she met her husband when she was nineteen and he, an already prominent dermatologist, was twenty-nine. They moved to Los Angeles and she raised her family while her husband achieved international fame. She came to class to begin memoirs for her grandchildren, memories of her beloved husband, hospitalized with Alzheimer's disease.

says anything or not, you'll be able to feel in his hand that he is hearing you."

"If you say so, I'll do it," she answered, unconvinced.

The following week she came to class with a story of her experience at his bedside.

I Read My Story to Lou
by Helen Winer

As I enter Crescent Bay Convalescent Hospital, I notice one of my friends, a patient, coming toward me in her wheelchair. "Do you wish to hear my latest story?" I ask. "My teacher said I should read it to Dr. Winer and see his reaction."

"Ya, sure. I like your stories. I'll listen even if he doesn't," says Mary, "because he probably is only half here." We go into his room and he is half-awake. I start my story.

"Show me the way to go home.

I'm tired and I want to go to bed . . ."

Lou stiffens. I can see he hears my voice. I take his hand. As I read he begins to smile. By the time I read about the floozy girl who tried to pick him up, he is grinning from ear to ear. "It's OK honey, I never looked at another woman. Just you!" Lou says and then dozes off. I smile at Mary and put my story in my purse.

I go home and hug myself.

— • • • —

We can learn a number of things from Helen's experience. If we have relatives or friends who are seriously ill or near death, we need not give them up as lost. They may not be awake, but they are accessible. Talking to them when they are in an unconscious state will be good for them whether they seem to respond or not. Writing about an experience that has been shared, bringing back the good times of the past, and reading the moment to them rather than merely talking about it is all the more powerful because we have taken the time and energy to shape the experience artistically.

When someone is a long way away and we intend to make contact with him or her, we can write about the experience we wish to share. The more vividly we write, the more deeply our loved one will be touched.

The healing power of "writing from within" is enormous for the writer. The power of the story can push deep into the unconscious of even those who are very sick and infirm. Likewise, if we can awaken searing memories from the past, as does Joanne Baumgart with "Christmas 1944" (see page 248), bringing the story to life as vividly as possible is a way of removing it from the part of ourselves that is haunted by the past. The more fully the story is written, the more complete the release from our past and, therefore, the greater the possibility of healing ourselves from this terrible wound. (Remember Diane Hanson's story "Double Trouble"—and why she wrote it.)

A Profitable Merger: Fiction Writing and Life Writing

Although a number of my writer friends consider life writing to be a poor stepchild to the high art of writing fiction, some of them have changed their minds after taking my writing workshops. "Writing my life stories brings an honesty to my work that I can't seem to get anywhere else," says Mar Puatu, a novelist and screenwriter. "There is a grittiness, a texture to my life stories that I am able to get into my fiction only when it is based on some kind of life experience."

Over the years I have noticed that when my life writers attempt fiction (and I encourage only those who are skilled at "writing from within"), the first few efforts don't ring true. They often overwrite, embrace clichés, or write from their heads rather than from their guts. Gradually, I bring them back to the simplicity of life writing, to the directness of feelings and the focus on physical sensation, and their fiction becomes more honest and believable.

Most of the skills learned in life writing translate directly into the fiction medium, such as the way we uncover character in "writing from within" by stressing the very real difference between the narrator's concerns and the character's concerns. If the character is a young child and his or her innocence must be respected, then the narrator must lay in details in such a way as to establish rather than to undermine the belief in the character's understanding of what goes on.

Another crossover skill is using action to portray character. Too often in fiction we see a lot said *about* the characters by the narrator.

Too seldom does the writer simply *allow* the character's actions to reveal who he is.

These techniques, when practiced in the writing of our own life experiences, will help us write more authentic, more believable (and more salable) fiction. At the very least, the sketches we create when writing life stories enable us to draw accurately from life. After all, Leonardo da Vinci created thousands of sketches before he committed anything to canvas or wall. Even if our sketches are nothing but short, single-page vignettes of people we know, they become the source material for longer, richer stories.

On a visit to the British Museum some ten years ago, I was fascinated to see how many half-size sketches for his famous "Sunday Afternoon on the Island of La Grande Jatte" impressionist painter Georges Seurat created before he did the final work. In sketch after richly colored sketch, each tiny point of pigment creates a sense of the life at the river's edge. That's just what we do when we write and rewrite our stories. In each moment, we find a changing color . . . and a different quality of honesty or grittiness as our light passes over the surfaces of our characters and their struggles.

Bringing the Family Together

This book began with a brief statement about the way in which our society has developed a certain rootlessness over several generations. Fortunately, our society has turned its attention once more to the stabilizing influence of family and roots in preserving and developing some of the qualities that lead to fulfilled lives: a sense of belonging, enhanced communication, freedom for growth, and the need for support and encouragement.

Life story writing practiced "from within" can be one of the factors that leads to a more harmonious family life. Writing one's most vivid early memories brings many members of the family into the arena of one's life. Writing about significant characters gives unusual members of the family the opportunity to be seen and understood. Writing from several points of view allows family members to compare notes about important moments and to experience events each in his or her own way, knowing that most of the family will disagree about both the facts and the meaning of any given circumstance. Pursuit of family history allows family members to glimpse stories from the past and the relationships out of which those stories have come. Additionally, this pursuit serves to help those who are shy know how important such revealing is to other members of the family. In sum, life story writing allows the many points of view within a family to be heard.

The actual process by which stories are exchanged may be a fascinating story in itself. Distant families in which little sharing takes place can begin to dissolve some of their barriers. Closer families in which bonds are stronger may develop more of a sense of who each family member really is.

Life Story Writing and Values in the Twenty-First Century

The United States is an increasingly pluralistic and multicultural society. Our schools, legal, judicial, and welfare systems strain under the unfamiliar customs, habits, and language of those coming into our systems as well as the poor, homeless, and drug-damaged dwellers in our urban areas.

What common ground do all of these people have? How can we as a society work toward common goals with such diversity around us?

Seventy years ago the goal of every immigrant was to learn the language, customs, and habits of this country and to melt into American society while keeping some traditions alive. This is not the main goal of most immigrants today, nor of the poor and the homeless. America's money, power, political freedom, and material opportunities are still desired. Its ideological and judicial elasticity are quite puzzling. Its humanistic concern for a highly developed, personal ability to grasp ideas and express them vigorously is little understood.

Storytelling is one thread that can weave all these diverse needs and desires together. The poorest and wealthiest touch one another through stories of struggle, humor, suffering, and compassion.

Storytelling cuts across all boundaries. Christian fundamentalist and existential humanist alike communicate through stories. Older adults touch the lives of children not through insistent and didactic moralizing, but through stories of life's mysteries.

Every child in every classroom across the country can learn to tell and to share stories of his or her significant experiences in life. These stories are as precious to the child as a substantial bank account is to an adult. Each child needs to know how to put stories in and take stories out of his or her memory bank. For too long, storytelling has been forgotten as a part of our educational system. From the lower grades through college, storytelling through life story writing will help build positive values and enhance self-esteem. (For teachers who wish to employ some of what we have been exploring in this book, please see my book *In Your Own Voice* [Alameda, CA: Hunter House, 1993].)

I recently spent several months working with a group of people in recovery from alcohol and drug abuse. I introduced them to the idea that perhaps each of them carried inside a creativity that had gone undiscovered or neglected over a lifetime. Almost everyone responded strongly to this idea and wrote vivid, expressive life stories. It became clear to me that these former addicts (mostly young men who came from lower middle class, very macho families in which the fathers were highly critical and contemptuous of creativity as too feminine) yearned for that which would allow them to be more creative in their lives, and not be criticized for it.

In subsequent conversations with their counselors, I learned that several of those with whom I had worked were, in fact, further exploring their life stories and were apparently much more focused on their recovery than before I began working with them.

Every segment of society profits by the ability to tell stories effectively. The homeless win refuge, abused children win safety, teachers win community support, and the disenfranchised win representation. Stories told well support each person's claim to truth and importance and win for each storyteller growing self-esteem.

Plato tells us that everything we need to know already exists and that our job is to penetrate through to our awareness of the truths that lie within. A central question asked by one of the popular human-growth-potential organizations is, "What is it that you know that you are pretending not to know?" Parsifal, the great warrior-knight of the Grail Quest of the middle ages, was on this very path. His name (sometimes spelled Perceval) means to pierce through or to see through. His is the story of the warrior who sees through conventional definitions of what a warrior must be and discovers compassion in order to be reunited with his father. Family stories remind us of such values, conveyed in an entertaining way, without insistence.

The stories of our personal past, even if we are small children, form the mythic path we are to follow for the rest of our lives. Some family stories lead to family traditions of compassion, dedication, self-sacrifice, and idealism. Others lead to family traditions of honest public service. Personal and family stories help produce citizens who are not molded by popular culture alone. A society in which personal and family stories are developed is a society in which survival values are strong.

I hope we will return storytelling to a place of honor within the family and in the classroom.

Conclusion

Writing our life's stories has given us the opportunity to approach events and experiences creatively, perhaps for the first time. We have learned that writing is not so magical a thing that only a few can do it. We *can* create. We *can* write. By softening our critic, by seeking helpful feedback, and by becoming aware of our own process when we work, we can continue to grow as writers and storytellers. Little by little we are discovering our own authentic voices as writers. By first looking at life through the innocent eyes of the child who still dwells within us, we can write stories in a way that is fresh, direct, visual, and emotional. Our critic is at rest.

CHAPTER 20

Putting It All Together,
Making a Book

Having finished the story of your life, an undertaking of many months, perhaps even years, you will want to put it together, or "package" it, in a way that will give you a sense of accomplishment and have a pleasing effect on those who read it. You've tackled the project as seriously as any artist would, and your work deserves to be properly displayed. Here are some hints about "wrapping it all up": illustrating your work, presenting each page in the most readable way, using calligraphy and ornamentation to enhance the text, reproducing and binding copies handsomely, and selecting an appropriate cover.

Just as we anticipate with pleasure what will be found inside a nicely wrapped gift, the little extras we add to our finished volume will give our readers a sense of anticipation and delight when they pick up our work.

Page Design and Layout

Your narratives are worth preserving and should be as readable as possible. Unless you have very legible and artistic handwriting, format your stories on a word processor or on a computer using word-processing software. If you don't have a laser or ink-jet printer, look into renting the use of one at a copy and print shop or a computer rental store.

If your work is typed, earlier drafts should be double-spaced, but the final version can be set with less line space; a common setting is one and a half lines of space. Allow approximately a one-inch margin on three sides of the page, with an inch and a half for the left-hand, or inside, margin to accommodate the binding.

Choose an appealing, readable typeface for the text and perhaps a bolder font for the heads. Treat special elements of the text, like poetry and quotations, in a distinctive way. One common technique is to indent these sections an extra half inch from the left margin. Remember to indent the beginnings of new paragraphs, though it is not necessary to leave an entire extra line between paragraphs.

You might consider finding someone with an understanding of book design and typography to help you design the basic page layout. And if you have the book professionally typeset, hire a book typesetter, not someone whose main experience is with advertising, newsletters, and flyers.

Titles and Headings

Treat the first page of each story a bit differently. Book designers frequently use ornamental capitals or special sizes and typefaces for chapter headings and openings. As a basic page layout, you might start the title of the story one or two inches from the top of the page, and start your first line of text about two to three inches below the title—but feel free to get as creative as you wish! For examples of some of the design elements we have talked about, study the treatment of titles, chapter openings, and page layouts in this and other books.

Another way of giving your narrative a nice look is to use calligraphy in appropriate places. Calligraphy, which is elegant, stylized handwriting, can be used to nice effect as chapter or story headings, as in the following:

Cracking Open the Door to the Past

Calligraphy or special designs can also be used as ornamentation to give style to the first letter of a chapter or text:

HISTORIANS of art like to present the turn of the century as an epoch and begin a new chapter even when describing northern painting.

You may think calligraphy and ornamentation are too fancy for your narrative, but in fact they are entirely appropriate: they add a personal, handcrafted feel to a volume of stories and experiences that is itself very personal and handcrafted.

A good way to find calligraphers and obtain advice about graphic design is to consult the list of course offerings at your local adult school, community college, art school, or the art department of a local high school or college.

Illustrations

"A picture is worth a thousand words" is the cliché, and it truly will enhance your work to add photographs, drawings, and even carefully chosen memorabilia to the pages of your book. If you plan to have a number of copies of your life story made, you might tape the photographs onto the printout and then make photocopies of the story. For better quality at a slightly higher cost, you could order duplicate photographs, or ask your local small printer to make you "photostats." Be sure to leave room in the text for the photos as you are typing it or printing it out, or ask a local graphic artist or graphic arts student to scan in the photographs, which can then be easily sized, shaped, and placed in the text.

Handmade drawings make delightful illustrations. One creative idea was suggested by a student who was writing the life of her mother. As she finished each story, she had her young daughter illustrate it. The illustrated collection of stories was given as a present to the student's mother on her birthday, and a second installment at Christmastime. It was a deeply heartfelt experience shared by three generations of a family.

Reproduction, Covers, and Bindings

Photocopying allows one to reproduce one's work fairly inexpensively. Likewise, inexpensive, attractive covers and bindings may be obtained at most copy and print shops for a few dollars and will lend a nice appearance to your work. Two commonly available binding options are *velo binding,* in which the pages of the book have punched holes and a plastic strip is attached on both sides to hold the pages and covers together, and *comb* or *spiral binding,* in which the pages and covers are held together by a broad comb, making it look rather like a spiral notebook. Velo binding is generally neater and stronger; comb binding is better for thick books and those that need to open flat. To see examples of these and other inexpensive binding options, such as Docutech, visit your local copy shop.

More expensive binding options include *perfect binding,* in which the pages are glued together inside a cover, and *case* or *cloth binding,* which uses a hardcover case. These are generally too expensive for one, two, or even fifty copies of a book, but if you are interested, look in your local yellow pages under "bookbinders" or ask at your library for the name of a library binder.

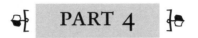

PART 4

Life Story Writing Selections

The stories that follow are selections from works written by students in life story writing classes in Los Angeles from 1990 to 1996. They were written using the techniques outlined in this book and serve as effective examples of the methods—and rewards—of "writing from within." I hope you find them enjoyable. They may stimulate in you recollections of a similar kind, recollections that you may someday want to write.

Blind Lemon Jefferson Sings the Blues
by Eddie White

"But I thought for sure that Blind Lemon Jefferson was born in Shreveport, Brother Johnson."

"Naw, Suh! Naw, Suh! Blind Lemon was born in Wortham, Texas, in 1897. They say he was born with a guitar in his hand, and he weren't a-bawlin' for milk, he was bawlin' the blues, Brer Jackson. Blind Lemon was born singing the blues and pickin' that mean guitar."

"Yes, Lawd! Heh! Heh! Heh!" laughs Brother Johnson.

The word is being said all over Ruston that Blind Lemon is gonna stop off in Ruston on his way to Monroe, Louisiana. Everyone is looking forward to seeing and hearing Blind Lemon Jefferson sing the blues.

My Granny says that, "It ain't the kind of music I just like to hear, but it is so filled with something—I just have to hear that poor man sing."

Time passes. It seems like Blind Lemon will never come.

"Granny, is Blind Lemon Jefferson ever going to come to town?"

"I right 'spect he will, chile. I right 'spect he will, effen it be the good Lord's will."

We work and wait. We wait and wait. "Granny, do you think it's gonna rain, it's so cloudy looking?"

"Naw, Suh! I don't think so. Just kinda looks like that."

"Granny! Granny! Listen! Don't you hear somebody singing? It's a long way away, Granny, but it seems like I can hear somebody singing."

"Shhhhh! Shhh! Chile, I believe that must be Blind Lemon Jefferson. That must be Blind Lemon." Granny takes off her apron in a hurry, and puts on her bonnet.

"Come on, Sonny, come on," she tells me.

I hurry outside. It seems like a stampede, a wild horse stampede. The people are running, just running running to see and hear Blind Lemon Jefferson.

We children join the grownup chase. We can't keep up, but we are not far behind. I can hear Blind Lemon real good, but I cannot see him. "Hey, Lawdy Lawdy," he moans and strums his guitar. "Since you been gone—I BE SO LONESOME AND SO ALONEOWN! But one day WO-O-MANNE, you AIN'T go worry my life NO MO!"

Blind Lemon sings like he knows what the weather looks like on this cloudy, rainy-looking afternoon. Blind Lemon throws his head back and howls.

A big tall man looks down at me, picks me up and puts me on his shoulders. "I want you to see and hear something that I hope you never forget," he tells me.

Blind Lemon howls so sad; it's almost like a funeral.

"YOU TREATS ME MEAN-and aruh so low down. Sometimes Ah feels lak I ON DE EH groundHOUND, but someday WO-O-Manne-DAS RIGHT!" he shouts. "YOU AIN'T GO WORRY MY LIFE NO MO!"

It's one day in May 1927 I will never forget! Blind Lemon has on a dusty-looking brown suit. His shoes look new but they are dusty-looking too, as they should be. Paved roads are few, and the few paved roads are mostly for white people. A few white folks have come to hear and see Blind Lemon Jefferson, but they stay way in the back because white folks and colored folks are not to get too close together. That's against the Law. When the white people go to see Grambling College play football, they stand on the tops of their cars on the nearby highway. I look back, way back, and see some white people standing on the tops of their cars, seeing and hearing Blind Lemon Jefferson.

One day, white people will learn to sing and play the blues because they sure do listen to them. One day I will think—if one does not like the blues they must be dead. Granny goes to church but she likes Blind Lemon.

A young man stands near Blind Lemon. They say that he is some kin to Blind Lemon. The young man also leads Blind Lemon Jefferson around. A tin cup is at the end of Blind Lemon's guitar. It will be passed around to pick up whatever money the people can afford to give.

I hear one person say, "He sho goin' to make a heap er money when he go to Monroe, and I sho hope he do!"

Many people witness and say soft-like, "Sho do hope so! SHO DO!"

Another says, "Even if he ain't blind, he sho do deserve all the money he can make—because that man, Good Lawd, Good Lawd! Blind Lemon Jefferson sho nuff sing the blues."

Twilight is coming on. Blind Lemon has stopped singing. I guess he is going to go on to Monroe now. Everyone is kind of silent and quiet-like now. It is a feeling as though we have just come out of church. The Doxology and Benediction have been read, Amen! Amen! With each head, it

WRITING
FROM
WITHIN

216

seems, a little bowed, we begin our journey home with silent thoughts.

The sun has set. Nighttime comes in a hurry to a small country town. The nightingale and whippoorwill sing their blues in the night, while a few lightening bugs try to make us feel not so blue.

As we walk along, Granny and I hear two men talking loud. At first we think they might be angry at each other.

Then we hear them laugh.

"They don't mean no harm, they just joshing with each other," Granny tells me. We listen. Oh, it's the voices of Brother Johnson and Brother Jackson.

"Weren't that sho nuff something, Brer Jackson?"

"Sho was, Brother Johnson! Sho was!"

"It were like the singing of angels on wings of thunder and lightning, Thunder and Lightning!"

"Right! Right! You right as rain, Brother Johnson."

"It just seemed like the stars were gonna fall right down outta the sky," Brother Johnson continues, "the heavens resounded! Can I get a witness?"

"I'm right HEAH!" yells Brer Jackson.

"The moon, the sun, and the stars turned to silver and gold," Brother Johnson throws back his head and hollers—"Heh! Heh! Heh!" and raves on in a singsong voice—"and the silver and gold turned into diamonds, and the diamonds became a lake of fire! And the lake of fire became rubies and pearls—and the rubies and pearls are placed on the necked breast of a whole heap of colored virgins, fifty thousand ebony maidens whose warm black thighs have advised them that the time done come! Come enter in and let your soul find its moon mad bliss when Blind Lemon Jefferson sings the blues. Let no soul stand still. You gotta be moved out, inside-outside-inside because the TRUTH done come! The soul Truth done come!"

"And you sho' ain't wrong, Bro' Johnson!" shouts Brother Jackson. "You sho' ain't wrong!"

"Sonny, I hope you tried to turn your ears from all that wild talk of Brother Johnson and Brother Jackson," Granny says.

Granny goes on, "Everybody thought that Blind Lemon is mighty fine, but the way those brothers carry on it's a shame before the Lord, Uh! Uh! Uh! I wonder if Brother Johnson and them have been drinking some of Grandma Bradshaw's moonshine? Uh! Uh! Uh! It's a shame before the Lord!"

EDDIE WHITE   Raised in Louisiana, Eddie came north to Cleveland, Ohio, with his family in the years after World War II. He studied music and tried boxing. At five feet four inches, he decided he was a bit undersized for a pugilistic career. Coming to Los Angeles, he befriended many of the greats of jazz including Buddy Collette, Charlie Mingus, and Chico Hamilton. He retired recently after working for the post office some thirty years.

The Overhead Bridge
by Eddie White

I love to walk to the post office and pick up our mail. The post office is about two miles from Granny's house in downtown Ruston, Louisiana. Our box number is Box 107. I remove the mailbox key from the string around my neck and open our mailbox. Ahh, Ooooweee! I yell to myself. I count to myself. Granny sure has a lot of mail today. Because my mother is a school teacher and helps me with all of my school work along with her two youngest sisters, Baby Lowell and Sally Brooks, I learn to read very good and I have a very good knowledge of words and a better than most kids' understanding of the language. With three good teachers any kid can learn fast, at least something. Since I was three years old, I read better than most kids. I am seven now. Oh! Here is a letter from my Mother Dear; wonder if she has any money in it for Granny and me? One is from Aunt Brookside, another from Baby Lowell. Bet they want something. They are away at school, college or something!

Ooooo, here's one from Aunt Anna. She hasn't written in a long time; this one is from Aunt Tee (Lucyellen). I don't know why we call her Aunt Tee. And here is the last one—a letter from good old Uncle Charlie, Granny's oldest son. This should make my grandmother happy, six letters in all, but I know what she will say when I get home. Sonny, we didn't get no mail from Little Brother. Everyone calls Uncle John Glover Harvey either Little Uncle or Little Brother or the Baby Boy. Lawd! Lawd! Why don't he ever write just to let me know how he is getting along. I keep so worried all of the time wondering if something has happened to him. My baby got his leg cut off riding them freight trains when he weren't but nine years old, and has been a-hoboin' ever since, just ridin' the rails all over this land. He's been in every state in the country, I 'spect. Lawd! Lawd! Have mercy!"

It seems that Granny would know by now that Little Uncle only writes to her or anyone else when he needs some money or something. We see him once in a great while. One day Little Uncle will come home for a day or so, then he will leave just like he came, like Santa Claus. Only Little Uncle won't bring anything but himself. I just cain't stand to hear a freight train whistle blow. I just have to put on my travelin' clothes and go. That's what Little Uncle tells everyone.

Hey there boy! One of the mail clerks hollers at me as I am walking out the door of the post office. Tell your grandma that sure was a good chocolate cake she mailed to her daughter. Be sure to tell her to make a bigger cake next time so everybody in OUR post office can get some. He laughs real loud. HEH! HEH! HEH! I turn and look back at him. He kind of throws back his head a little. He has a very RED face, a big throat, and he is the one I have seen up close with the wrinkles in his neck like a turkey. I say nothing as I wonder to myself, Is he one of the kinds of people that the "rich white" people call "cracker trash"? I am getting close to the old Overhead Bridge. It is made and shaped like a big rainbow. I have to cross the bridge going to and from the post office. Trains going out of and coming into town pass under the Overhead Bridge.

Sitting on an old cane-bottom chair at the bottom of the crossing is a very old, gray-headed white man. He is talking to a very big white boy as he kind of rocks back and forth in his chair. As I get near them I see that the boy is about Baby Lowell's age, around seventeen or so, and he is not old and ugly looking like the old man. The boy is bare-headed. His hair is short, light-colored and sandy-looking. The old man has on a dirty pair of raggedy-looking overalls and an old straw hat that has a hole in it. Neither of them have any shoes on, just like me. Because both the old man and the boy are poor-looking, I think that they must be nice and not mean white people, like that old post office clerk who ate up Baby Lowell's chocolate cake that Granny had baked and mailed to her.

As I walk by the two, the old man and the boy, I kind of smile at them, thinking they are nice people.

Wait a MINUTE! shouts the big boy, real mean and ugly-like. WHATCHALL EN YOU HANES? He drawls out nasty and slow.

It's mail for my Granny, I whisper, kind of scared but not too much because the ugly old man is nearby. Gimme dat dare mail, he drawls, snatching the mail from my hand. I look kind of long at the ugly old man and wait for him to make the big boy give me back our mail. Being little and the boy being big, I know that the ugly old man will be on my side and will make the boy give me back my mail. The mean old gray-headed man just grins his toothless grin and watches me. Tobacco or snuff spit drools down the corner of his ugly mouth which seems to sit almost in the middle of an ugly, odd-shaped face. He has greenish bird-eyes that shift from me to the big boy. He reminds me some of a chicken hawk.

The big boy now begins to open my mail. He takes his time and reads the letters very slow to the old man, and they laugh at anything they think is funny. Because Granny cannot read or write, all the family members know that I read the mail to her. They write large and clear, and are sure to use words that I can understand.

The big boy stumbles across a word that he cannot pronounce. It is an easy word, at least for me. He begins to stumble and spell out the word. Let me see, he stumbles, ppp-rrr-o-gram? Prigrin-UH! Wonder what the hell is that?

It's not prigrin. It's PROGRAM. Don't you know what a program is? I ask him.

LISTEN HEAH! YOU SHUT UP NIGGER! Don't you even dare to make a fool out of a white man! Do ya heah me, nigger boy?

Yes! I answer.

WHATTA you mean YES. Don't you know you be talkin' to a white man? Yo folks better teach you yo manners 'fo you grow up an gits lynched. We love ta have necktie parties for you smart uppity niggers. They want to teach you to grow up RIGHT and RESPECT WHITE FOLKS! YOU HEAH ME, BOY? Yes, sir, I answer. Tears begin to run down my face to the hot ground. It is not the word NIGGER or saying YES SIR that makes me cry. It's reading of our MAIL OUR MAIL GRANNY'S MAIL. He puts all of the mail in the right envelopes. I think he is trying to let me know that he can read as well as I can, but I know that he can't. He gives the mail back to me. NOW YOU GIT!!! I WANTCHA TA GIT!! GIT TA RUNNIN'! DON'T YA DARE LOOK BACK! He slaps his hands hard and loud, and kicks at me. I jump back. He misses. I run almost all the way home. I am mad and scared as I run home. Two miles is a long way for a seven-year-old, so I run some but trot most of the way. I think of the old man and the big boy. How they stink. I think it is a very hot day and both of them are mean and stinking. But the UGLY OLD MAN STINKS WORSE THAN THE BOY I say to myself. Maybe it's because the old man has been meaner and stinking longer than the boy. There is a difference between the postal clerk and the mean two. The postal clerk must be what rich people call cracker trash, and the mean two must be what rich white people call POOR WHITE TRASH. Granny works for a real rich white lady sometimes, and Granny tells me that when Mrs. Satterfield leaves her home for any reason, she tells Granny, Now Lucinda, effen any niggers at all come by heah a-beggin' for food while I'm gone, I want you to be sure and feed the niggers but effen any poor white trash come by heah for anything at all, I want you to call Sheriff Thigpen and get them the hell away from my premises. Don't give THE TRASH a damned thing! Let the trash starve to death! That's what they deserve. They been free all their born no-account days. Now do you heah me Lucinda? Yes'm I heah you, Miss Satterfield. One day I asked Granny, What do you do when the beggars come by, Granny? Do you do what Mrs. Satterfield tells you to do? GOD DON'T LOVE UGLY, CHILE. I just feeds them all who comes by begging for food. I feeds them all, black and white alike.

I am finally home. It seems like I have been gone all day. I hurry into the house. Granny can tell I have been crying, and I am a little out of breath. Why what's the matter, chile? What's the matter? Tell your Granny.

I tell Granny all about it. The South bein' what it is, nothing can be done about what happened to me. Granny pulls me to her and whispers, We will just have to take it to the Good Lord in prayer. He will wipe away all tears and he will wash away all sorrow. Let us try and forget about it. God changes things, Sonny.

I think to myself just before getting ready to go to bed, Granny is right. Granny is always right. My Granny is always RIGHT? There are no more tears, and no sorrow and no anger.

Now I look back and laugh at it all but how CAN I FORGET?

Doctor, Oh Doctor
by George Small

My mother is standing next to her teacher's black grand piano. She is wearing her best shiny dress, the bracelet I gave her for Christmas and long earrings. Her mouth is covered with her favorite ruby red lipstick. She says it makes her look glamorous. Her singing can hurt my ears, especially when she does the real high notes. Sometimes I go into another room and cover my ears.

Tonight I have to be on my best behavior. Mom wants me to be "a little gentleman" and sit quietly in the library while she takes her voice lesson from her teacher. Her teacher is an old German man who speaks with a strong accent. He has long gray hair and wears thick glasses. He never is nice to me, he never smiles. His hands are giant, bigger than my dad's. His hands are thick, rough, and covered in gray hair. He has gray hair everywhere. Coming out of his nose, his shirt collar and going up his neck. Some hairs in his nose are still black and stand out more than the gray ones. He spits when he talks too, always wiping his mouth with his big hands. You can see the spit build up on his lips and watch it fly when he talks. I try and cover my face when he talks with my arm, but Mom always pushes my arm back down and makes me take it like a man.

I'm afraid to take my shoes off tonight and play on the couch in the library so I play on the floor with my metal airplane I always bring with me. My plane is a silver B-29 with propellers that can spin. It's my favorite plane because it's small and I can take it wherever we go. I like to put it out the back window of the car and watch the propellers spin fast.

The singing is very loud tonight, especially Mom and Ray's duet. Ray is my mother's best girlfriend. They love to listen to *Madame Butterfly* and make faces, cry, and hold each other. Everything with Mom is a big deal. She's very dramatic.

I'm playing war with my plane when Mom and Ray come into the library. "Hi honey, how are you sweetie, did you hear Ray and me singing, did you like it, Georgie?" Mom starts to straighten my clothes and brush my hair to the side. "Let's go out and take a smoke break, Georgie come along." Mom grabs my arm and leads me through the house to the backyard. The yard is very dark. It's so dark you can't see anything in it. Mom and Ray light up and start smoking and talking, sometimes humming and doing melody from their duet. "Mom, make the cigarette glow," I say. Mom takes a deep drag off the cigarette so it glows bright orange, lighting her face up in the dark. Sometimes when we are driving late at night Mom lets me play with her cigarette and make circles in the dark.

I'm standing next to Mom touching her skirt, feeling the material on my shoulder and smelling the smoke from their cigarettes when Ray asks, "Do you like music, Georgie?" "Yes, I like . . ." Mom interrupts me and says, "He loves music. I think it's in the blood. You know at home on Sunday mornings his dad will play his favorite classical recordings on the hi-fi and Georgie will get up on the kitchen chair and conduct to Toscanini and Bernstein, he's so adorable." She always talks for me and tells me it's because she so proud of me and thinks I'm a perfect ten-year-old doll.

All of a sudden two girls come running out of the dark yard. "Georgie, this is Gail, she's the daughter of our friends the Levines. And who's your friend, Gail?" And Gail says, "This is my cousin Cindy, she lives with us now, she's nine years old and I'm eleven years old yesterday." "Oh, happy birthday, Gail," Mom says. Gail is a good foot taller than me and Cindy. She has long legs and arms with white skin that glows in the dark and beautiful blond hair with bangs that flop over her face. I've never seen anybody with such long arms and legs before. Gail and Cindy are full of energy, holding hands and hopping around us while the adults talk. I try to keep busy looking at Mom and Ray. I don't know many girls outside of school. Girls are different and they never seem shy like me. Gail interrupts and asks Mom if they can play with me in the yard. Mom thinks for a minute and says, "OK, but Georgie don't get your new pants dirty. Don't get into any trouble, please Georgie, be your best." Gail and Cindy grab one arm each and lead me off into the dark yard.

Gail takes hold of my hand and leads me around the patio furniture into the steep hill that becomes the yard. Gail looks right into my eyes and says, "Let me take you to our most secret place." She holds my hand and squeezes it tight. Her face is large and white, lit by the moon. "I've never shown our place to anyone else before," she says. "He's a boy, he'll ruin it, it's supposed to be our secret," Cindy says. Gail just ignores Cindy and takes me searching for the small trail behind the bushes and along the fence. As we get deeper into the yard my eyes adjust and I can see more. When I look up I can see a million stars. The house seems so far away now.

Gail stops me and points through a large hole in the fence. "We can go in there if you want, we do it all the time." My eyes turn away from hers. "Isn't that the neighbor's yard," I say. "We do it all the time," she says. The girls are both looking at me. "I don't want to, I want to stay in our yard." She turns away from me. Cindy and Gail start to whisper and I hear Cindy say, "He's a chicken." I look back through the hole in the fence and wonder if I can do this. The girls keep on whispering and ignoring me for a long time. Finally Gail turns around and grabs my hand. She leads me back to some stairs and shows me how they make a bush into a secret place by hanging old clothes from inside the bush, making it private and secret.

Gail is older and bigger than me, but she's very nice to me. She's like a boy in some ways but she's still a girl. She doesn't get dirty like me, girls never get dirty. But now I'm getting dirty and I'm worrying about ruining my pants. I try to dust off my pants a little, and Gail says, "Can you play Doctor?" "I never played Doctor before," I say. And Cindy says, "He can't play Doctor, he wouldn't be any good." Gail looks at me and asks me if I can give a shot. She picks up a twig and shows me how to give her a shot. She pushes the stick between her two fingers with her thumb. She hands me the twig and they lead me to their secret doctor's office on the side of the house, barely lit by the small bathroom window. You can hear voices inside the house and an occasional flush of the toilet as the girls start to move old tables and patio furniture around to make the doctor's office. They know exactly what to do; in a minute they move everything in place. There is a short wall to lay the patient on. Gail lies down on the wall, stomach first. She says, "I'm so sick Doctor, can you help me, I think I need a shot, Doctor." Cindy takes Gail's hand and says, "It will be just a minute." Then she says to Gail, "You must prepare yourself for the shot, and you must be brave." Gail moans and lifts her cotton dress above her waist and tells me where to give her a shot. Cindy insists that I give Gail a little shot first in her arm. Gail is moaning and says, "Please Doctor help me take my panties off, pull them down here," showing her white thighs. I pull her panties down while she wriggles to help me pull them all the way down to her knees. Her panties are silky and soft like her white skin. Her butt is the biggest part of her body. Gail moans, "Oh Doctor I'm so sick, please help me get well, please." I try and speak like a doctor, in a low voice, "Yes little girl, I can help you, but it will hurt." Gail moans and wriggles uncomfortably on the wall waiting for the shot. Cindy takes a little piece of cotton and wipes the spot on her butt where she wants the shot. I don't think Cindy likes me. I'm too slow for her, I don't know what to do, and I never played Doctor before. I take the twig and press it into the softest part of her butt. Cindy puts baby powder on Gail's butt and wipes it with cotton. Her butt smells sweet like babies, soft and mushy. My stick presses into her deep down leaving a red mark. Gail moans and asks for another, and another and another. The harder I press the more she likes it, but I'm afraid I will hurt her. I try not to press too hard, but she scolds me, "Harder, harder," she cries. Her butt is full of bright red marks. She wriggles on the wall moaning and groaning, "Oh Doctor, oh Doctor." Now I'm getting the idea and I look for new places to give her a shot. She likes that and for a minute I know how to play Doctor.

All of a sudden the porch lights go on and voices come from inside the house. I turn around and see Mom and another lady staring right at us. Mom is mad. I've never seen her so red. The other lady screams at Gail and Cindy, "Get your dress back on you brat, you brats." Mom looks at me with shock. "How could you, in my teacher's house, with my friends all here, how could you, why?" "Mom, I didn't do anything," I try to tell her, but she grabs me by the arm, picking me up off the ground, dragging me through the house. She's pinching and hurting my arm all the while she's saying, "How could you, how could you?" She never lets me tell her why. "Mom, it was their idea, I didn't want to play," I say. "Don't lie to me Georgie, I saw you enjoying it, playing with little girls, naked, how could you?" She gathers up our things in the house and stops to speak with her teacher at the door. He doesn't even look at me.

I know Mom won't listen to me now, nobody will believe me now. Mom and I start to step down the long flight of stairs to the street below and she stops us. "This is not the son I raised, you are not going to ever do anything like that again, do you hear me." She spanks my butt six or seven times and goes down a few steps more, stopping to look back at the house, and then hits me again, "I'm so embarrassed by you, my only son, how could you?"

When we finally get down to the sidewalk Mom won't even look at me and she won't let me try and explain what happened. I feel so bad, my heart is beating so fast, my head is buzzing, and I'm short of breath.

Mom puts me in the back seat of our '52 Chevy and slams the door in my face. I know I can't talk to her. I know she's going to tell Dad. She takes my plane out of her purse and throws it into the back seat of the car. "Don't bother to play with your plane now, just sit there and think about what you've done to your mother." We drive off, she lights up another cigarette and I watch the houses on the hills go by. Mom turns the radio on and I sit back in the seat, burying my face in my arms, smelling that baby smell on my shirt and wishing I was back in that doctor's office playing Doctor.

GEORGE SMALL   George is a painter, actor, teacher, and now writer. Owner of an art school in Santa Monica, he divides his time between Santa Barbara and Los Angeles. For many years George has been Bernard's next-door neighbor. Over-the-fence conversations led George to join the Sunday writers group.

Where Is Mother?

by Chung Mi Kim

"I wanna go see Mother," I cry out.

"You can't," says my sister Bok.

"Why not?"

"You don't know where she is," my sister says so calmly, as if she doesn't even miss Mother.

Outside, everything is covered with snow. The ground, the roof and the trees—the sky is gray. It's windy and cold. I see no one around. I don't know where we are. The vast field and the mountain look pretty with snow but cold and lonely. It's been five days since my sister, Bok, and I followed the peasant host to this home—a man whom my parents knew well. On January 4th, the North Korean Red Army invaded South Korea again. My family decided not to stay together. My older brothers and sisters went south because they could not risk being captured by the Red Army. Taking the young ones, my father and mother decided to hide in the rural country north of our home. My father and my little brother went to Antogol, while my sister and I were to wait for Mother to join us at this peasant's house. We will then join Father and my little brother.

I came here with no books. That night when we left, we were in a hurry. Following the stranger, my sister and I walked on the dark mountain roads. There was no moon or a lantern. I wished I were an owl. Several times we had to cross brooks, stepping on the rocks. I slipped. My feet got wet. How cold I was! Whimpering and limping, I walked for more than twenty *li*. When we finally arrived at the stranger's house, it was past midnight.

The first night, I did not cry. I didn't want the strangers to think I was such a whiner. But then I couldn't help it the second day. My sister and I fought over something. She didn't want to play with me. If I cried, calling my mother, she only scolded me. At twelve, how could she behave like a grownup? Since then every day I've been crying, waiting for my mother. The grownup host family are nice to us but I miss my mother so much. After all I am the youngest daughter who followed Mother everywhere. This is the first time I ever got separated from my mother.

"Don't you miss Mother?" I ask. My sister doesn't answer, cutting a piece of cloth with a large pair of scissors. She is three years older than me. She wants to make Korean socks.

"Let me try it," I ask. "I can do it, too."

"No. You can't."

"Please, show me how to do it then," I plead.

Bok doesn't answer and keeps cutting away the cloth. I snatch the cloth from her out of spite.

Instantly, she hits my hand, yelling, "Stop pestering me!"

Angrily I throw the cloth at her.

"I wanna see Mother!" I cry. Suddenly, I feel like an orphan.

"Stop crying. You're such a cry-baby. Behave yourself, this is not our home, you know," she scolds me.

"That's why I'm crying—because I miss our home! I wanna go see Mother!" I run out of the room. I hate to be in this tiny, stuffy room anyway.

Next to the house, there is a big tree on a small hill. I don't know what kind of tree that is. It has only branches on which snow sits pretty. It's windy and cold. I run up the hill and stand by the tree. From there I can see down the road far away. I want to see if my mother is coming. The winter field is empty with everyone inside houses. And because of the war, many people left home, I'm sure. Just like we did.

I think of my mother. I miss her. I cry. I wait. My feet hurt from cold snow. I jump up and down to keep my feet warm. I cry again.

The peasant host comes out of the house and sees me.

"Why are you out in the cold? Please come inside," he says.

I keep crying. He comes up to me and pulls my arm. "Come inside. You're gonna catch a cold."

"Where is my mother?" I cry out. "Please, take me to my mother!"

"Your mother is coming soon. Come, come," he coaxes me.

"You say that every day. This is the fifth day!" I cry louder.

"She must be busy. She'll come tomorrow—maybe."

"Take me to my mother, please," I plead, crying. "You know where she is!"

The peasant host stops for a moment and then clicks his tongue.

"You've been crying every day, little girl," he says. "If your mother doesn't come tomorrow, I'll take you to her. I think I know where she is."

"Really, you will?" I look up at him. He nods.

"It's quite a distance, though," he says.

"I can walk. You know that."

"All right. Don't cry, and come inside."

Wiping tears with my sleeve, I follow him.

A ray of sunlight is coming down through the clouds, and the snow glistens. I feel better. I can hardly wait for one more night.

Where are you, Mother?

CHUNG MI KIM   Chung Mi was a refugee during the Korean War, which displaced her entire family. After the war, she came to the United States where she learned the language and began writing. She is now an award-winning author of poems and plays.

Mom's Trip North
by Bernard Selling

"Your mother wants to see you," says Mr. Stoner, my teacher. I look up from my desk and see Mom standing at the doorway to my classroom. It is 1950 and I am eleven years old, in the sixth grade class in Winter Park, Florida. Mom has a funny look on her face, all smiles. *What's she doing here?* I wonder to myself. She motions me to the door. I get up and go to her.

"We're going to take a trip," she says. Her eyes are bright, excited. She leads me out of school.

"What about my class?" I ask her.

"Oh, don't worry about that," she laughs.

A few moments later we get in our old '36 Packard. My sister Lee is already there. We start driving north, out of Winter Park. She's driving very fast, like she's trying to get away from something. There aren't any clothes in the car that I can see, so we can't be going too far.

Mom turns toward me and grins. "We're going to Uncle Cully's." It's like she's read my mind. Lee in the back seat says nothing.

"All the way up there?" I ask. Uncle Cully lives up in Virginia, near Washington, D.C. "Why go up there?" She doesn't say anything. I know she doesn't like it much here in Florida. We only came down here because Dad had a heart attack in Detroit and almost died. He needs to be where it's warm. Even now he coughs a lot in the winter. Maybe they had a fight or something. I remember sitting on the stairs with Lee, watching Dad yell at her, "If you don't . . . (something or other) . . . you know what I'll do?" Neither of us could figure out what that was.

As Mom drives, she laughs and sings and talks to herself. This isn't like her at all. She's usually sort of quiet and friendly and interested in other people. Never has anything bad to say about anyone or anything. But now she's talking to herself, like I'm not even here. She scares me.

After we cross the Georgia state line, Mom pulls into a gas station and stops. She takes us inside and makes a telephone call.

"Hello, Lowell, it's me," she says, all smiles. "We're going up to Maine. And you can't get me. Ha, ha, ha." I stand in the corner, shifting from one foot to the other. She's in another world. I want to talk to my dad, except sometimes he gets really mad at me. I wonder if he's mad now.

She hands me the phone. "He wants to talk to you," she says, still laughing.

"Hi, Dad," I say, real soft. I'm close to tears.

"Hello, Butch," I hear him say. He is very calm. It's really good to hear his voice. "Are you OK?" His voice is very soft. He's not angry or upset, just . . . I think, worried. Like I am.

"Uh, huh," I say.

"Don't worry. Everything'll be OK. You'll be back home soon," I think he says.

"OK," I say and give the phone back to Mom.

A few moments later we are on our way again. I wish I could talk to him more. I wish he'd just come get me and Lee.

That night we stop at a fancy hotel in Georgia. The room is big. I'll bet it costs a lot. We eat in a big dining room. Then she gets on the phone and starts talking and talking. I go to sleep wondering what's going to happen to me and Lee. She usually talks all the time but she's been quiet the whole trip.

The next morning Mom is on the phone again. We don't do much but sit around and eat. After a couple of days, a man comes to lunch. Then I hear her on the phone talking to a lot of different people. I think she is trying to get money. We buy some clothes. It seems like we're here forever. I hate it here.

Now we're in the Packard again. I love it in the car. It smells like Dad's cigars. And there's a St. Christopher medal pinned to the visor. St. Christopher protects travelers.

Mom is driving along really fast. A policeman pulls up behind us, then waves us over to the side. Mom pulls over.

"Hello, officer. Did I do something wrong?" She gives him a big smile.

"Lady," he says, "you were going sixty miles an hour in a thirty-five-mile-an-hour zone."

"Oh, no," she laughs. "That's not possible. This car is so old, it won't even go over forty."

"Not true, Mom," I say. "You were doing way over sixty. The speedometer said seventy." She gives me a scowl, then laughs. The policeman gives her a ticket and she has to go into a town and pay it.

In a few more days, we get to Uncle Cully and Aunt Marge's house.

"Hi, Butch," says Aunt Marge, coming out to greet us. "It's good to see you again." She's pretty friendly though I don't like her much. She watches her kids, my cousins Tommy and Mary Ellen, like a hawk. They have to do exactly what she says, all the time. I know 'cause we stopped here last summer on our way to Maine.

Uncle Cully comes home. He's real nice looking with wavy hair. He smiles and goes out into his woodshop. When we visited last summer, he never said a word. Just smiled.

At dinner that night we have to cross ourselves and say grace at the table and stuff like that, not like at home where Dad and Mom encourage me to do what I want. "It's called 'wholesome neglect,'" he says, then laughs. So does Mom, when she's not in her room, lying on her bed, looking at the wall. But Dad's funny: he plays the saxophone really badly and laughs. Then he puts on a funny hat and plays the bugle, and sucks in his fat tummy and his pants fall down. Nobody laughs much here.

Now it's Friday and I am standing in line outside the church. I have a headache and I am very cold. We are waiting to go into the church for confession. Everyone in this sixth grade class has to go.

When the nun isn't watching, I slip back to the end of the line, hoping they won't see me.

The thing is, I'm not Catholic. I shouldn't even be in this school.

Mom's gone up to Maine, to our summer home, and so Aunt Marge has put me in this school. I've been here all week and I hate it.

The line gets shorter and shorter. Finally I'm the only one in it.

"Come on along," says the nun. She shoos me into the church. We walk up to the place where the altar is. There are two chairs. A priest stands next to one of them. He motions me to one and sits in the other.

"Now then," he says. "What sins have you committed during the past week, my son?" I shake my head. "What did you say?" He leans closer.

Nobody's asked me if I've committed a sin since I was six years old and went to communion classes. They talked about sin a lot and I was glad when Dad told Mom I didn't have to go any longer. I can tell this priest thinks I've committed a sin by not going to confession. I wonder if it's a big sin. *What is a big sin?* I wonder. *Maybe I'll go to hell. Will I go to hell? Oh, oh.*

"No . . . er, none, nothing," I answer.

He looks at me sort of surprised but not smiling. "No sins to confess? My, haven't we been a good boy." Still he doesn't smile. He has kind of mean eyes and real thin lips. He looks like a wolf out looking for food. I don't like him and I want outta here in the worst way.

"Now then, when was your last confession?" he asks.

Oh, oh! I think to myself. That was a long time ago. When we were in Detroit. I couldn't even remember the Lord's Prayer. *"Hail Mary full of grace, the Lord is with thee . . ."* I hear my voice in my head.

"I said when was your last confession." He sort of licks his lips and his eyes narrow into slits.

"Ah, I guess, ah, about . . . maybe six years ago," I say.

"What? Six years. . . ." His eyes get smaller and meaner. He looks at me like I've committed a crime.

What would the Green Hornet do? Or Sky King? I think. *". . . blessed is the fruit of thy womb Jesus . . ."*

He gets up and hurries down the aisle of the church. Boy, I'm in trouble now. What kind of punishment will I get? I know they hit kids in Catholic schools. I want to run out but I can't. The nun is standing nearby. I feel real alone. I hate this church stuff.

The priest comes back with three other priests. They stand over me. I want to die or disappear.

"Now then, tell them what you told me," he says. They all lean in. I smell peppermint. I say nothing. Seems like I can't see daylight anymore, only black, the color of what they're wearing.

"How long has it been since your last confession?" asks a sort of fat one.

"About . . . ah, four years," I say in a small voice.

"How long?" asks the first priest.

I'd love to jump up and punch him in the nose. But then that would be a big sin.

"Ah, about three years," I say in a real small voice.

"Is that the truth?" says the third one leaning on the back of the other chair. "Huh?"

What do they want me to say? I'm not Catholic!! I'm only here because my aunt made me? My mom is not making sense, and my aunt and uncle haven't done anything about it!

They all shake their heads. They talk among themselves. I'm afraid of them. Maybe they see something really dark and evil in me that I don't see, that I don't know about. Maybe I'll go to hell. Naw, there isn't any hell. I know Dad doesn't believe in a hell. But then his parents were Jewish. I wonder what they're gonna do.

They look at me and point, then they all walk toward the door. The nun takes me to the door of the church, shakes her head then disappears.

I go outside and wait for the school bus. I'm alone again. I don't really know how I feel, kinda numb I guess. But I stood up to the priests and told the truth. I could have lied and told them what they wanted to hear. But I told the truth, even if I did fudge a bit. I feel good. Maybe I have some courage that I never knew I had.

P.S. By the weekend, Lee and I were on a plane and flown to Jacksonville, Florida, where Dad picked us up. Looking back, I wonder why he hadn't come up to Virginia to get us sooner. Maybe he didn't know where we were. I always wondered why my aunt and uncle didn't get us back to Dad as soon as possible. It seems like they were pretending Mom wasn't sick.

But I've heard members of the family say that Aunt Marge came to Detroit to take care of me and Lee when Dad had his heart attack and Mom had her first manic-depressive break, so they had to know. A few years ago my cousin Mary Ellen said her mother felt Lee and I were better off with them rather than with my dad. (He was Jewish after all, and they were good Catholics.) After I heard that I became really furious with that side of the family.

When this unhappy trip was over, Dad never asked me how I felt about what had happened. I wonder why he didn't. I needed to talk about it. This was Mom's second manic-depressive break in four years. The earlier one I don't remember.

When I think about Mom during this whole experience I feel very sad. Sad for her because she had demons inside that she never shared with anyone. I have felt angry at her for leaving us to these narrow-minded relatives with their mean-spirited prejudices. I have felt angry that she burned up the car that I was looking forward to having when I got old enough. Mostly, though, I feel sad for her for all the years when she wasn't herself, and for me, not having the safe, secure mothering I deserved to have.

Throughout these hard times my father was calm. He never blamed anyone. He had a temper and no doubt Mom suffered from it. He wasn't easy to live with. But the tougher things got, the calmer he became.

What did I learn about myself? Well, I see the origins of this painful, sinking feeling I have had many times in my life, that I am not in control of what's going on around me, that I am being judged, that I have little protection against it.

As I reflect on being judged by the priests, I realize that I have never believed in heaven, hell, and judgment; in sin or damnation; but inside I have fears of it all.

More than any other memory of my childhood, this is the memory that brings back the most aloneness, pain, anger, and confusion. What made Mom go off the deep end? It has caused me to ask over and over, what went on between Mom and Dad when I was eight and he had his first heart attack and she had her first manic-depressive break? I remember nothing. Where was I?

As I read over the story I see in myself a quality I hadn't known existed in me at that time. At every point in the story, I am asking questions: "Why is this happening? When is this going to end? Where are we going?" It is a quality I value and possibly the quality that has served me best in the crisis times of my life.

For no reason that I can discern, I learned somehow not to ask emotional questions in my family. Intellectual ones, yes. But not emotional ones. That I've had to learn for myself.

• • •

As I rewrote the story, knowing what the audience needed to know, many details of the past came back to me, particularly Mom taunting Dad, "Ha ha, you can't get me," and feeling so surrounded by the priests that "I can't see daylight anymore, only black, the color of what they're wearing."

This was the final moment that I added to the story:

> But I stood up to the priests and told the truth. I could have lied
> and told them what they wanted to hear. But I told the truth, even if I
> did fudge a bit. I feel good. Maybe I have some courage that I never
> knew I had.

As I look back on the story, I realize that what has always been a terrifying story of being at the mercy of my mother's craziness and the domination of the church is actually a story of gaining courage.

This story and these reflections are virtually the last things written for the new edition of this book. It has taken several years of writing the book before I could get to this story and its meaning for me.

BERNARD SELLING   Bernard is a writer, director, musician, and teacher in Los Angeles. He is the creator of several educational films and nonfiction books. He is currently at work on a novel of fifteenth-century Italy.

Kumander Aguila
by Mar V. Puatu

Father is packing his clothes. His bus for the US navy base in Olongapo, Zambales, will come soon. The base at Subic Bay is about 200 kilometers away. I cling to his pants, while munching a star-apple.

"Why can't I go with you?" I put on a grieving face, even some tears.

"Now, Nonino," my father looks at me straight in the eye, "you know I have to work there. Somebody's got to look after your mama and your sister." He wipes at the violet stain of the star-apple on my mouth. "You're eight years old, so you're elected."

"I still dream of the Japanese in the big house." The sweetness of the star-apple becomes acidic. "They tortured the prisoners." I spit the pungent taste.

"The war is over," Father says. "It's been over for almost a year."

"But I still see the prisoners stretched on racks. The Japanese broke their ribs. They tore the nails from their fingers. Ugh . . . I can't sleep without hearing their screams."

"Well, you can sleep with your mama and baby Cris," Father says. "You can sleep and at the same time, you can protect them from Kumander Aguila."

"The bandit?" My eyes widen.

"The villagers call him that." Father carries his luggage, and walks to the highway to wait for his bus. "Aguila was a guerrillero, a freedom fighter. He fought the Japanese, and now refuses to lay down his .45 pistol and his garands."

"He scares me." I shiver, remembering his picture in the newspaper. "He has a big scar down his cheek. He's like an eel."

"He is wily, all right. He holes up in the Sierra Madre mountains with his men. Somehow they know when the government will strike, so they transfer to the Caraballo mountains near our village."

"The government hunts him as a common thief, huh, Father?"

"Yes, but he imagines himself as Robin Hood."

"Like Errol Flynn in the movies?"

"The newspapers paint him as such. He thinks all rich men are corrupt, so he takes their money. He pretends to give all the money he's stolen to the poor because they are downtrodden."

"Downtrodden?"

"Yes, Aguila upsets the masses because he says that the government oppresses them. But he's terrorizing the towns, pillaging for food, ravaging the church for gold and silver."

Father's anger makes his temples throb.

"His men kill the priests, denouncing them for their faith. He rapes women left unprotected by their menfolk."

"Please go slow, Father." I scratch my head. "I don't understand."

The bus comes chugging up the road. My father hails it, and boards the rickety vehicle. "Remember, I'm counting on you."

My father's palm on my cheek reassures me. The truck rattles on like a sick dog. It coughs black smoke. I cover my nose to keep from belching and wave to my father.

That night, after saying the rosary, I ask my mother, "Why does Father have to work at all? Isn't he the overseer at Grandfather's hacienda?"

"Your grandfather and he had a falling out." Mother prepares my bamboo bed, pats the pillow, and puts on the mosquito net.

I unhook the bamboo pole that supports the windowsill, and close it. It is cold outside. I jump into bed. "Is that why we have to live in this hut, and not at the big house?"

She nods, and tucks me under the thick, *Ilocana* blanket.

My mother has tender, rough palms. She smoothes my face, smiles, and joins my sister Cris on the bed close to mine. "We have our own lives to live."

"Grandfather is wrong," I call out to her. "He's a snob."

Mother chuckles a little. "Don't let him hear that."

My father marrying a laundry-woman does not sit well with Grandfather. He ridicules her as the daughter of a fisherman who did not catch many fish when he was alive. The sun darkens her skin. To Grandfather and his Castilian amigos, she must look like an Aeta, an aborigine. Begrudgingly, he confesses that mother looks like a Moorish *La Maja Desnuda*. In school, I sneak into the library and discover what the Spanish words mean. My heart beats with pride. My mother is a pale imitation of Goya's masterpiece, *The Naked Maja*. My cheeks blush to see the nude model. But then, I am relieved to know that Goya painted the same model with all her clothes.

Later that night, as I turn over in bed, I hear my mother gasping for breath. She must be suffering from a *bangungot*, or nightmare; the thought quickly passes through my mind. Many people die because of this oppressive dream. No one ever wakes up from this frightful sleep.

The kerosene lamp flickers by the bamboo bed on which Mother and Cris lay. I take off my blanket and open my mosquito net to wake her. She is struggling with a man with a wide straw hat. He clamps a hand over her mouth. She claws at his face.

Sleep still in my eyes, I run to the window. I pull off the supporting bamboo pole, take up my mother's mosquito net, and lunge at her attacker.

My puny arms are weak, but with all the strength I can muster, I strike the man at the back of the neck. I knock the straw hat off his head.

The man's eyes blaze at me. The fiery balls burrow into my face. I back away, wanting to escape. A bristled beard half-covers the scar on his face. He turns into the dreaded half-man, half-horse smoking a long cigar that my mother warns me about when I do something bad.

I recognize him. The papers splash his picture on the front page everywhere. Kumander Aguila. Aguila, the eagle. Aguila, the hawk. Aguila, the buzzard.

He grabs me by the neck. My eyes bulge. The room about me begins to go blue, then gray, then black.

"Please . . ." My mother tugs at the man's hands. "I beg you, don't . . ."

Kumander Aguila loosens his grip. Air rushes back to my lungs. The dreaded bandit looms above me.

"Brave little man." The bamboo pole makes a raw mark at the back of his neck. A swelling grows on his nape.

Chuckling, he gets hold of the bamboo pole. He snaps it into halves with his knee, and throws it away. "Brave little man."

My mother embraces me, protectingly.

"Don't worry, Onen." The man shakes off the mosquito net that entangles us. Then, he strides across the room and barks orders to his men who stand guard. I hear the muffled answers of the men. My mother tightens her embrace.

"I'll see you again," Aguila says. He picks up the straw hat, straightens it, and puts it on, hiding the scar on his face. With a mock bow to my mother, he salutes me, "The next time, you won't catch me with my back turned." He disappears into the night.

"Mother," I pry loose from her. "He called you by your first name. Do you know . . ."

"No," she hugs me and cries. "I don't know him."

My five year old sister, Cris, snores in the corner of the bed.

"At least, you're out of danger." I stand my ground, with my pride intact. "Father will be proud of me."

"Don't tell him about this," my mother sobs.

"Why not?"

"Aguila's very cruel . . . he'll kill your father . . . all of us!"

I look at my mother. She says she's afraid for my father, but I wonder. . . . Anyway, when Father comes back, I'll tell him about Aguila. My father will avenge his honor, just like I did this night. He sure can count on me.

MAR V. PUATU Mar was born in Manila, Philippines. After graduating from the University of the East, he worked for J. W. Thompson and other international advertising companies. He wrote, acted in, produced, and directed for Philippine radio, television, stage, and cinema. A six-time winner of the prestigious Palanca Award and the Arena Playwriting Contest, he now resides in California. In 1995, he won the PALM (Philippine Arts, Letters and Media Council, in Washington, D.C.) short story contest. He has published a semi-autobiographical book of short stories, *The Girl with One Eye*.

Gloria

by James Dybas

Friday Night Socials at the Russell Square Park Gym in South Chicago are really cool. Most of my eighth grade class is here and so are some of the guys and girls from St. Michoslaw's.

"Did you say I've got a lot to learn? Well don't think I'm trying not to learn. Since this is the perfect spot to learn . . ." Gloria Wisneski and I are dancing real close.

"Teach Me Tonight." She's wearing a real tight black skirt with a kinda flare at the bottom, bobby socks, ballerina shoes, and a pink sweater. Her brown hair is pulled over to one side and her pink lipstick is way over her real lips. She looks kinda like a small, Polish Rita Hayworth. All four-foot-eleven of her is pressed up against me and it feels like we're glued together. "Should the teacher stand so near my love?" she sings in my ear. It tickles but it feels great. "Graduation's almost here my love," I sing back in her ear.

I can't believe that my eighth grade graduation is happening next week. Our feet are barely moving, one uh two, three uh four. Oh man, I'm nervous and excited. Our eyes closed, holding each other tightly, swaying, turning, spinning.

Stop, hold. Gloria giggles. "What's that I feel?" she whispers in my ear. I start to laugh a little because her whisper tickles. I don't say a word.

She knows what it is. She's fourteen. One uh two, three uh four, buh dum, "Teach Me Tonight."

"Ya wanna take a walk? We can go over by the swings," I say, my heart beating like a tom-tom.

"Sure, I'll be right back," she says as she winks at me and heads towards the little girls' room. I wonder if she likes to . . .

"What are you doin' here? I thought you said you had to study."

Oh shit, it's Alice. She must have had kielbasa for supper. She smells like garlic, and as she snarls at me she doesn't know it but there's like a little black thing wedged between two of her bottom teeth. It makes her look weird. I think it's a caraway seed or maybe a bit of *kishka,* otherwise known as blood sausage, which is what I'm gonna turn into if I don't think fast.

"Oh, hi, Alice," I pretend to be happy to see her. "I got through with my homework faster than I thought and I tried to call you but there was no answer."

I'm lying and it feels as if the poodle that's sewn onto her skirt is gonna jump off it and bite the hell outta my nose, which is getting as long as Pinocchio's.

"Oh yeah, what time did you call?" she says, trying to catch me in my lie.

"Oh, about twenty minutes ago," I say, hoping that Gloria doesn't come out of the little girls' room and I can get Alice over to the other side of the gym.

"Hey look, there's Stash, standing by the record player." Even though Stash Grankowski doesn't see me I wave at him pretending he does. I grab Alice's hand and start to walk over to him. A plan of action pops into my head. "I'm gonna go to the john, Alice. I'll meet you over there by Stash."

"OK," she says sweetly; the black thing between her teeth seems even bigger.

I hightail it back to where the little girls' room and the john are. Gloria is walking towards me with that little wiggle of hers. She even smells like a movie star. She's screwing the top on a little blue bottle, which she puts in her purse.

"Oh Gloria, you smell beautiful."

"Evening in Paris, my favorite," she whispers as she touches that little spot behind her ear. The spot that when I blow on it, drives her crazy. I wish I had a staircase to run down just like Gene Kelly did with the real Rita Hayworth in that movie *Magazine Girl*.

"Come on, let's go out to the swings for a while," I say.

I gotta strike while the iron is hot. It's now or never. I take her hand and we start to walk to the side door of the gym. She takes tiny baby steps and can't walk too fast, cuz her tight skirt with the flare at the bottom keeps her legs together.

"Hey, where the hell do you think you're goin'?" Oh please God, Matka Boeze, ALICE!

I turn around.

"Yeah, you! What are you doin' with that whore?" she snaps.

"Who are you talkin' to? You fat Polak bitch!" Gloria spits at her. Oh no, oh God, how could this happen? It's like a dream, a nightmare. All of a sudden they're pushing each other. A circle of guys and girls start to gather around us and all I can hear is Buddy Morrow's *Night Train* playing. My and Gloria's favorite that we dance real sexy to. Now Alice and Gloria are slugging it out. Buh Dum, Buh Dum, Buh Dum, Buh Dum, Buh Dum, Buh Dum, Buh Dum, Buh Dah Dah, Pow! Pow! Pow!

People are yellin', "Get her, Gloria." "Knock the shit out of her, Alice," and I'm trying to pull 'em apart. Oh please God no, no.

I see Stash running over.

"Hey man, help me get these two apart," I yell. Gloria's hair is all messed up, her sweater's pulled out of her skirt and there's tissue paper all over the floor. Her Evening in Paris bottle is on the floor. I snatch it up, put it in my pocket, pull her around the waist and separate them again. Alice's fluffy slips are down around her knees and some of them are torn. They're still screaming at each other.

"Hey, you guys, here comes the cops," someone shouts, and everyone scatters. Gloria is in my arms and we run out the side door. "Are you OK? Are you hurt?"

"No, I'm OK," she laughs. "Where's that fat bitch, I'll kill her. Did I get her?"

"Yeah, you got her," I say lovingly. She looks in her purse, pulls out her lipstick.

"Oh no, I lost my Evening in Paris."

"No you didn't, I got her here in my pocket." I pull out the little blue bottle and give it to her. She unscrews the cap, puts a little splash on that spot behind her ear, and we start to walk over to the swings.

> "The sky's a blackboard high above us, and if a shooting
> star goes by, I'll take that star to write I love you, a
> thousand times across the sky."

JAMES DYBAS For more than thirty years, Jimmy has been a noted singer, actor, dancer, and musical comedy performer. In 1996 he was offered a part in *Sunset Boulevard* and is now performing on Broadway.

Grass and Trees

by Rosalyn Cron

With Vi Burnside wailing on tenor, Tiny Davis tearing up the place on trumpet, and Pauline Braddy making the walls move with her drum solo, the International Sweethearts of Rhythm brings *Sing, Sing, Sing* to a close.

We're in Seattle—a jumpin' city in 1944. It's early Sunday morning, 4:00 A.M., and the Sweethearts, an all-female big band (and all colored except for Toby Butler and me), just played the last tune of a successful one-week gig at an after-hours spot called the Club Kazam. We say goodnight to a cheering crowd and pack up. In a few hours, we move on to another city.

Meanwhile, Mr. Townes, the club manager, has invited everyone in the band, plus some Seattle musicians, to meet in a back room to hear a new '78 recording by Billie Holiday, which includes a new tune called *Strange Fruit*. The record has been banned and is being bootlegged around.

I dry and pack away my horns and head for the back room where I find everyone seated in a circle, and in the middle is a turntable sitting on a wooden box.

"Hey, Roz, sit here," Saine, the other alto player and my good buddy, yells over to me. I squeeze in between her and a man who introduces himself as Fred, a bass player in the Seattle area.

Everyone is talking in low voices. This is a serious scene. Some people are smoking what looks like a homemade cigarette and the thing keeps traveling from person to person—rather unsanitary, I think. I'm looking around to see who's there when I feel an elbow nudge me and I turn to Fred.

"Here, Roz, have a drag," he says in a voice that sounds like strangling.

I look at the funny-looking cigarette and think, "Doesn't anyone in this crowd have enough money to buy proper cigarettes?"

"I'm sorry, Fred, I don't smoke," I tell him.

"Hey, kid, this is no ordinary cigarette. This is reefer—good stuff. You don't have to know how to smoke or to ever smoke in your life to enjoy this baby," Fred says with a kind of silly grin on his face.

"It's okay, Roz," Saine tells me. "I tried it once and it was kind of fun. You know I don't drink or smoke, either, so this gave me a real pleasant feeling. Come on, try one."

Well, I think, it's such a little cigarette, one puff can't hurt and at nineteen I feel grownup enough to try it.

"Go for it, Roz, while I roll us another spot of tea," Tiny Davis, our own Bunny Berigan of the trumpet section, calls out to me.

As I reach for the cigarette (or is it a reefer?), I glance at Tiny and all two hundred pounds of her are hunched over a little piece of paper into which she's dropping what looks like dried-up grass after the lawn-mower is through with it. I put the slightly damp reefer into my mouth and pull on it, as Fred instructs.

My God, I'm choking! My mouth and throat feel funny and I'm coughing so much, I can't yell for help. Everyone is looking at me and laughing. I don't get the joke. Willie Mae Wong (Rabbit to us), our serious half-Chinese, half-colored baritone sax player, hands me a cup of water and looks at me with disapproval on her face. Whew! I'm better now, but I feel a little different. Must be because the room is so smoky and smells so funny.

Here comes Mr. Townes. We becomes very quiet as he says, "It wasn't easy getting this record and I won't tell you how I got it. Just listen to Billie's voice and the words she sings. I'm going to keep playing the track over and over again and I can tell you, this song hits hard. Some day those ofays (that's what colored folks call us whites) will hear it on the radio and they won't even understand what she's saying."

He puts the needle on the track and the first sound I hear is a piano chord followed by a couple of measures of powerful notes soaring out of a trumpet. Tiny whispers, "Charlie Shavers." Then, an exquisite, haunting voice sings:

> Southern trees bear a strange fruit.
> Blood on the leaves; blood at the root.
> Black bodies swinging in the southern breeze.
> Strange fruit hanging from the poplar trees.

My God, what is she singing? Am I hearing her right? She's singing everyone's nightmare! My eyes travel around the room. No one is moving; eyes are closed or looking at the floor. This woman is singing with such truth and power in her voice that I can hardly bear to listen. I can feel the tears coming.

There's only a piano behind her. She pauses at the end of each phrase—as though to make sure her listeners really understand what she's saying. She bends her notes—making them sound like tears from her soul. There's a little rasp in her throat—like the words hurt her throat as they pass through. The last word of the song, sounds like a real cry to heaven. It's followed by a few guitar notes and a closing thump from a bass drum. That's it! One chorus; no repeats; no steady beat; just a lady telling a story too painful to hear and, evidently, too powerful to be heard by the white folks of this country.

Mr. Townes immediately puts the needle back in the groove and it begins again. Tiny starts another of her little cigarettes around the room and when it gets to me, Billie is singing, "the bulging eyes and the twisted mouth." I take a big drag and hope these green weeds will soften the hurt I feel.

We've heard Billie sing her story about eight or ten times now. Someone else has started one of those funny cigarettes going around. The air in the room is heavy with smoke and pain. There are tears in some eyes—including mine.

I sit back in my chair and close my eyes. Some people are starting to talk again. There's nothing I can say. I may be the ofay in the crowd, but I've also experienced all the humiliations, fears, and pain of these people. We share a closeness in this room tonight. I can only pray that the poplar trees will one day no longer bear strange fruit.

I'll just sit here for a while with my eyes closed and hang onto the quietness I feel flooding over me, since the smoke from the dried-up leaves in the funny cigarettes invaded my mind and Billie Holiday touched my soul here in Seattle.

ROSALYN CRON   Born in Boston, Roz fell in love with the saxophone at an early age. By the time she was seventeen, she was on the road with Ina Raye Hutton's all-girl orchestra. During World War II, she toured the United States and Europe with the only all-girl, all-black (except for Roz and one other girl) swing band—the International Sweethearts of Rhythm. The band was the subject of a PBS documentary some years ago. Recently, Roz and the other living members of the band were honored by the Library of Congress.

Christmas 1944

by Joanne Baumgart

I have no idea what the Germans have in mind when, in mid-November, 1944, in Auschwitz, we, a group of women, are detained after the morning roll call. They encircle our group with SS men, machine guns, as usual, and tell us not to move but remain in rows of fives. After counting and counting, they command us to march, this time out of the gate, out of Auschwitz. We are forced to walk for seven days, and seven nights, through small towns, over mountains and mountains, with short rests in between to receive our small portions of bread, to an undisclosed location.

Many, many of the women perish on this walk.

We bury the bodies in shallow graves with our bare hands. Sisters and friends of the deceased try to hang on to them, but we, the rest of the prisoners, do not let them. We beg them; we tell them, "Do not cry, do not admit that they are yours."

By now we know the mentality and the methods of the SS too well. They do not like to separate families they say, and it would not surprise us if they kill their next of kin.

Exhausted and more dead than alive, we arrive at a brand new camp, a different concentration camp than anything else I have seen in all the years. There are no watchtowers, no electric wires, just miles and miles of sandy grounds, and a primitive little house.

There, we receive, for the first time after this exhausting journey, our first hot soup. which is almost inedible.

Soon male prisoners arrive. They seem to be in a hurry; they do not look at us. They carry bundles and bundles of straw into these houses while we are still standing outside in the cold. As silently as they arrive, so they leave. Suddenly cars with bright lights and SS men appear. I do not see the usual entourage, no machine guns, no dogs.

"You are here to work, you will be led by your overseers to and from your workplaces. You may not see fences or wires, but do not try to escape. You won't go far, we assure you," says one SS officer. "You may go to your rooms now."

About sixty women are assigned to a room bare except for straw on both sides of these long cement floors. Two small windows are at the end of the room. The smell of the damp cement walls and floors is awful—grey, cold, musty.

We do not have a chance to orient ourselves when SS women with their rifles and their whips enter the room.

"Attention, attention. These are your quarters, the straw by the walls has to be kept in perfect order. The walkway in the middle has to be at all times kept clean. Never let us see a strand of straw. The consequences are deadly. You soon will learn to keep the room neat and clean and the straw in perfect line."

By this time each of us has to step forward and each of us is handed a broom, and a paper bag neatly folded with a white cord to pull together on top. "There are no blankets." *As if we had blankets before,* I think without saying a word. "But here are your bags."

The SS woman opens one bag and demonstrates the bag to us, and how to use it. "You sit down and pull it over your body to your neck, keeping your arms inside so you will use less room. If one of you does not wake up in the morning, it is the duty of the person next to the deceased to pull the bag over the head of the deceased and tie it together. The body has to be brought out to the roll call and put down on the ground."

Until that moment I do not realize that these are bags for the dead, in which dead soldiers are taken away from where they have been killed or wherever their bodies have to be shipped to. I take my bag into my hands and move on. I swear to myself, *I will not put this bag on.* I can't stand to be covered up and tied to or into something. No, I won't put this on. I don't know what I am going to do, but I am definitely not crawling into that bag.

Otherwise, I find this camp livable. There are washrooms, toilets where one can flush. I hope I have not forgotten how to do that. I encourage myself. It does not bother me that we have cold water only and it is cold. Icy cold in this place. I wonder if we are still in Poland? We will soon find out, I console myself.

It is evening. I don't know what time it is. We lie next to one another on damp straw. I see the women slipping into their bags. I unfold mine but I do not slip into it. I put it on top of me. "What are you doing Joanne?" someone next to me asks. I turn my back. "Why do you do that?"

"Never mind," I say. The dim lights go out. To keep warm we move closer to each other. I hear some bags tearing. I remember an old Jewish saying, "When one puts a garment on, one is supposed to wear it in good health." I want to laugh.

I am proud to be Jewish, I say to myself, we are a smart people. Even these bags prove it. Better to wear them in good health than to be put into them dead. . . .

I have to survive, I vow to myself. *I have to prove them wrong. I must, yes, I must survive.*

The next day after roll call we are marched off to work.

We walk and walk. We do not see a living soul. The air is so clean, so crisp. Where are we? I can't believe that something so beautiful still exists. Beautiful forest everywhere I look, nothing but pine trees, everywhere pine trees. What a sight. I am elated. This must be paradise. We can walk here and breathe. The Jews must have a prayer for this too. I am sure but I can't think of one. Instead, I think of a German song: "One asks who has created you, you beautiful forest it can only be a grant from above, only you, master of the universe can be praised, only you." I am afraid to move my lips but my heart sings.

We walk and walk for a long time. I don't mind. I cherish every moment until we hear the harsh sounds.

"Halt. Stop." Again we are counted and are told, one by one, to walk into an underground building. Who would think that under this beautiful forest, in this far-away place I never saw before, the Germans would build an ammunitions factory.

No one would ever suspect or think that under these pine trees is a factory in which hundreds of men and women are worked and starved to death.

The noise is unbearable. Machines, motors, men, women, grotesque-looking people with pale, sweaty faces, moving quietly back and forth.

"Oh my God. What is awaiting us here?" Above us, life. In this factory . . .

By now, we are a few weeks in Gebhardsdorf, Sudetenland. This long, twice-daily walk through this forest to and from work keeps us alive.

Sometimes when we walk so very early in the morning, the moon is pale but still visible and the majestic trees, their branches heavy with snow, and the silence all around us, make me truly believe in peace on earth.

I pretend that this is my world—no war, no one disturbs me. I can look as far as I want and see nothing but trees. And for such moments during these awful times I am grateful.

One afternoon, on our way back from work, it is a windy day. I see broken branches all around us. I can't resist. I bend down and pick up a branch. What a feeling! The long, soft green needles, I caress with my fingers. I suddenly realize that since fall or winter, 1939, I have never touched a flower, a leaf, or a branch.

I will bring it to our room, my mind wanders, *I will let the girls touch the needles.*

Too soon, I rejoice. One of the SS women who walks us (and I am sure never noticed what I did) stops me. "What do you have there?" as if she does not see it.

"A Christmas tree branch," I answer, knowing quite well that this is not really a Christmas tree branch. She pulls it out of my hand and throws it on the ground. I bend down and pick it up. She lifts her arm with the whip and she strikes out, but the whip does not touch me. I am too low or the whip is too high.

How badly do I want this branch? I know what she is going to do to me and yet I have it in my hand again. I look at her and I say, "I want this because it is Christmastime, Frau Auperchim."

"What did you say? You want this for Christmas?"

"Because it *is* Christmas," I correct her. She is surprised. "You are a . . . ?" She does not end her sentence. By now I have the situation well in my hand. My mother is German. I, too, do not finish the sentence. I could tell her my stepmother was a German Jewish woman but I don't say that. Let's see how this works, I think to myself.

"Do the other women know that?" she asks, as she now walks beside me.

"I don't think I am the only one."

We do not talk about it. She is silent and holds the branch. I can sense that she is too long by my side. She moves away from me. The girls look at me. I do feel what they are thinking, *You stupid fool. This is not the end of it and for what? For a green branch.*

I, too, feel that this is not the end of it, but I am not afraid. My mind is already far ahead of me. . . . Among our inmates is a young, very pretty woman. She has the most beautiful voice I ever heard. That voice has a special quality. Sometimes when we are able to persuade her to sing, we always say, "Aguisha, sing please, we promise not to die during the night." We also know that many of us pray. On rare occasions, she does sing. I really believe that everyone wants to live.

As soon as we are in our room, I look for Aguisha. We sit down on the straw and I tell her what happened on the way home. "Joanne, you are crazy, crazy, crazy. Why do you get yourself in trouble?"

"I don't know," I say. "I just felt like it. Aguisha, will you let me teach you to sing the German words to *Silent Night, Holy Night*?"

"You know them?" she asks. I know I have her approval.

"Yes, of course, I know them." I don't know if I wished for anything more at that moment than a pen and piece of paper. This is impossible, but I can teach her and she will sing—that is important.

For a Polish-speaking person it is not easy to say these beautiful, old German words but after a few times she can say them. When she comes to *"shdat in himmlisher Ruh'"* ("sing in heavenly peace") tears are running down her face and mine as well.

The next day, on the way to work, I see the same SS woman. Does she remember me? I wonder. This time I purposely do not walk with my sister in the same row just in case. I say to myself, *let her be out of it.*

On the way back, the German SS woman is looking for me. "You may take as many branches as you can carry. Let the girls help you. After roll call, I will come to your room," she says.

Oh, my God. What did I start? I only hope that I did not go too far, but I do pick up some long branches and some of the girls do too.

After roll call that very night, the SS woman arrives at our door with a tin container to put the branches in, and orders me to tell the girls to help me to form a Christmas tree. She promises to bring white tissue paper to make some curtains for the windows. One of our women, a real artist, calls me aside and tells me, "Joanne, ask her to bring a pair of scissors and some tape, I can make something very beautiful."

"I don't believe so," I answer. "You know we are not allowed to have anything, they consider scissors weapons."

"Ask her anyway. Go ahead, ask her, Joanne."

"Alright, I will," I promise, "I will." The SS woman does not object. The very same evening she brings the scissors and tape. Martha starts knitting and creates a masterpiece. The girls are so enthusiastic to help, I think for a moment many of us forget what hell we are in.

While all this is going on, Aguisha tries to rehearse the lovely chorus. What thoughts come to my mind: Do I endanger everyone here with my crazy adventures? How do I bring a Christmas atmosphere into this Jewish concentration camp, to my people who are suffering? Will they doubt my true intentions? I, whom they trust so much; I, who has developed a reputation—"talk to Joanne" or "ask Joanne, maybe Joanne knows." What am I trying to do here, trying to convince this pale, uneducated rough SS woman, that I am half German? I am sorry that I picked up that branch, sorry that I have made this German woman bring all that stuff in the room. May God help me. At this moment, I am very unhappy.

The next day we work only half a day. It is December 24, 1944. It is Christmas Eve. As I walk through the woods I think of my homeland, of the gifts we handed out to our employees, of the hustle and bustle that goes with this holiday. How I loved it when at midnight all the church bells started to ring. When I was still a child, I tried not to fall asleep, so our maid could take me to the midnight mass at the church. I enjoyed watching people so fashionable-looking. I enjoyed listening to our maid, when every year she told me the same story—not to talk to the animals because after midnight they can talk with human voices. You should really not talk to them.

Could this world (of hate) really disappear? Will it ever end? Will I live to see that? Has religion brought such hate? I can't, I won't accept this.

We get this horrible smelling and even more horrible tasting soup. After the usual roll call, we are, so to say, on our own. The SS woman comes one more time to the room. She brings some foil paper and hands it to me. "Trim the tree," she tells me.

I walk over to Malka, the artist, and show her the silver foil.

Will I ever stop being a fool? My worries are already forgotten. "Malka, I say, do you think we have enough foil paper to make a star?"

"A star?" she looks at me. "A star?"

"Don't you know, the star of Bethlehem."

"Joanne, are you alright? You want me to make a star? A star of Bethlehem?"

"Yes, Malka," I say, "Make a star of David, our star, our Jewish star, the star of David. Please Malka, do that for me," I beg her.

She embraces me half crying, half laughing, "You are something, you are really something, Yes, I will make a Star of David."

It is evening. Girls from other rooms come in and admire our room. It really looks different. The tinfoil with the rest of the white tissue paper, Malka draped it softly around the can and the star. . . . Everyone says, "Our star, our Star of David, who did that?" We are laughing.

"It's our secret, do you like it?" Malka says.

At nine o'clock, no one can be in the halls anymore. Each of us has to be in her assigned room. It happens quite often that SS men or women come to check, with flashlights in their hands, that no one moves, that everyone is where they belong.

"Aguisha, please sings us to sleep," the girls beg her. She sings a lovely Jewish lullaby and I can't see, but I know that many tears are shed. We listen. We hear heavy steps in the hallway.

Aguisha changes her tune, she sings "Stille Nacht, heilige Nacht." One must hear angels' voices to listen to her.

The door opens. Our SS woman steps into our room and turns the lights on. She does not say a word. She stays next to the door. She looks for me. I get up and walk closer. She calls me out. "Come with me," she says. I must admit, I am scared, but, of course, I follow her. "That is beautiful," she says. "Just beautiful." I would like to say something myself but at the moment I do not know what to say.

"Is the girl who sang, also a *mischling*?" (A *mischling* is the offspring of parents of different religions.)

"I don't know, Frau Auperchim."

She walks again into our room and admires the beautiful cutouts on the windows. She likes what we did with the branches and sees the star. "It looks odd," she says. "It is empty in the middle."

"Yes, of course," I say. "That is the Star of Bethlehem, that is as the shepherd who saw the star."

"I never saw it that way," she says.

"Well, Frau Auperchim, that's all the foil we had."

"I see, I see."

"I am sorry that is all the foil I had."

"Don't be," she answers.

"We are satisfied and we thank you."

She does not ask who the girl is who sang so beautifully. Is she afraid to meet another German?

She calls me out again. "I am so sorry for you," she says. "You know what is going to happen to all of you, once the work is finished here?"

"No, I don't. What is going to happen to us?" I ask.

With a very calm voice she says, "Oh, I can't tell you, but it is not good."

"You mean they are going to kill us?"

"Yes, they will, you see." I think she wants to excuse the Germans for what they are doing.

"Impossible," I say to her. "Frau Auperchim, they can never kill all the Jews. Impossible. They will always live, they will."

"Why do you say that?" she asks, with not such a certain voice any more.

"Because Jesus is a Jew, Frau Auperchim."

"Jesus, a Jew? How can you say that?"

"Because I know." It amuses me how calm I am. "Jesus is a Jew. The history was written three hundred years after he died and not by him."

"Really?" she asks.

"Really," I answer.

"Oh, my God, I never knew it," she says. "But you had a nice Christmas, didn't you?" she asks.

"Yes, very nice," I answer. "And I thank you for it."

"I have to go now," she says.

"Thank you Frau Auperchim, have a Merry Christmas." She leaves me standing before the door and walks off into the night.

I return to the room. "What did she say?" the girls ask.

"Not much. I think she believes I am not Jewish and I wished her a Merry Christmas."

"What???"

"See," I say to the girls, "when I lie, they believe me; when I say the truth, no one does." I really wished her a Merry Christmas. I repeat, "Good night, girls."

This was December 1944. Gebhardsdorf, Sudetenland.

The bells did not chime and the animals did not talk, but it was a memorable Christmas.

P.S. The movie *Schindler's List* has made its impact on me. Almost every newspaper I pick up has something to say about it. The film tells more in three and a half hours than the world has realized in fifty years about the destruction of the Jews during the Holocaust. "We are dealing with the unthinkable, the unimaginable, the incomprehensible, we do not have a vocabulary to communicate the scale of the hate and horror unleashed by the Holocaust," says Ben Kingsley, as he describes the events he has tried to portray in the movie. Not for me, is it unthinkable. To me it was just yesterday, when I, as I always do around Christmas, let my thoughts take me back to Christmas 1944.

JOANNE BAUMGART   Born in Poland, Joanne survived years of internment in the War-
saw ghetto and, later, a number of the concentration camps set up by the Nazis. Fluent
in German, she stayed alive, and helped many others stay alive, by outthinking the
Nazis. She is one of the true heroes of the
Polish Resistance. She came to the United States shortly after the war ended.

Johnny and Me
by Georgia Lowe

My mother answers the phone on the first ring. She frowns and hands me the phone without a word. I know it must be Johnny.

First thing Johnny says is, "I have to go to this classical music concert tomorrow night. It's a drag, but it's an assignment for Music Appreciation and I've got two tickets. It's the L.A. Philharmonic Orchestra at the auditorium downtown. Would you like to go?"

I'd go anywhere with Johnny, but it's not cool to sound too eager. So I hesitate a little and say, "Classical music? Really?"

We both snicker. We only listen to jazz. At Sardi's or the Haig.

Johnny is a jazz musician. He is very cool. He plays saxophone in the big band at City College. He also plays gigs around town with Julius Wechter, Jerry Williams, Kenny Grieg, and Jim Hendricks. Johnny sounds just like Paul Desmond. The guys all play great and they're cute and hip besides. Sometimes I go with them to a gig and sit up front pretending to be the singer with laryngitis.

"The conductor is somebody named Wallenstein," Johnny says. "I don't know what the program is, but I need to be there by 7:30 to watch the musicians set up. Are you going to come with me or not?"

Johnny sounds a little cranky so I tell him I'd love to go and we hang up. My mother shakes her head and doesn't say a word. She doesn't need to.

You'd think my mother would finally catch on that Johnny and I are not children anymore. After all, we've been going together for two years. Johnny's in his first year in college now and I've graduated from high school and work full-time at Security National Bank as a bookkeeper. My dad treats us like the adults we are and he likes Johnny besides. But not my mother. Oh, no. She ignores Johnny when he's here and harps at me about him all the time when he's not.

My mother thinks Johnny's some sort of subversive because he's an intellectual and hates Joe McCarthy. She blames him because I argue with her about religion all the time and tell her I'm an agnostic. She also seems to think that all jazz musicians are drug-crazed sex fiends and that he takes advantage of me. Ha! If she only knew.

Johnny picks me up at 6:30. He is wearing his gray flannel suit with the one button roll, blue knit tie and his dark blue suede shoes. He looks very cool. I have on my new red Jonathan Logan dress and black heels. I think we look neat together.

As soon as we pull away from the house, I slide across the front seat of the Pontiac and sit as close to him as I can. I kiss his ear while he's driving and he puts his hand on my leg. I feel very warm inside and say, "I can't wait until later." I can see he feels the same way.

We stand together on the sidewalk on Grand Street in front of the auditorium and beat one last weed before we go in. I feel very hip.

"Excuse us, excuse us." We slide across the aisle and find our seats. The musicians are wandering onto the stage setting up their instruments. They are all dressed up in formal clothes and look very elegant. They are laughing and talking to each other as if the audience doesn't exist. Finally they are all seated. A note is sounded. I look at Johnny and he whispers, "That's the oboe. They're tuning." The musicians start tootling away. It's a terrible sound. Then it's silent.

The audience is rustling a little; I hear a few muffled coughs and the conductor sweeps onto the stage. Everyone claps. He bows to the audience, turns to the orchestra and lifts his arms. The most wonderful music I've ever heard fills the air and surrounds us. Johnny and I reach for each other's hand and we hold tight. Tears are running down my cheeks. I feel my heart will break from the beauty of it. The music is *Appalachian Spring* by Aaron Copeland.

When it's over we applaud until my hands sting and I know I will always remember this night.

One day at work Mr. London, the manager of the bank, calls me into his office. "Georgia, you're careless in your work," he says. "You're not punctual and you call in sick too often. It's not fair to the other girls. One more slip-up and I'll have to let you go."

"That does it," I think, "I hate this job anyway." So I quit right on the spot.

My dad works at Lockheed and helps me get a job. Department 82-83, Blueprint Control. My job is to deliver blueprints to the guys on the line either by bicycle or roller skates. It's a lot more fun than sitting at a bookkeeping machine at the bank with a bunch of gossipy girls all doing the same thing over and over. Besides, some of the guys in the plant are really cute and nice.

My parents are fighting nearly all the time now and decide to separate. Naturally, I stay with my dad. Johnny is playing gigs nearly every night and is still going to school during the day. He's always tired and whenever we go out he falls asleep. It feels like he doesn't care much about me anymore and I'm not sure what to do.

"Johnny," I ask one night, "do you think we'll ever get married?"

He shakes his head. "Jazz players don't get married. They have to be on the road. It wouldn't be fair."

"I'm nineteen, Johnny, I should be married."

"I'm sorry," is all he says.

It's true. He doesn't care about me. All he cares about is being a musician. I want to cry, I want him to feel bad to see how he's hurt me. But I don't.

"Guess that's the way it goes," I say and turn away. I don't ever want to see him again.

I feel lost and alone, but before long a very cute guy at work named Dick asks me out. He has just joined the navy and is waiting to go to boot camp. He's had a terrible life and I'm sure all he needs is the love of a good woman. Me. After three months he's assigned to Guam so we decide to get married. That way I can go to Guam too. My dad wonders why I want to marry a sailor. My mother seems relieved he's not a musician.

It's June and in a burst of excitement Dick and I go to Las Vegas. I'm old enough at nineteen to get married, but Dick isn't twenty-one yet so needs signed permission. My father comes along to give the bride away. Dick's mother comes along to sign the paper. They drink, we get married.

Now it's January and I finally arrive in Guam. The weather is hotter and more humid than I believed possible, but who cares? Dick and I are together now. We listen to *Quiet Village* by Les Baxter on the record player and feel very romantic. It doesn't even matter that we live in a Quonset hut or that there's an eel in the toilet. I don't even mind the lizards in the cupboards. I tell myself it's very picturesque and write humorous letters to my folks and friends back home describing life in the tropics. But Dick and I begin to fight a lot and he's not home much and I'm very lonely.

One hot day in July I'm struggling to iron perfect creases into Dick's navy whites when a letter from my mother arrives. I rip it open and a clipping falls out. It's a wedding announcement and a picture from our local newspaper back home. The picture is of Johnny and a pretty girl. I know that girl. That's Marilyn. She lived right down the street from him. They are all dressed up and are arm-in-arm coming out of a church. The caption reads, Mr. and Mrs. John Lowe. My mother writes, "Looks like jazz musicians get married after all." I put my head down on the ironing board and start to cry. Dick hates it when I cry and he slams out the door.

"God," I think, "why Marilyn and not me? What's wrong with me?"

The weeks go by and Dick and I argue all the time now, over who knows what. Finally one night at dinner he says, "I don't want to be married anymore."

I choke on the green beans and cry, "What's wrong with me?"

He says, "Nothing, nothing, it's me, not you."

I don't believe him and feel ashamed and embarrassed. It hasn't even been a year. I agonize and write home. My mother writes back. Come home, she writes, come home. And so I do.

Time flashes by, then slows and takes a beat while I fall in love and marry again. Now time takes off and hurtles by in a blur of babies, toddlers, teenagers, college, a family business, a cancer scare. When I look around it's 1990 and I'm fifty-five years old.

My long marriage is over. I'm newly divorced and terrified. And exhilarated. The kids are grown up and gone so I decide to sell my big house and move to the mountains. It's a new life.

For weeks I sort, sell, dump out, and get down to basics. Then one day, as I sit cross-legged on the floor going through a box of costume jewelry, I find an old and tarnished copper pendant. My God, it's the pendant Johnny Lowe gave me when we were kids. Oh, Johnny, my first love. How I remember Johnny Lowe. I'd love to see him again. I wonder if he really became a musician. I wonder if he's still married. Maybe I should try to find him. No, don't take a chance. But, somehow I feel guided. I need to do this.

I call an old friend who might know about Johnny. He does. He asks if I know that Marilyn had died?

"My God, no, I didn't know. When?"

"Seven or eight years ago."

He says he hasn't heard from John since then, but he has an old address. He gives it to me. I write a letter.

It's nine in the morning two days later when the phone rings. I answer on the first ring.

"Hello?"

"Georgia?" The voice is deep and warm sounding. "This is John Lowe, is it really you?"

"It is." And then, and I don't know why, "Oh God, I'm so relieved." I'm babbling on. "Did you get to be a musician?"

He laughs, "Oh, yes, I haven't had a regular job since 1956."

Then he says, "I tried to find you once, thought of hiring a detective, but got scared. Now you've found me. It feels like a dream."

"To me too, John. I'd love to see you."

We make a lunch date for Tuesday. Five more days to wait. After thirty-six years five more days shouldn't be such a long time to wait. But it is. The days creep by ever so slowly.

It's Tuesday, at last, and I'm early and standing on the corner waiting, watching. Do I look all right? Am I too fat? Too gray, too old? I watch the men move by me. No, please God, not him, or him. But who is that slender, very attractive man walking toward me? That cool, long stride, slouchy, very hip walk. I remember that walk. Now silver-gray hair, perfect silver-gray beard, tweed jacket, gray slacks. Blue knit tie. It must be.

"John?"

We're laughing, hugging, talking all at once. We finally make it to the restaurant. John is a mature man now, he's no longer Johnny. He's handsome, charming, urbane, and very funny. He tells me about being on the road with big bands and about working in the studios. I tell him about my life and my children. We can't seem to stop talking. Lunch segues into dinner. We see each other every day for a week and then I move to Mammoth.

My new condo is cold; the wind howls over the crest of the Sierra and pushes hard against my sliding glass door. Evil-looking gray clouds scud over the mountaintops. I'm surrounded by piles of boxes. My big dog Sonny looks up me and shivers. I sit down next to him and hug him. I can guess what he's thinking. Same as me. "What are we doing here?"

There's plenty of firewood, but the wood stove is a complete mystery. I open the little door and pile in four or five pieces of wood and throw in a match. Nothing happens except the wind blowing down the chimney snuffs it right out. Again and again. I stuff in newspapers, throw in a match. The papers blaze into life, the room fills with acrid, eye-stinging smoke, the fire fizzles out. I give up and put on my hooded down jacket.

The new phone rings for the first time and echoes in the cold, empty space.

"Hello?" Even my voice is shivering.

John, in that rich, warm, voice asks, "Georgia, do you need some help? I can be there tomorrow."

"Oh, please."

The condo is finally warm thanks to Thomas Edison and Company. I shower and get somewhat presentable. John arrives. Hugs, a few tears—mine—a few glasses of wine and we're out for dinner. With salad he puts his hand on mine and says, "You know I still love you." With coffee he holds my hand and says, "Will you marry me?" "Yes," I say, "Yes. I don't ever want to lose you again."

I call my daughter and tell her the news. She says, "Mom, this is a gift from God. Don't wait."

My son, Tim, the outdoorsman, says, "Does this mean I have to wear a suit and tie?"

I wonder what my mother, who died so long ago, would say now. "Marry in haste, repent in leisure?" Hardly haste, I think.

Summer arrives in a blaze of wildflowers and deep green meadows. At last John and I marry to the tune of *It Had to Be You*. We're surrounded by a flurry of old friends and best wishes.

We live in Mammoth most of the time now. Hiking, playing tennis, loving the warm days and starry nights. John only goes to town when he has a work call.

Sometimes I dread Service calling, but this time Ann says the call is with the Philharmonic at the Hollywood Bowl. John takes the job and I decide to go down to L.A. too.

We arrive at the Bowl early; John introduces me to some of his cronies, and Irving Bush hands me a ticket for a house seat. I slide across the aisle, "Excuse me, excuse me," and find my place. Couples are talking softly, glasses clink, the last of the wine is poured, picnic baskets are stowed away. The night is warm, a light breeze barely stirs the trees and I lean back to look up at the twilight sky to find the wishing star. I can't think of another place I'd rather be.

The musicians are wandering onto the stage setting up their instruments. They are all dressed up in white dinner jackets and look very elegant. They are laughing and talking to each other as if the audience doesn't exist. There's John. He's laughing and carrying on, probably telling jokes while he's setting up his clarinet and bass clarinet. He is still so cool.

Finally the musicians are settled. The oboe sounds a note. The orchestra tunes, then silence. The audience is rustling a little, I hear a few muffled coughs. Then the conductor sweeps onto the stage. Everyone claps. He bows to the audience, turns to the orchestra and lifts his arms. Wonderful music fills the air and surrounds me. It's *Appalachian Spring.* Tears are running down my cheeks and I feel my heart will break from the beauty of it.

When the piece is over I applaud until my hands sting. Through my tears I can see John up there on the stage smiling out into the audience and I know that he remembers that night so long ago too and that his smile is for me. I lean back again and look up at the starry night sky.

"Thank you, God," I say, "Thank you."

GEORGIA LOWE Georgia is a businesswoman, mother, and writer in the Los Angeles area. Her husband, John Lowe, was one of the top studio musicians in Los Angeles.

Bittersweet Remembering
by Bill Peterson

It is a bright blue skies morning, July 15, 1988. I put on my blue seer-sucker suit, a white shirt and tie that I think look like Monet might have designed. This suit is the one that Eric and Laura laugh at and call my "old man" suit. It hurts that they laugh at it, but I try to ignore it, and kid them back to show that it doesn't matter. Anyway, I won't see them today, so it really doesn't matter. I get in the car and drive to work. It is eight o'clock in the morning, traffic is light, and I feel pretty good.

Last night I came home to find my son Eric lying on his bed with his baseball cap on backwards. He is on the phone, naturally. He is wearing a tank top and a pair of baggy shorts which display his muscles and a pair of strong, hairy legs. Both muscles and body hair are an important consideration to him and his buddies, and he is doing well in both areas. He is laughing and talking with animation, and even though I try not to eavesdrop, I can hear him lower his surprisingly deep voice down to a persuasive soft pitch; and say something like, "Well, sure I'll come see you—maybe this weekend." He finishes his call, as I come to the doorway.

He looks up to say, "These long-distance romances just don't make it, Dad."

I ask, "The girl in Palm Springs?"

He nods, and says, "Yeah—you know these long-distance romances just don't make it. I guess I'll just have to go up there and see her."

"You mean, go down there—Palm Springs is south of here," I correct.

He grins at me, and says, "Whatever."

He springs up off the bed, grabs up his Magic Johnson basketball, and asks, "You want to shoot some baskets?"

"Sure," I say, and follow him outside to the backboard that we erected on the sloping roof, just over the garage door.

We play Horse and of course he wins, then we play a little one-on-one. I guard Eric with about the same amount of success I would have against Magic. After a bit more of my athletic futility against my jock son, I wander back in the house for dinner. Eric comes in, sweaty and happy.

I ask, "You staying for dinner?"

"No, I've got to go." His face breaks into a smile. "You know how it is—places to go, ladies to see."

Eric gives me a nudge in the ribs, then as he often does, he impulsively gives me a hug and a kiss on the cheek. His beginnings of stubble scrape my cheek.

He tells me in a breezy tone, "I love you, Pop!"

I know it's his way to lighten the display of affection he has allowed; after all he is going off to the University of Arizona soon, and he has to let me know he's a man now, too.

It was just a couple of weeks ago, just before graduation (thank God he's not too grown up to ask me for advice) when he asked, "What do you think this essay by George Bernard Shaw really means?"

He hands me the essay and I am surprised to find my son has chosen this topic as I find myself reading about the death and cremation of Shaw's mother. I am amazed to find that Shaw, the great self-proclaimed atheist, tells of experiencing his mother's spirit. He says she is looking over his shoulder, as he watches the cremators gather up her ashes.

Shaw says that his mother's spirit asks him, "Do you really think that's me down there in those ashes?"

I finish reading Shaw's essay, and watching Eric's reaction, and I say, "Well, I must say, I think your analysis is correct. It's Shaw's way of telling us that the spirit of the person that dies does not die with her, but goes on."

Eric grins, "That's exactly what I thought you'd say. That's what I think too."

"Why in the world did you choose this subject out of the twenty you had to choose from?"

"Because it interested me, Dad!" he says in his remarkable deep voice. Then he says, "Hey, Dad, check this out," and reads a quote from Raphael Sabatini's book, *Scaramouche.*

"Isn't this a great description?" asks my literary offspring. "See, Dad, Sabatini is describing Scaramouche, and he says, 'He was born with the gift of laughter and a sense that the world was mad.' Isn't that cool?"

"Yes, that's good, and it was me that lent you the book!"

"Oh yeah, that's right, I've got to get that back to you. Well, I've got to go!"

He goes out the door, and I turn on the porch light against the oncoming dark of evening. Eric stands under the porch light, turns and looks at me, and turns on that wonderful smile. No words, just that big smile, as if to say, "Aren't I something?" and "Isn't life great?"

I watch his little red Toyota pull away, and I feel the joy of having this combination of playing basketball with my kid, then having a literary discussion to boot. How good can it be?

I drive to work in my blue "old man" suit, climb the stairs to my office and start the day's work. My secretary, Bess Garcia, comes to the door. Her face is serious, as she says softly, "It's Rita."

My ex-wife calling? What does she want? Maybe she wants to swap weekends. I haven't much left that she would want. Rita got the condo on Maui and our big old Spanish house with my studio; but those are only "things." Most of all, she got custodial custody of the children, her biggest victory in a bitter divorce. I have lost the primary privilege of raising my children, and the everyday pleasure of their company, except for the three evenings a week that I drive over and pick them up. I bring them to my house, cook dinner with them, and do homework with them. I also get to have them every other weekend, in the house we moved out of because it was too small. I am still angry at having so much that I worked so hard for, and loved, taken away. I am trying to do what everyone tells me—you know, the advice you get from all the pop-psych paperbacks, such as, "Get on with your life" and "The best revenge is living well." Yeah, right! But after all the time we shared, it's so painful to drive over to our—no, her home. She will almost never bring Eric and Laura over, or pick them up. When I drive away I feel like all that counts I'm leaving at a house I can't even enter. I'm like a stranger at the gate, excluded from everyone and everything I've loved. When I drive back to my small house in North Hollywood, where our children were conceived, I feel so alone and sad because the house has so many resonances of two little kids who were so excited when I would come home; so many memories and laughter. As I wait for Bess to go back across the wall and transfer the call, I reflect on my children.

Laura, my beautiful, sensitive, daughter, is a junior at Grant High School and Eric has just graduated from the Cleveland High School's Gifted Magnet program. They are a very big part of my reason for living.

Eric is a very bright kid, and a very talented basketball player who was always on some all-star team or other. He has been accepted at several University of California campuses, as well as some universities back East. However, he and his best buddy, Brian Chernow, have chosen the

University of Arizona. Laura and Eric are never out of my thoughts for more than a moment. I reach for the phone.

I punch the button to receive the call and say, "Yes, what is it?"

Rita's voice is tight yet matter-of-fact. "There's been an emergency. He's been taken to the same place."

The phone clicks off, the line is dead; no more than that, she's hung up. It's cold and matter-of-fact, but I don't know what the facts are. I bang the phone down, put my coat on, and grab the car keys. I remember that last year at this same time Eric had a seizure and she had him taken to Sherman Way Emergency Room, then I had him transferred to St. Joseph's. I hesitate, then decide to call Mary McManne's number. Mary is the lady to whom Eric introduced me. She was his English teacher when Rita started in her determination to end our marriage and break up our family. Mary and I have been engaged, but we have broken up. Still, I feel I should call her. I get her answering machine. I leave a message: "Something has happened to Eric. Please meet me at the emergency room."

I drive fast through Hollywood, out the freeway, and get to the hospital. As I drive I decide that perhaps he's had another seizure; maybe he's banged his head in a fall. I hope against hope that he hasn't injured an eye. I figure I'll have to get on him if he hasn't been taking his medicine. I pull up in front of the emergency entrance, jump out of the car, and move quickly to Mary, at the door, still in her jogging outfit. Her shocked expression scares me. There is something more than what I've guessed; something is terribly wrong. The words seem to tumble out, "What is it, Mary? What happened? Did he fall and hurt his head?"

She looks at me and says, "Oh Bill, the doctor will have to tell you . . ."

I turn and sprint for the door. Just as I get inside, a young doctor in full ER green moves to meet me. He says, "I'm sorry, Mr. Peterson, we did all we could to save him."

I cannot understand him. What the hell is he telling me? That he couldn't save Eric? Is Eric . . . is he . . . ?

I follow him to where Laura is standing, sobbing. She is in her mother's arms. I put my arms around them both. Mary is right at my side. She holds my arm as I ask the doctor, "Where is he? What happened?"

Rita's explanation stumbles out. "He was taking a shower. It was taking too long, I could hear the water running so I knocked on the door, and when he didn't answer, I went in. He was down in the shower. I called the paramedics. They came right away. They got him out on the floor and tried to revive him . . . then they brought him here."

I follow the doctor into the emergency area. He leads me behind the curtain which encircles a gurney; on it is Eric. His beautiful green eyes are shut, there is an airway in his mouth, and there are white round patches on his bare chest from which small wires still dangle in a futile way. I stand next to him, and take his hand in mine. His hand is still warm, his skin roughened from baseball bats and weight lifting. I say, "Eric—oh Eric."

I guess I start to cry, as I touch his face, his cheek, and his forehead with my hand. It only seems a breath ago that I saw him born, a millisecond ago that we brought him home from maternity. At three he was hitting a big blue ball with a plastic bat. It seems like yesterday he was throwing fastballs past opposing batters, or going three for four as a hitter. This cannot be. I plead with God—let him wake up now; this is just a bad dream, isn't it? I mean, barely two weeks ago he wore his cap and gown proudly as a graduate of the gifted magnet program at Cleveland High, and after the ceremony I watched with my heart bursting with pride and love and the shared expectation of his days in the sun. He has grown and matured into this young man, handsome, charming, who is both a talented athlete and a good student. And now I stand here in horror and disbelief, trying to bargain with God. All I can do is to hold his hand, and say, "I love you, Eric."

It's a week after. Both Eric's mother and I are in shock, and I go through the awful business of looking at gravesites. Mary reminds us of Eric's essay; it seems so wrenchingly sad that this is something we can both agree to. He will be cremated. My daughter Laura and her best friend Ali, Mary, his mother, and all the family and friends overflow the Chapel of the Hills in Forest Lawn. Today is to be the celebration of his life.

Marilyn and Irving Bush are my best friends. Irving has the Pacific Brass Quintet playing Eric's favorite music, Bach and Mozart. Marilyn has somehow gotten a large snapshot of Eric enlarged. It rests on an easel, surrounded by flowers. A single rose lies on the frame below the picture. Just a month ago, the Bushes and their lovely daughter, Nicole, who is in her mid-twenties, go to dinner with Eric, almost twenty, Laura, who is sixteen, and me. I'm fifty-seven. Anyway, we come out onto the sidewalk. Eric sees something, and says, "Wait a minute."

He dashes off, and comes back with a rose for each of the ladies. They smile and accept his gift with, "Thank you, Eric!"

Later when we get home, Eric asks me, in that offhand, man-to-man manner, "How do you think Nicole feels about younger men?"

I try not to smile, and say, "Gee, son, I just don't know."

Now, I return from my memories to see one of Eric's best friends, Steve Boxer, get up to the lectern in the chapel to speak. I don't know if Steve will be able to do it, but he smiles at all of us, and I feel relieved. More than anything, I want Steve to tell me something—anything—about my son that I didn't have the chance to know or experience while he was alive. I am not disappointed. Steve is a tall kid with both brains and charm, and he shows great inner resources as he is able to talk about his buddy with a smile.

Steve says, "Three years ago, Eric and I and some of our classmates got to tour Europe. Eric's dad gave him a Walkman with two headsets. We are on the tour bus, listening to Basie and Sinatra's rendition of *Fly Me to the Moon,* while Fiona, our nice English tour guide, drones on for an hour about this monument or that bit of history that has happened in the streets of Brussels. Finally, all of us are trying to be polite, but we're pretty tired of the lecture; the whole busload of us have kind of drifted off in a half-unconscious state.

"I guess Fiona must have felt she lost us, because she stops. Eric sees what's happening; he stands up, takes off his headset, walks down the aisle, smiles at Fiona, who is really shocked, and respectfully but firmly takes the microphone from her hand. Then he turns to this busload of kids—who are mostly strangers to each other, from all over the U.S. Eric grins, takes a deep breath, and launches into *Fly Me to the Moon,* solo, a cappella. I start to break up and then the entire bus starts to laugh and applaud, including the teachers and Fiona. Eric has broken the ice for the group, and we all start to talk and have fun, as Eric hands Fiona her mike and grins at her."

Steve finishes, and I feel like laughing and crying all at the same time. A friend gets ready to sing, but my friend John Rodbyll's synthesizer simply refused to play anymore; it will only snap, crackle and pop. I look up at Eric's picture, and say to myself, "Well, Eric, I wonder if you are here, doing this?"

Bob Grabeau, the singer, says, "Well it looks like I'm going to have to sing this the way Eric did, a cappella."

Bob sings *Fly Me to the Moon,* and changes the line from "darling love" to "please, remember me." The celebration finishes. Laura and her friend talk quietly with her and Eric's friends. People come and hug me, and say whatever it is that people say. I walk out into the bright sunshine, hold my daughter in my arms, and then drive back to my exwife's house, a home that was once filled with a family's love and happiness, and now is only a terrible reminder to me of what once was, to toast Eric's unfulfilled life.

Coda

The hurt of losing Eric is not so raw now, but it will never go away. Laura has just graduated from the University of California at Berkeley, after attending the University of Oxford in England on a work-study program for a semester, and NYU. Her dual major is history (she became vitally interested in Russian History) and art, but she has many film production courses to her credit also. She wants to eventually produce documentary films. She is beautiful and sweet and smart, and has a special something about her. She has wonderful friends to whom she is very close, and life is good for her now.

But for me, the best thing is, she always says to me, "I love you, Daddy."

Whenever I think of Eric, which is every day, I am grateful for the twenty-one years I had of his company, and know that he had "the gift of laughter, and a sense that the world was mad."

I try to remember too, what he taught me, when he had me read his essay, about how spirit never dies.

Go well, my son.

BILL PETERSON   Bill is a graduate of UCLA and for many years has played with bands in Los Angeles. As a young married man, he played in house bands in and around Lake Tahoe, backing such well-known headliners as Frank Sinatra, Nat "King" Cole, Jerry Lewis, and Sammy Davis Jr. He later became a respected Hollywood studio musician, and he is currently president of the Professional Musicians Union Local 47.

The End
by Rebecca A. Harmon

It's funny the thoughts that go through your mind on a five-and-a-half-hour drive. Maybe he didn't go to L.A., maybe he'll be at the house waiting for me, maybe he'll change his mind about the divorce, maybe . . . this is all a bad dream.

"Hello, is anybody home?" I call into the house as I put my luggage down. I already know the answer. Maybe I just want to see how it feels, hear it said out loud one last time. My voice seems to echo through the empty rooms. I am alone.

I walk over to the phone. He's left me a note. I read it once quickly. Then I do it again trying to find a deeper message, hoping for some sense of "feeling" beneath the words, searching for hidden clues, like a needle in a haystack.

"The porch light is out. The garbage cans are in the garage. I left you some packing boxes in the second bedroom. This is the phone number for a local storage facility. Also, the realtor may be calling, he wants to bring some people over to see the house."

He doesn't even sign his name. I set the note down and go turn on the heat. I wonder if I will ever feel warm again.

As I start to unpack my suitcase, I remember that I was supposed to call to let everyone know that I arrived safely in Monterey.

"Hi Mom and Dad, it's me. I guess you're out. It's 4:30. I made it. Talk to you later."

I'm glad they aren't home. I really don't want to talk to anyone. I am so overwhelmed with emotion right now. I feel paralyzed and mute. On the drive up from L.A., I wondered how I would feel when I got here. So, here I am. It's strange. I'm home . . . in my house. It feels so good. I have space all around me. I walk from room to room. The paintings that I love hang on the walls, the antique desk from Nana is filled with my papers, my clothes hang neatly in the closet, the roses are blooming in the garden.

"I'm home," I yell, then collapse onto the couch. I can't stop crying.

Although everything looks the same as I left it four months ago, something is missing. There is no warmth in this house, no laughter, no love . . . no soul. This isn't my home anymore, it's a tomb. I go to turn up the heat. I put on James Taylor and start to pack up the boxes. I feel like I am watching myself in a slow-motion movie. A sad-looking woman with pulled-back hair and swollen eyes sits on the floor of a dimly lit room. She is surrounded by boxes. As she picks up each object, she holds and caresses it, looking lovingly at something only she can see. Slowly, painfully, she carefully wraps each piece and places it in a box. I want to call out to her: "Hey, this isn't real. This isn't your life. This wasn't supposed to happen." Why can't she hear me? There is nothing else I can say to her, nothing else I can do. The only thing left is to help.

I jump when the phone rings. As I reach to pick it up, I see that it is 8:30 the next morning. I'm still dressed in the clothes I wore yesterday. I don't even remember falling asleep.

"Hello," I whisper.

"Hi. When did you get in?" he says flatly.

"Last night about 5:00 P.M.," I answer.

"Oh, did you get my note?" he continues. No feeling, no emotion, just business as usual. His indifference is like a rude alarm clock. Well, I guess I had to wake up anyway.

"When will you be back up here?" I ask. I remember when he used to say "Why, do you miss me?" (yes) "Do you love me?" (yes) "Okay, keep the bed warm and I'll be home as fast as I can."

"I'm not sure," he answers, "probably on Sunday around noon. Look, I've got to go. I'll talk to you later." I end up saying good-bye to a dial tone.

The phone rings again. It's got to be him. He feels bad. He wants to apologize for being so curt. I knew it. He still has a heart.

"Hello," I answer, a bit too happily.

"Hi, it's Mercy."

"Hi," I reply with some disappointment. Still I'm glad to hear from her. She is one of my closest friends. She lives four blocks away and has offered to help me pack, keep me fed, and generally offer lots of moral support. Thank God I have her to help me through these next few terrible days.

"Listen," she says, "I'm sorry I didn't call you sooner, my dad died yesterday. So, how are you doing?"

"Oh, Mercy, I am so sorry. Don't be ridiculous. How are *you* doing?" I can't believe this, I think to myself, she's worried about me. I mean, I'm just getting divorced, that's nothing compared with someone dying.

"Is there anything I can do? Is Joe there with you? Listen, don't worry about me, I'm fine. You go over to your mom's, I'll call you later. I'm so, so sorry Merc. I love you. Bye."

I'm crying again, for Mercy, but also for me. Life isn't fair. Nothing is making sense anymore. Will anything ever feel right again? Back to packing. No more tears. I have work to do and not a lot of time. So, I continue to box up the memories from the past ten years. How did we ever get from there to here?

I've finished packing up most of the kitchen. He already told me that he wants the Dansk Mesa dishes, so do I, but I guess I should keep the Verushka china that we got when we were married. I'm definitely taking the blue Mexican glassware, he never really liked it anyway. I put the things I'm not sure about in a corner on the floor, and the "mine" and "yours" piles on the dining room table. It is all very organized so we can go through everything when he gets here. The linen closet is next. He wants the blue and gray towels. I guess I'll take the burgundy and mauve sets. At this point, I don't really care. I don't want anything. It hurts too much. Every single thing holds a memory of what we had together but now it's become an ugly reminder of what I've lost. I start to sob. I can't keep doing this, it's slowing me down. The movers will be here the day after tomorrow. I have to keep going. We haven't decided yet who is going to keep the bed. I divide all the sheets equally. Cotton blue stripes for him, the pink flannel for me. I want to be fair about this. My friend Nancy thinks I am being too nice.

"After everything he's done . . . all you've been through," she says angrily. "He's been horrible to you, in fact a complete asshole. Just take everything. Screw him!"

As I'm pulling out my travel case, I see a package of condoms stashed behind it. I get a knot in my stomach. He told me he stopped seeing "her," that it was over between them. I feel like someone just threw a bucket of ice-cold water on me. I'm not feeling too nice anymore. In fact, I think I'll open them and spell out "fuck you" on the front door. That will be a nice greeting for him when he gets back on Sunday. Welcome home dear.

Am I going crazy? One minute I'm raging, and the next I'm in tears. Later, I stand in his open closet and squeeze all of his clothes together in my arms. I try to feel him, smell him, and somehow hold him. Dammit, I still love him. Yes . . . I am definitely going crazy.

"Hello," he yells, as the door slams.

My heart pounds. I haven't seen him in two and a half months. I want to run into the living room and hug him, tell him how happy I am that he's home. I keep forgetting. I walk out slowly. He's plopped down on his back in the middle of the floor. Even in Levi's and a sweatshirt, with his hair blown out by the wind, he still looks good to me. I hate that.

"The traffic was terrible," he says, clearly frustrated. "There was a big pileup because of the fog. Finally I couldn't take it anymore and I pulled off in Pismo to wait it out." He rambles on but I don't really hear what he's saying. I just stare at him, trying to see through the exterior shell. On the outside he looks the same, it's the inside that has changed. Where is the heart and soul of the man that I have loved for the past ten years? Is he still in there somewhere? God, I miss him so much. Meanwhile, he hasn't even looked up at me since I came into the room.

"Well, let's get to work," he says and suddenly jumps up. He grabs some masking tape and starts making more packing boxes.

For the rest of the day and night, we dance around each other like two strangers. The space between us is so heavy . . . it's suffocating. Is this how it happens? Can two people who were once so close, now be so far apart?

We work quietly, interrupted occasionally by some question like "Is this yours or mine?" or "Did you want to save this or can I toss it?" I proceed with this torturous job in total disbelief. I want to grab him, shake him, even slap him. SNAP OUT OF IT! Then, in those rare moments when he smiles, laughs, or glances my way, I hoard them in my mind and heart like a hungry beggar stealing crumbs. How sad that I am so grateful when he shows me even the slightest bit of kindness. There has been so much bad lately, I guess I just want to hold onto a few nice memories at the end.

Later that night, totally exhausted, he goes to sleep in the guest room. In our room, I am wide awake. I listen to him breathe, hear him shift around, realizing that this is the last time we'll be in the same house. Here, in our king-size bed, wrapped in our down comforter, the heat on full blast, I am freezing. I slide my hand to his side of the bed. I felt the empty space. I am alone. Alone, except for the ghosts of happier days and all my memories.

In the morning he leaves early. No "good-bye," no "good luck," no "nice knowing you, have a good life."

I run after him. "I HATE YOU!" I scream, but he is already gone. I take a long shower and cry.

Funny the thoughts that go through your mind on a five-and-a-half-hour drive. What now? I still love him. I don't want to be divorced. I'm so scared. I have to get a new job, find a place to live, start all over again. Tomorrow night is Lauren's party. Maybe I should go. Even if I don't know anybody it could be a chance to network. Hey, my birthday is next week. I should celebrate. I'll go shopping with Nancy and buy something fun to wear. I'll call some friends. Maybe we'll go dancing. Would you look at that view, the ocean is so calm today, it looks like a giant mirror and the sky is so blue, not one cloud. What a beautiful day.

"Hello, is anybody home?" I call into the house as I put my luggage down. I already know the answer.

"Hi honey, are you okay?" my mom says as she hugs me. "I missed you."

"Welcome home," my dad says.

I am not alone.

REBECCA A. HARMON   For a number of years an events planner for the Monterey Museum of Art, in California, Rebecca moved to Los Angeles after her divorce. At present she is employed by Sony Corporation. Rebecca is the granddaughter of Anne Freedman.

My Mother's Death
by Stephanie Bernardi

My mother is dying. Cancer has eaten away at her. Today she weighs sixty-eight pounds.

As I sit and watch her, she stares off, fixed on the painting hanging in the corner. His picture hangs over her chest of drawers. It always has. His blue eyes catch me as they call out, "I still am."

The thick knife strokes of paint add depth to his three-year-old cheeks. He is rosy and animated and forever three.

My brother. The one I never knew. Thirty-five years ago he drowned. He is never spoken of. This has only added emphasis to his missing place in our large family.

When I was eleven, our family dog was hit by a car. As I sat on the beach sobbing in front of our house my mother came slowly down the steps. She told me she was worried about Dad. He was crying. I guess she thinks girls cry all the time because she didn't seem to even notice my tears.

"I have never seen him cry since Gary drowned thirteen years ago," she says.

Not to cry for thirteen years. I am afraid of the pain that caused this.

"Mom, how did you ever get over it?" I once boldly ask her.

"You don't ever get over the pain, you just learn to live with it," she replied. End of conversation.

And now today, as she lies dying in this rented metal hospital bed continually staring at the painting, I am aware that we are not alone. In the silence between us, I can feel his presence. It surrounds us. It always has.

"What do you see, Mom? Is someone there?" I ask her. There is no response, just that quiet. "Mom, is someone there?" I repeat.

"Yes," she says. "Mama is here."

I don't doubt this. I just want to hear more. She has not spoken for weeks. She drifts in and out. Occasionally she babbles. My father says it's from senility, from the cancer in her brain. I don't believe him. Something more is going on. In the hospital last week, when I sat with her, it seemed she was talking to someone, but when I asked her about it, I could get no response.

"That's wonderful, Mom. Is anyone else there?" I ask.

"Yes . . . Gary . . . and Helen." I am not surprised about Gary. But who's Helen? Helen . . . Helen? I think Grandma had a sister named Helen, I don't remember any special relationship though . . . at least she's never mentioned it. Maybe a childhood friend named Helen?

"What do they want, Mom?" I ask.

Of course, I know what they want. Here she lies in her suffering, shriveled up to nothing more than a faded memory of the mom she was. Her gestures are infantlike now. The fingers curled. And the hands. The part of her body that hasn't changed. I used to hate those hands. They were wrinkled beyond her age. My hands are the same. Now they are the only familiar part of her. I reach for them. Somehow when I touch them and close my eyes for a moment, it is all forgotten: the feeding tubes up her nose, the diapers, the look of childlike innocence on her face that is pathetic from her. My once elegant mother even picks her nose and scratches herself.

However the antiseptic smell does not hide when my eyes are closed nor does the sound of the plastic mattress cover the sound of her thick breath.

"How does Gary look, Mom?" I ask.

"He looks wonderful because of his beginning and the place he is in," she says.

His beginning. He didn't get very far did he? So untouched. I know the place must be heaven. Where else would a three-year-old be? I am curious.

"Mom, do you want to go with them?" I ask. I know what the answer is. I don't blame them. This is not a life. But I still need to hear it.

"Yes, but they do not want . . . to steal the family," she tells me. This shocks me. But I don't know why it should. I mean, I clearly understand this. My mom is the center of this family and with her gone who knows what will happen . . . maybe we'll all drown.

Already my father and I are not speaking. He hates me. I do not agree with him. And he does not like that. I try to understand him but I am angry that he does not treat her with respect. He lifts her roughly to put medicine on her bedsores. He talks in front of her as if she is not there. And worse, being a radiologist himself, he won't stop radiating this dying woman.

He says it's to keep her from pain, but the only pain I see is from the side effects. I just learned a new word today, "fistula." That is the hole that was just burned through her rectum into her vagina. Yes, I hate him too. Why won't he let this poor woman die? Forty-five years of marriage and he does not see what he is doing.

He is crazy with grief. Because I speak up, he has shut me out. He ignores me when I come to visit. I help take care of her in the day while he is working. I know she will not last much longer so I refuse to let him push me away. Last week I left him a birthday present hoping to make peace. It still sits in the entry unopened. He refuses to accept it. So there it sits for everyone to see his rejection of me. But I know she knows what's going on here and so do they.

"Mom, they're not stealing the family. Because of you, we're strong. We'll get through this. Your love will live on in all of us. We're all just scared right now but it will be OK," I lie.

"We must transcend this," she says.

Transcend? This is not my mother's type of word. I have never heard her use this expression.

"Mom, I want you to tell Gary that we don't blame him for wanting you now. We've had you all these years. Now it is his turn. Tell him how much we've missed him in our lives and how much he's loved by all of us. We just wish things had been different . . . he could have been here."

"Every family has a beginning and he was our beginning," she says.

I grab a pencil and paper and take notes. No one will believe this. I've got to put down exactly what she says so I don't forget it or reword it. Her phrasing is odd but the power in her words . . . it's like I've got this window through to the other side. Gary being the beginning? He was not the first child; he was the second. So his death was a new beginning? Is that why they had five more kids?

"Just give me twenty more minutes," she is begging.

Now what's going on? What is she talking about? To live? To keep this communication open? Don't die! We're not done yet . . . I'm not ready.

"Mom, what's going on? Are you OK?" I ask. There is no answer. She is talking within herself. "Mom . . . Mom, are you still with me?" I ask.

Slowly, I see action return to those eyes. She is coming back.

"Unfortunately I have to translate for us, and that's why, it is difficult to translate these things," she says.

To translate things? What is the form of communication? Just keep going. Say everything you need to say, Stephanie.

"Mom, I want you to tell Gary something else. I've always felt specially close to him because of being born on the same date that he had died. I also think the reason I was a girl and not your fifth boy was because of his help. He made that sad day a special day for you and it's always made me feel special," I tell her.

She is studying me. What does she see? So often I hide my sadness. I don't even wear makeup to visit her anymore; too often I leave with black eyes. I wonder, does she notice? I know she hates the perms. Always says it looks healthier without one . . . I think she sees my strength. That's what she sees.

"You are special, because you have chosen the source," she says.

The source? Mom has never said that word either . . . referring to God as the source is not from her Catholic thinking. And calling me special because of choosing the source. Amazing.

"We've learned a lot together haven't we, Mom? It hasn't always been easy, has it? But look how far we've come. How close we've gotten . . . I love you," I tell her.

"The chance to learn is the only point we have in life. And we are only given one chance to learn it," she says. What is she saying? Learning to love, is that what it's all about? Her words are confusing but the feelings are clear.

"Mom, you still haven't told me yet, do you want to go with them?" I ask.

"Yeah," she says as she looks at me. Am I imagining the relief I sense in her with those words? It's probably my own selfish relief that this won't keep going on week after week . . . "But something is holding me here," she says.

"Who? Me?" I ask.

"No."

"Is it Dad?" I say.

"No," she says. There is quiet. Then, "The whole bunch," she tells me.

She is right. It's all of us. The name on our boat for the past twenty years has been *The Wild Bunch*. She even signs her Christmas cards that way. She is looking tired. I don't blame her. We're a big group to worry about. She's got to let go and so do we.

"Mom, it's like I said. We're just scared, that's all. It doesn't mean we want you to stay on suffering like this. It's OK for you to go, Mom. The only thing you need to know is how much you are loved and that we will be OK. Alright? We will survive," I say.

I feel strong and I am proud. If I can say this so clearly and without tears, then I know it's true. And if Gary and her mom are waiting for her, then won't she be waiting for me, too? There is relief in this.

"Will you be there for me, Mom, when I die?" I ask. She giggles. Her curled fingers flex as she studies them. She reaches for the tiny stuffed dog that hangs from the metal pull-bar over her. He has the St. Augustine medal pinned to his neck, the saint that is supposed to help get us safely to the other side. She bats at it like a three-month-old. She cannot grasp it, but it fascinates her. Now I understand why. She knows its red-and-white checked bow around its neck, its barking happy expression that tells her not to be afraid.

"How can it be? That would make me one hundred and eighteen?" She smiles slyly. Her sense of humor never really leaves. I wish she would be serious.

"No, I mean like Gary is there for you, Mom. Will you help me cross to the other side?" I am crying. She smiles. I wait. "Yes, I will," she whispers. "Yes, I will . . . but now it is my turn," she says. I can hardly hear her.

Her arms try to reach me so I help wrap them around my neck. Her hands flop on me as she tries to stroke my hair. I climb in bed with her. We cuddle, my mom and I, something we've not done in years. Just my mom and me. For this moment, I am her baby again.

Out the window the day is crystal clear. The bay water is oily smooth. The large tree is no longer bare of leaves. Winter has ended here and, for the first time, I am aware of the early signs of spring. Those branches, that were so empty and cold to look out at, are turning green again.

Inside my head, while wrapped in my mom's still-warm body, I am rapidly calculating that my mother, my supposedly senile mom, has just figured out that I will be eighty-eight when I die. Does she see the future in this state, too? She tries to tell me something about my father's red Porsche and about the estate, but they are not clear. I am losing her now. I won't know until I die if she saw the future or not. But what I do know is someday she and I will be together again. Also, I now know, someday I will finally meet Gary. And then there will be no more sad goodbyes, just hellos.

STEPHANIE BERNARDI   A mother of two small children, Stephanie assists her husband in his business and writes to keep her mind active. Earlier drafts of this story appear on pages 102–106.

The Beach
by Tamara J. Randall

In the darkness of our *palapa* (beach hut), I awaken to the sound of the ocean waves crashing upon the beach. The air is rustling the palm leaves of our beach hut. I roll out of my hammock, landing upon my hands and knees in the soft sand floor.

Our hammocks are strung out from the center pole of the palapa like a Ferris wheel. I hear the brothers beginning to stir now. I have two brothers and three sisters. I am ten years old, the oldest in my family, and living in Mexico with my mother.

"Eric," I say, "help me open up one of the walls." Eric and I each grab one of the long forked poles that are used to hold the walls of the palapa open during the day. We spear the bottom corner of one wall with a pole and push it out and plant the poles in the sand. The ocean breeze rushes in and I can taste the salt in the ocean spray. The sea is blue green, edged in a clean white foam. The waves thunder down on the moon-shaped beach and I feel the earth shake with each wave.

We are living on a sandbar called Barra de Navidad (Bar of Christmas) that separates the ocean from a peaceful, island-filled lagoon. In the background, I hear a jungle buzzing just inland. I see the rock cliff and hillside rising up on the other side of the tip of the sandbar, making a canal which the lagoon fills and empties with the tides. At midday when the tide pulls the water out of the lagoon and back into the sea, we kids go down and jump in and are rushed by the current out to the sea waves crashing at the mouth of the canal. Then we pull ourselves out and run back to the lagoon side for another bubbly ride. I love living in a palapa, sleeping in a hammock, opening the four walls to the warm ocean breeze, and I am crazy about the outdoor shower, an old oil drum that sits on stilts.

As I stand under it and pull the rope, fresh water falls on me. I love it so much that I take several showers a day. I love never being cold, day or night. I run free, swimming and playing all day long. This is a peaceful, beautiful paradise and I feel so natural here, without a worry in the world.

Our palapa is the last one at the very end of the sandbar. We have been here for a few months now. I don't know when we are going to go back home to Ajijic, and right now I don't care. Yesterday, the old grey-bearded gringo with the hole-filled straw hat, who lives in a palapa just down from ours, shared his breakfast of oatmeal with all seven of us. This morning, though, is different from yesterday. I can't remember whether or not I had any lunch or dinner yesterday and I am starting to wonder if we are going to get any breakfast this morning. Mama is not doing anything. She just sits on the sandy floor of our palapa with my baby sister in her lap. Her light-colored curly hair falls in ringlets down around her beautiful, sad, worried face. Her blue eyes seem calm. The other kids are looking around at one another, but no one wants to be the first to ask.

"Mama, I'm hungry," my little six-year-old brother Chris says at last.

Mama looks around and takes her time answering. "I don't have any food to feed you today," she answers sadly. After a moment, as the words of "no food today" set in, she says, "All I have is this LSD. I guess we could eat it. It is all I've got to give you." We all agree we should eat the LSD. This is not the first time I have eaten LSD. "Turning on" has been a monthly event in my life for a couple of years now. Mama pulls a little container out of her purse, takes out a little white capsule and opens it up. She sprinkles a bit of the white powder from the capsule onto her baby finger and as I lick it off of her finger, I get a little shiver. It tastes salty and tickles my nose as I swallow it.

Each of us gets our share, including Mama and my month-old baby sister Sara. My sister Jill and I are playing at the edge of the lagoon. My brothers Eric and Chris and my sister Rachael are playing together nearby as Mama watches. In and out of the lagoon we move, the sun blazing down on us. As the hunger pains melt away and I forget about food, Jill and I play, laughing and giggling, rolling in and out of the lagoon. We make castles and mud pies and splash in the water. Endlessly, we play and play and play.

In the afternoon the water in the lagoon empties with the tides and so we all go down to the tip of the sandbar for our ritual of jumping in on the lagoon side and letting ourselves be rushed out by the sea waves. As fast as I can, I jump into the water, bobbing up and down in the bubbly water. I giggle and giggle and laugh loud, screaming, my body tickled all over by the rushing water as I am pulled and tossed out to meet the crashing sea waves at the great mouth of the sea.

The world is shiny, glistening, a million colors and patterns . . . the water and sky blend. I cannot tell where one thing begins and the other ends. I melt into a sea of everything.

After what seems like forever, I begin to feel tired of all this running, jumping, splashing, swimming and laughing.

I stop and sit. One by one, my brothers and sisters pull themselves out of the current too. We all sit at the tip of the sandbar with Mama and watch the world move, everything is breathing life.

At last we walk back over to our palapa. I stand under the old oil drum, pull the rope and am refreshed by the warm, clear, sweet water pouring down on my head. It washes through my long golden brown hair, over my body. I feel as clear and sweet as the water pouring over me; I have become sweet water.

It is late afternoon now, and everything has become very quiet and still. We are sitting next to the lagoon again. My family is all silence and peace. I lay in the sand next to Mama, looking up at her as she holds sweet little Sara, her golden hair in ringlets softly surrounding her beautiful, strong, tender face. "Mama," I say, the first words I have spoken to her all day, "you are so beautiful."

I see in my mother such beauty and tenderness, and I hold in my heart such love for her! She looks at me, and shiny blue eyes smile the most wonderful smile I have ever seen! She doesn't say a word. She doesn't have to. I am filled with her and love. I look around at my world. I see Eric standing knee deep in the calm smooth lagoon. He is watching the water.

Suddenly he yells out, "Look!" He is pointing at the water in front of him. All of us kids scurry to the water's edge to see what he is pointing at. "A big old fish!!" he exclaims. "Right there!"

I can see it now. It is just swimming in circles right in front of Eric. Eric suddenly leaps out to the water and runs as fast as he can down the beach to the palapa of a fisherman.

He comes running back, with the fisherman running right behind him, and his big round net hanging over his dark arm. *"¡Andale! ¡Corrale! ¡Mira aca! ¡Un pescado grandismo!"* ("Hurry! Run! Look here! A really big fish!")

The fisherman steps up to the water and the fish is still swimming around and around right where Eric first spotted him.

The fisherman looks very serious in his big straw hat tilted to the side and his pants rolled up past his thighs. I can see his blue blood running right through his dark brown skin, his muscles and veins tense as he prepares to cast his net.

Everyone is hushed as he steps into the still lagoon. His dark eyes follow to where Eric is pointing. *"¡Alli!"* ("There!") Eric whispers to him.

The fisherman waits for the right moment, then throws the net up and over the spot where the fish is. The circular net flies, twirling through the air, splashing down upon the flat smooth surface of the water, the fisherman pulls the net slowly and soon lands the biggest fish I have ever seen! We all gather around to get a better look. This fish is huge. It is flipping and flapping back and forth. My brother Chris gets a little too close and gets a good fishtail whack across the ankles, knocking him right off his feet.

"Wow!" he yells as he speedily gets back onto his feet.

This causes everyone to laugh great big belly laughs. The fisherman smiles and laughs too and is missing a lot of teeth.

The fish lies on the wet glistening sand, his silver scales shining out rainbow colors. He is dying slowly and isn't moving much, only his gills move as though he struggles for a breath.

"¿Que tip de pescado es?" ("What kind of fish is this?") Mama asks the fisherman.

"¡Es una Lis Grande!" ("It is a Big Lisa!") he answers.

"¿Y como se cocina un pescado tan grande?" ("How do you cook such a big fish?") asks Mama.

"En hojas de platano, en la arena," ("In banana leaves, in the sand") he replies.

Soon after that we all begin to help dig a big hole in the sand. The old gringo who has come to help is making a big bonfire in the sandpit with wood that the fisherman has brought. We kids run down to the back edge of the lagoon where there is a grove of banana trees in somebody's back yard and we are allowed to pick some leaves from them. We take them back and wrap the fish well in the leaves and secure them with some string. Soon the coals are ready and the old gringo spreads the coals out flat and he and Mama lay the fish over the coals and cover it with sand. The sun is setting and we all begin to wait for dinner. Hours pass, the night has come, and the old gringo has come to help us pull the fish from the sandpit. Mama and the old gringo carry the fish up into our palapa and we begin to wake the other children as they have fallen asleep waiting for the fish to cook. "Hey, everybody, the fish is done!" says Mama. "Come and eat. Come on." Slowly, rubbing the sleep from his eyes each child eats fish. The old gringo is very impressed by the flavor of the fish. It is the best fish I have ever tasted, especially since I don't even like fish! I feast on fish and then happy as can be fall into my hammock and sleep, thinking, "What a great ending to a great day."

P.S. I can never forget that great day on the sandbar, the innocence and the fish that came to us when we needed it. It was pure magic! From that day on, whenever I found myself in a difficulty of some kind, I always carried within me a strength and an undying faith in a power beyond what I could comprehend, and it was always there for me when I needed it.

TAMARA J. RANDALL   Tamara's mother, a 1960s hippie, took her very young children to Mexico, where they lived hand-to-mouth for fifteen years. Tamara's stories are filled with the mystery of native religion and folkways of Mexico. She is the mother of two children.

A Day at the Races

by George Small

I'm sitting in the Hollywood Race Track dining room on the second floor. In front of me is a small TV screen showing the horses outside. It is a miserable day. Sheets of rain are pouring down on L.A. The bitter wind is cold and blows through the grandstands, forcing the bettors inside to the dining rooms. This room is stuffed with gamblers gulping down steaming hot coffee and nervously eating lunch while they watch and play each race from the TVs. It's just about time for the fifth race to go off and people are lining up at the windows inside to make their bets.

The whole city has been in a downpour for days. The track is sloppy. The jockeys wear heavy rain gear over their colors and big goggles to protect their eyes from the flying mud. The horses are lining up at the gate. Track hands draped in green raincoats and large rubber boots place each horse in a numbered gate. The men slip and slide in the mud. Some of the drenched horses are calm and relaxed, but others seem anxious and resist going into the gate.

My track buddy, Tony, sits next to me putting Equal into his coffee and grumbling, "They're all crooks. The riders, the stewards and especially those trainers, all sleazy bastards."

Tony always cuts to the point of things. He's been around. He used to own horses. That was some time ago. Times have changed, but not his view of the world.

I'm watching the horse and I say, "Hey, Tony, look at that Number One. He's really nervous. He won't go in the gate."

Tony sighs, and with his usual dry tone says, "Ah, that one is a loser. He'll use up his juice, he can't win."

In these moments right before the horses go into the gate there is much to be observed. Gamblers will be watching intently. Last minute clues or hunches can lead to bets of thousands of dollars in those last few seconds before the race. I'm also very intense. I'm watching several horses from the TV that are waiting to enter the gate. That stubborn Number One is digging his hooves into the soggy earth. His legs are stiff and his body is rigid as four track hands push and shove him into the gate. Another horse rears up. He throws the jockey off into the deep mud right on his ass.

"Tony, I think we got a lotta screwed-up horses in this rain and shit. Man, I would hate to be out there in that shit with a skittish horse. What a shit job," I say.

Tony is glued to the TV and snaps back sarcastically, "Don't worry about them, they make big bucks or they wouldn't be out there."

Over the loudspeaker the announcer calls, "And there goes Number One into the gate. He's a little hesitant . . . but there he goes."

My eyes search all the waiting horses for clues. As I scan the TV screen I focus carefully on one waiting horse. The jockey on this horse, Number Eight, crosses himself in a religious way and turns his head out toward the grandstands. He looks out and smiles as if he's looking right at someone. His sheepish smile is all-knowing and confident.

"Tony, did you see that? That son-of-a-bitch crossed himself and I swear smiled at someone in the grandstands. What the hell's going on here?" Tony looks puzzled. He scans his racing form and studies Number Eight, Nutcracker Man. He concentrates on the form for a few seconds and says, "Well, let's see. This horse hasn't won a race in two years. He's a loser and Ortega rides on top. Two losers. I don't know what the religious thing is all about but he will need all the help he can get from above and that ain't more rain, I'll tell you that."

Well, I'm hooked. I can feel something in my gut, a hunch I guess. I look at the form and the stats on the horse over and over. I think to myself out loud, "He's a loser. His weight's the same, never won at this track, lousy rider and he's a cheap horse. No way, no way. But goddamn, he's twenty to one, what a long shot." I look back at Nutcracker Man standing in bullets of rain, his wet body relaxed just waiting for his turn. Ortega is set, whip in hand, feet in the stirrups and goggles on. For a moment I feel sorry for the men and horses. Especially the horses. They didn't ask for this life and there probably isn't a lot of reward for the losers. Horses or jockeys.

I say, "You know, Tony, it's a pitiful sight out there, but I got a hunch. Somebody knows something. Ortega knows something, I know it. Is there still time to bet?"

Tony responds, "Well, you better get to the window. Hurry, because if he comes in you'll never forgive yourself for not doing it."

"I know. I know. But he is such a piece of shit on paper," I say as I get up from the table and run to the betting windows.

Tony yells out to me, "Don't forget the five. Moongate with Stevens, that's your winner, I guarantee it, and take that to the bank."

I run to the windows and look for the shortest line, thinking to my-self, "I've been a loser all day. Lost every race. What I need is a miracle like this to pull me out. Make some big bucks and pay off some of those pain-in-the-ass fuckin' credit cards." My hands are filled with forms, programs, pens and money. I can see the screen behind the teller. The eight is now thirty to one. No one is betting the horse. I start to figure, "Let's see, at thirty to one, a hundred to win could pay a few thousand. I can bet exactas, triples, doubles, trifectas and even more to win. This could be an easy twenty grand. I'll make a killing."

The lines are clogged, moving very slowly. Many people have gone to the windows at the last minute. I jump from line to line and find the last window with one person in line. A very large, obese woman takes up the whole window. She leans into the window making her bets from the program figuring her bet out as she goes.

This is all a "no-no." Never but never figure out your bet at the win-dow, be prepared. Don't take other people's valuable money.

There she is leaning in the window, taking her time and rethinking some of her bets while the horses are almost in the gate. I'm right behind her looking over her shoulder as she finishes and then starts counting out her money. I'm so frustrated. The sight of this giant woman dressed in her Sunday best, her huge frame precariously balanced on tiny high-heel shoes, filling the entire window with her gross body, is driving me nuts.

People are so stupid and inconsiderate. Never but never count out your money in line. Always have your money ready, use big bills and don't look for exact change. "Jesus." I look at other lines. They're all busy, she is my only chance.

"Oh, come on lady, move it along, please for the rest of us who want to make a bet," I say.

Another man who is behind me now and wants to make his last-minute bet yells out, "Come on lady, get with it," then in a softer tone under his breath says, "fat bitch."

But she never budges. She seems untouched by our rantings while she still searches for the exact change. "God!!" I glance up to the TV screen behind the teller and I see the last horse go into the gate.

"Please, lady, I beg you, I need to make this bet now! Please hurry up, for Christ's sake."

That got her attention. She turns around and says, "When I'm fin-ished it will be your turn and Jesus Christ has nothing to do with it."

I'm dying here. I'm about to collapse with a heart attack or something when the old bag finally moves from the window. The teller looks at me sympathetically.

I yell out "a hundred-to-one on the eight," when the bell goes off and the horses leave the gate. The betting machines automatically shut down and the betting is stopped. Over the loudspeaker, I hear the announcer call, "And they're off!"

I never get my bet in. "Oh fuck, shit shit shit," I yell out loud.

The teller tried but the machine shut down, fucked again. The teller closes the window in my face. I turn towards the big TV camera and watch Moongate takes the lead while the other horses trail and Nutcracker Man falls to the back out of sight of the camera.

The announcer calls out, "Moongate is moving to the front setting a quick pace followed by Hipster right behind and Honey Bunny on the rail gaining an inside position. The other horses are closely packed together with Nutcracker Man trailing with more than twenty lengths to the leader."

Then the announcer adds, "Nutcracker Man will have his work cut out for him today."

For a moment I feel relieved. Maybe that fat bitch saved my stupid ass. Maybe I saved myself a hundred bucks after all. God sure does work in some funny ways.

As I return to the table and watch the race continue I see Nutcracker Man start to close in on the pack. My stomach takes a little dip.

The announcer calls ". . . and coming around the far turn just burning up the track is Nutcracker Man, coming like a freight train."

I can see him now. It's incredible. There is Ortega soaked from head to toe with flying mud. He passes the lagging horse on the outside and then joins the group, weaving his way in and out, closing right behind the leader Moongate.

As Nutcracker Man enters the near stretch Ortega gives him a tap on his behind with the whip. The horse responds, lengthening his stride and digging down deep into the soft track. Now both rider and horse are completely covered with mud as Ortega lowers his body into the horse's back, stretching out the horse's neck for the finishing line.

"Tony, do you see that? That son of a bitch. I was right. He knew he was gonna win. He's gonna win and fuck me at the same time. Why me? What lesson is this?"

Dramatically I throw my hands up in the air and look away from the screen. "I can't stand this. I can't look. Why me, God? What have I done to deserve this pain on earth?"

The sound of the crowd grows into a chorus of yells and screams as the horses near the finish line. People yell for their horse right to the end. My stomach sinks again. I know now that the son of a bitch will win at the last second and I will lose everything. And it's all because of that fat bitch in line. That concrete pillar of bone and flesh that manages to block me and my life whenever it can. Her stinkin' words ring in my confused mind: "It's my turn now, you will have to wait for your turn."

My stomach burns deep down and I think to myself, "Oh yeah, you fat bitch. Your turn. It seems to me that for my whole life it's been your game. It's always been your turn over mine. You've squashed me whenever you could."

Over the noise of the crowd the announcer yells, ". . . and Nutcracker Man is closing in with every stride. It's going to be a very tight one folks. Here he comes, closing, closing, he's closing. . . ."

Boom! They hit the wire.

"It's a photo, ladies and gentlemen. Please hold all tickets until it's official. I repeat, hold all tickets."

I'm sitting at the table exhausted. My emotions are drained, my body is spent. I'm dumbfounded. I stare at the TV screen.

"Tony, that fucker got him. Nutcracker got it didn't he?"

Tony leans over to me and whispers in my ear very confidently, "No, he didn't. Moongate nosed him at the wire. I'm sure of it. Your horse came in second just like I told you."

Tony is rarely wrong about finish-line calls. He's an expert.

And in a minute the announcer confirms. "Ladies and gentlemen, it was very close but Moongate with Stevens held on and won by a nose. Moongate is the winner. It's official."

That was a hell of a race. Almost a perfect ride. "Jesus." Everything set up for that rider and he still didn't win, what a disappointment. Will that horse ever get a situation like that again, where everything falls into place like that? Will he ever win or was this just a one-time deal? What happens to Nutcracker Man? Will they get rid of him in a cheap claimer race? Will he break down or will new owners drug him, run him into the ground and then sell him for dog food? He's not good enough for pasture or stud. What about Ortega? How long can he race without a winner? What little podunk track will he wind up on?

It's like all those old actors you've seen in all those old movies over the years. Do they ever get that chance again, or do they just disappear and go into oblivion?

My mood is sour. I feel cheated and frustrated. Will I ever hit the big one and have that story to tell? I feel despair all around me. I see it in people's faces all around me. Everybody is a loser.

I'm still sitting at the table. I take a deep breath and let out a sigh. I look over at Tony.

He's busy looking over his forms and papers and says, "Horses are like tomatoes. When they're ripe, they're ready. After that they turn bad, and let that be a lesson to you."

And then I think, somebody has to win. Between those poor creatures out there and the poor creatures in here somebody has to win.

"Hey, Tony, who do you like in the sixth race?"

GEORGE SMALL   George is a painter, actor, teacher, and now writer. Owner of an art school in Santa Monica, he divides his time between Santa Barbara and Los Angeles. For many years George has been Bernard's next-door neighbor. Over-the-fence conversations led George to join the Sunday writers group.

Now you have arrived at the end of this small journey. You have absorbed the techniques of writing from within, of writing in an authentic voice. You have reflected on the experiences and stages of your life, worked on your stories, and read a number of other stories that may have served as models for your own writing and rewriting. You have explored your own creativity—your ability to express what you have seen and felt in life—and have experienced the pleasure of writing well.

Perhaps you have also come to view the difficulties you've encountered in your life in a new light, gaining a new understanding of their meaning and a new respect for the ways in which you handled yourself in the circumstances. In the course of writing your life's stories you may also have given a great deal of pleasure to and provoked considerable thought and feeling in your readers and listeners.

Keep writing, and encourage those you love to do the same.

Appendix:
Developing Supportive Feedback

A key aspect of succeeding as a writer is knowing when and where to get guidance, support, and assistance. As writers, most of us need feedback from members of a writers' group, an editor, or some other trusted source. I want to suggest ways of getting and giving positive support and feedback and how to get the most out of it in order to continue to grow in your work.

We have all encountered criticism during our lives. We probably remember how stung we felt when teachers, parents, and even friends criticized us when we were doing the best we could. Such criticism felt particularly harsh when we were doing something artistic—writing, painting, drawing, or playing a musical instrument. Often, we simply stopped doing these artistic things. Gradually, we internalized this criticism and developed our own inner critic.

Now that we are doing some writing, we need to retrain this inner critic. Otherwise, we may not go on writing after the first bit of harsh criticism we receive when we share our work with others—*and we do need feedback.*

Retraining one's inner critic is no small or easy task. It can be accomplished, however, by patience, discipline, and a positive outlook. The same process can be used to retrain the critic within members of your support structure.

First, let us consider the kind of feedback we as writers would like to experience. Then I will outline a process by which the wild, undisciplined, even destructive critic within yourself can be converted to a purposeful, disciplined, insightful one.

What Is Supportive Feedback?

A group, or even one like-minded person, can help you get the kind of feedback you need. This person or group to whom you turn for support needs to develop a disciplined response to your writing, to protect you and make you feel safe while guiding you in the direction of better work.

That discipline involves adhering strictly to the following agreement, which each participant will make with other participants: feedback to each writer after he or she shares a story will be Non-Invasive, Non-Judgmental, Corrective, and Affirming (NINJCA for short). Each person giving feedback agrees to avoid any statement that sounds judgmental or invasive, no matter how innocently he or she intends it. During the early sessions of any group, one person may be appointed to be on the lookout for judgmental and invasive statements.

Typical judgmental statements are

- You *should* have. . . . You *could* have. . . . You *ought* to have. . . .

- If *I* were you, *I* would. . . .

- That (story, thought, paragraph, and so on) was too (sentimental, clever, abrupt, silly, slow, confusing, boring, and so on)

Typical invasive questions and statements are

- Why did (or didn't) you . . . ?

- Why were you . . . ?

- You sound like you were trying. . . .

- You often. . . .
- You always. . . .

Any one of these statements can discourage a writer. Instead, ask members of your group to try using the following:

Non-judgmental corrective statements, such as

- I would like to (see, feel, know, be able to follow, and so on)
- I had trouble seeing the picture.
- I had difficulty following the action.
- I needed to feel the character's feelings.
- I found my attention wandering.
- I needed to hear the characters talk to each other more.
- I had difficulty finding (or following) the spine.
- I didn't know what the central question of the story was.
- The key question was answered before I had a chance to get involved or get excited about it.

Non-judgmental affirming statements, such as

- I saw the picture clearly.
- I was right there with you the whole time.
- I knew what each character (or the narrator) was feeling from one moment to the next.
- The dialogue drew me in and helped me know each character.
- The balance of narrative, dialogue, and inner thoughts and feelings held my interest.

These are important considerations. A potential writer can listen all day to non-invasive, non-judgmental, corrective, and affirming comments. She can listen for only a few moments to invasive or judgmental statements, and then she will begin to defend himself, her creativity will turn off, and she will stop writing.

You may find that your support system is only one person, or perhaps you and a friend decide to write your life stories and share them. One person is enough if his or her feedback is non-invasive, non-judgmental, corrective, and affirming.

The great advantage of working in a group or with a friend is that the writer can stop being the critic and simply *create*. Each person can then be a responsible critic for the other writers when they read their stories. So keep looking for one or two people with whom you can share this special journey of self-exploration.

However, if the person you select to review your work simply says "I like it" or "I don't like it," and shows no inclination to go beyond this, get a new partner. Likewise, if he or she makes judgmental or invasive comments, find someone who is willing to provide NINJCA feedback. If you find yourself alone and unable to develop a writer-reviewer relationship with anyone, try to develop these NINJCA qualities in yourself.

If you are a teacher and you wish to encourage your students to write their life stories, it is important to develop habits of NINJCA feedback in them.

The exercises below will help you develop NINJCA feedback and may be tried alone or in a group.

1. Review each of the following stories.
   A. "Willem" (first draft) (p. 33)
   B. "The Goose Story" (first draft) (p. 87)

2. Give yourself and your friend or group at least one session per story, perhaps one or two sessions a week. Appoint one person to role-play the "writer" of each story. If you are that writer, you may *defend* what has been written any time you feel the feedback is hostile, judgmental, invasive, or superficial. When the critique of your work is over, tell the others what it felt like: who was providing NINJCA feedback and who was not.

3. If you are giving feedback, describe your responses to the story aloud. If you are doing this alone, talk into a tape recorder, or speak aloud, or, as a last resort, write them down.

Focus your attention on how you responded to the story rather than on how the story is written (for example "I needed more detail," "I found my attention wandering," and the like, rather than "It's too long, too confusing").

If the person role-playing the writer begins to defend himself, it is a clue that you or others in the group are being judgmental or invasive or superficial. Find a NINJCA comment that will make the point.

Remember, by giving NINJCA feedback, which focuses on your reactions to the story, you leave the writer room to make choices about what to change and what not to change.

Have each person in the group defend or absorb feedback for five minutes. Continue until each person has had a chance to role-play the writer. The comments may be repetitive, but the purpose of the task is to experience (1) being a writer under the gun and (2) changing your mode of giving feedback from judgmental or superficial to NINJCA.

4. Address the following issues:
   A. "Willem" (first draft)
      — Is the point of view child or adult?
      — Is the story written in the present or as a recollection?
      — Is the level of language child or adult?
      — Is the situation believable?
      — Are the writer's feelings clearly expressed?
   B. "The Goose Story" (first draft)
      — Is the picture clear?
      — Are the writer's feelings clearly expressed?
      — Where should the dialogue begin?
      — Where should the "setting the stage" material go?
5. When the initial critique of each story is complete, read the final version of the story aloud, again appointing a writer to defend or explain the work. Remember, there are no right answers to the issues. We are attending to the task of creating feedback and promoting lively discussions.
6. After the third session, you will be ready for feedback on your own stories. If you have not written your earliest memories yet, read the first two chapters in this book, and then follow the steps below.
   A. Tell your earliest memory aloud into a tape recorder or to your friend or group. Get a few NINJCA comments, then retell the story in the present tense: "I am five years old and I am" rather than "I was."

B. Write your story just as you have told it aloud. If the group is large or time is running short, do the writing at home, but try to do the writing immediately.

C. Repeat NINJCA feedback for each story.

D. Each writer in the group should repeat the storytelling/writing process until everyone is comfortable writing and receiving feedback. At this point, the writing can be done at home.

Each new person added to the group or class needs to be taken through this storytelling/writing process. New group members need to be encouraged to listen for NINJCA feedback and given a little time to develop the habit of giving NINJCA feedback. With practice and time the whole group's feedback—and unity—will be all the better for it!

Selected Readings

Writing Models

Aiken, Conrad. "Silent Snow, Secret Snow." In *Collected Short Stories*. New York: Schocken Books, 1982.

> *This story allows us to glimpse a young boy's fascinating and very private world from his point of view.*

Bierce, Ambrose. *The Stories and Fables of Ambrose Bierce*. Owings Mills, MD: Stemmer House Publishers, 1977.

> *The stories "Occurrence at Owl Creek Bridge," "The Boarded Window," and "One of the Missing" have superbly shocking, unpredictable, mind-teasing endings.*

Campbell, Joseph. *Hero with a Thousand Faces*. Princeton, NJ: Princeton University Press, 1973. *The Masks of God* (4 volumes). New York: Penguin, 1970, 1976.

> *The path of the hero in everyone is traced through quests and temptations, weaving its way through virtually all of the world's mythologies and religions.*

Doctorow, E. L. *World's Fair*. New York: Fawcett Crest, 1986.

> *Doctorow's novel, which displays a number of techniques of life writing, chronicles the events and experiences of his fictional hero's life.*

Dostoevsky, Feodor. *Crime and Punishment*. New York: Bantam Books, 1984.
> *The author interweaves first-person narrative, dialogue, and inner monologue in this classic story of risk-taking, crime, and conscience.*

Dreiser, Theodore. *The Best Short Stories of Theodore Dreiser*. Chicago: Ivan R. Dee, Inc., 1989.
> *The narrator's voice in a Dreiser story is often clumsy and intrusive, a legacy of the nineteenth century, yet the stories are well worked out and often gripping and ironic.*

Hemingway, Ernest. *Collected Short Stories*. New York: Charles Scribners Sons, 1938.
> *Hemingway's narrator remains as discreet and inconspicuous as Dreiser's is heavy-handed. The author makes his points dramatically through dialogue and occasional inner monologue.*

Ibsen, Henrik. *Complete Major Prose*. New York: New American Library, 1978.
> *The plot structure and problems Ibsen sets for his characters and the qualities he gives them make his plays forever interesting.*

Lang, Fritz. *M*. (Classic Film Scripts, a series). London: Lorrimer Publishing, 1973.
> *In M, we experience the forcefulness of pursuers, including the protagonist's own conscience, from the point of view of the criminal pursued.*

Miller, Arthur. *Death of a Salesman*. New York: Penguin, 1977.
> *The struggle of a character to achieve a goal and the way he pursues it when he cannot have what he really wants give Miller's play dignity and meaning.*

O'Connor, Flannery. *The Complete Stories*. New York: Farrar, Straus and Giroux, 1971.
> *O'Connor offers some of the most bizarre and interesting characters in modern short stories.*

Orwell, George. *Collected Essays* (4 volumes). San Diego: Harcourt Brace Jovanovich, 1968.
> *"Shooting an Elephant" is classic autobiographical writing: crisp narrative storytelling, a clear view of the objective world facing the writer, physical action, and reflection on the meaning of the actions one takes.*

Pirandello, Luigi. *Plays*. Middlesex, England: Penguin Books, 1962.
> *Pirandello's plays bring us into a series of delightfully separate worlds in which each character is convinced his view of the real world is correct and each character manages to convince us he is right.*

Writing Process

Capacchione, Lucia. *The Creative Journal.* Athens, OH: Ohio University Press, 1979.

Clurman, Harold. *On Directing.* New York: Macmillan, 1983.

Goldberg, Natalie. *Writing Down the Bones.* Boston: Shambhala Publications, 1986.

Rico, Gabriele. *Writing the Natural Way.* Los Angeles: J. P. Tarcher, 1983.

Stanislavski, Constantin. *An Actor Prepares.* New York: Routledge Theater Arts, 1989.

Ueland, Brenda. *If You Want to Write.* Saint Paul, MN: Graywolf Press, 1987.

Autobiographical Writing

St. Augustine. *The Confessions of St. Augustine.* New York: Mentor Books, 1963.

Dillard, Annie. *An American Childhood.* New York: Harper and Row, 1987.

Scott-Maxwell, Florida. *The Measure of My Days.* New York: Penguin Books, 1979.

Simon, Kate. *Bronx Primitive.* New York: Harper and Row, 1983.

Simon, Kate. *A Wider World: Portraits in an Adolescence.* New York: Harper and Row, 1986.

Wiesel, Elie. *Night.* New York: Bantam Books, 1982.

Wilde, Oscar. "Confessions." In *Complete Writings of Oscar Wilde* (10 volumes). New York: Nottingham Society, 1907.

Guides to Autobiographical Writing

Hateley, B. J. *Telling Your Story, Exploring Your Faith.* St. Louis: CBP Press, 1985.

Kanin, Ruth. *Write the Story of Your Life.* New York: Hawthorne Dutton, 1981.

Keen, Sam, and Anne Valley Fox. *Telling Your Story: A Guide to Who You Are and Who You Can Be.* New York: Signet Books, 1973.

Moffat, Mary Jane. *The Times of Our Lives*. Santa Barbara, CA: John Daniel and Co., 1989.

Collections

Walker, Scott, ed. *The Graywolf Annual Three: Essays, Memoirs, and Reflections*. Saint Paul, MN: Graywolf Press, 1986.

Zinsser, William, ed. *Inventing the Truth: The Art and Craft of Memoir*. Boston: Houghton Mifflin, 1987.

ORDER FORM

10% DISCOUNT on orders of $50 or more –
20% DISCOUNT on orders of $150 or more –
30% DISCOUNT on orders of $500 or more –
On cost of books for fully prepaid orders

NAME		
ADDRESS		
CITY/STATE	ZIP/POSTCODE	
PHONE	COUNTRY	

TITLE	QTY	PRICE	TOTAL
Writing From Within (paperback)		@ $14.95	
In Your Own Voice (paperback)		@ $13.95	
The Pleasure Prescription (paperback)		@ $13.95	
Write Your Own Pleasure Prescription (paperback)		@ $12.95	
Please list other titles below:			
		@ $	
		@ $	
		@ $	
		@ $	
		@ $	
		@ $	

Shipping costs
First book: $3.00 by book post; $4.50 by UPS or to ship outside the U.S.

Each additiona $1.00

For rush orde shipments (800) 266-

SUBTOTAL	
Less discount @ _____ %	( )
TOTAL COST OF BOOKS	

Ca
Sig

10/98

WFW3 12/97

GAYLORD S

ML